FORTY WEEKS

Letters From Prison

An Ignatian Path to Christ
With Sacred Story Prayer

With
Richard R. Roman

Foreword
Gregory J. Boyle, SJ

William M. Watson, SJ

ENCOURAGEMENT FOR THE INCARCERATED

Experiencing the love that bases the existence of every human being is the purpose of St Ignatius' Spiritual Exercises. I found a strong confirmation in the story told in Ritchie's letters from prison. Reading them is an invitation to travel that path open to every human being. It is an invitation to open the doors to the spiritual path that leads to the encounter with Jesus Christ.
Fr. Arturo Sosa Abascal, S.J., Superior General of the Society of Jesus

"I, Paul, a prisoner of the Lord, Jesus Christ..." reveals the point of origin for these important letters to you who are incarcerated in body and in spirit. The pilgrimage of prayer, begun in Paul, continuing through Ignatius Loyola, and now revealed in FORTY WEEKS... testifies to God's personal outreach towards you with Healing, Hope, and Help. Prisoners welcome letters. Always have. Now you have an abundance of mail.
Fr. Stephen Barber, S.J., Chaplain Emeritus, San Quentin State Prison

Find your own voice and story through the journey of this book. When you do, your story will be aligned to the affection of God for you and everything belongs in this glorious mosaic and nothing is a waste. For your story is magnificent and indeed sacred.
Fr. Greg Boyle, S.J., Founder: Homeboy Industries; author of Tattoos on the Heart

The knowledge of God through direct experience is available to anyone who seeks it sincerely, regardless of past actions or present circumstances. Those who choose to make such a journey always succeed and the fruits are eternal. May FORTY WEEKS - Letters from Prison, be this for you.
Michael Brown - Author of The Presence Process

Join Ritchie and Fr. Bill on a path to encounter unconditional love. Take the time to discover how you are loved beyond our understanding by a God who created you in his image and likeness. You were created with so many unique gifts and talents. As our attachments fall and we gain freedoms, we must gently recognize our brokenness and areas where we need healing. Take a chance like Ritchie did on a lifelong relationship with God: a God who will give you peace and will always have your back. This book is a gift that will keep on giving. Stick with it.

Karen Clifton, Director Catholic Mobilizing Network

"Nothing is more personal, valuable and heartfelt to an incarcerated person than their "inner landscape," esp. when the outer landscape of their cell and unit is so noisy, restrictive and depersonalizing. But it often takes quite a while for an imprisoned person's heart and soul to become a quiet and safe place that has clarity and is peaceful and hope-filled, as it is also at the same time a place of confusion, painful memories and frustrated longings.

God is the only One who can help an imprisoned person enter into the depths of their heart and soul, in order to begin a journey together in which he or she discovers their deepest and truest self and God's chosen purpose for their life's journey. It's never too late to begin that journey with God and experience what God has always had in store for those God loves—and God loves prisoners in a special and unique way. FORTY WEEKS and its exercises provide a sure and steady path while imprisoned to authentic self-knowledge and a transforming experience of God's unconditional love."

Rick Deshaies, S.J. Chair: American Catholic Correctional Chaplains

"To you who are holding this book, please know that your journey of prayer and writing can change your mind and open your heart....and stimulate spiritual transformation like it did for Ritchie. I know this too from 25 years of correspondence with inmates around the country-- mostly boys and men who have committed murder, and are seeking a way back into the light of the human community from the darkness that engulfed them in years gone by.

Allow yourself to meet Christ in written and spoken dialogue through

FORTY WEEKS. It will offer a path to your soul to make that journey. I will rejoice every day in the opportunity to prayerfully accompany you who take the journey."
James Garbarino, PhD, Author of Why Giving Teenage Killers a Second Chance Matters for All of Us

Do you want your stony heart replaced by a tender, responsive one (Ezek 36:29)? Enter the sacred Ignatian space offered to us by Bill Watson's SJ, new work, Forty Weeks: Letters from Prison. You'll have Bill and an incarcerated saint named Richard Roman, guide you out of your darkness and shadow of death into a land of peace. As a person who has worked with the incarcerated for many years, I say: Read this book. It will touch the secrets of your heart!
Michael E. Kennedy, SJ, Jesuit Restorative Justice Initiative

This beautiful book, which puts into action Jesus's call for us to minister to the imprisoned, is a series of open and honest letters between a Catholic priest and an inmate in a federal prison. By turns painful, heartfelt and inspiring, the communications between these two men, who are both seeking God in their lives, helps us understand how God's mercy never abandons anyone."
James Martin, SJ, Author of Jesus: A Pilgrimage and The Jesuit Guide.

"I was in prison and you came to visit Me," Jesus told his followers. In this inspiring volume Christ's love visits your prison cell through Fr. Bill Watson's Ignatian Examen and compassion-filled letters, and speaks back through the voice of Ritchie, a convicted man. The result is salvation for one human being, and a deep teaching not only for his fellow inmates but for all of us incarcerated in the self-constructed prisons of our minds.
Dr. Gabor Maté, author of In the Realm of Hungry Ghosts: Close Encounters with Addiction

I am no expert on how to live a life, but, my life has been changed from hearing the stories of the many men and women who are behind the walls. Use FORTY WEEKS ~ Letters from Prison to share your story, own your story, live your story. At the core of every story is a desire to love and be loved. I'm a grateful recipient and so will you. You who walk this journey are in my prayers.

Zachariah F. Presutti SJ, LMSW, Thrive for Life Prison Project

Congratulations on your decision to explore the nature of your unfolding story! Use FORTY WEEKS ~ Letters from Prison to learn to know yourself through self-examination. Let the Holy Spirit guide you on this exciting journey as your friendship with Jesus deepens. Be filled with peace and grace as you draw closer to God.

Douglas A. Sandvig, KM, Order of Malta- Federal Association, U.S.A., Prison Ministry

Real freedom begins in our hearts and minds. The Spiritual Exercises are a powerful way to connect with the One who came to set us free from all kinds of prisons. May your journey with FORTY WEEKS bring you to true freedom in Christ!

Fr. George Williams, S.J., Catholic Chaplain, San Quentin State Prison; President, Dismas Ministry

LETTERS FROM PRISON ~ WORTH OF SOULS

 FORTY WEEKS ~ Letters from Prison is collaborating with our award winning songwriters and singers on an album titled, Worth of Souls. Our record label, Stone Angel Music Inc. and Sacred Story Institute are still working to find a way to get this music to the incarcerated in prisons as *Letters from Prison* goes to press. In the meantime, we will provide a link for free downloads to interested prison chaplains and those who work with the incarcerated. Contact us at: https://sacredstory.net/forty-weeks/ and fill out the interest form under Prison Ministry.

Millions of you who are incarcerated have suffered life-long depression. Thousands have given up. The underlying cause of suicide is an unbearable pain derived from a pervasive sense of hopelessness, a loss or lack of connection to others and a life-long pattern of self-destruction.

Worth of Souls is a team of award winning recording artists who've produced an altruistic album of original and award winning contemporary Christian songs that promote the Savior's unconditional love and mercy. Music has been clinically proven to calm anxiety and ease pain and we hope it has that effect on you.

Because many of you who are incarcerated have been called unworthy and don't know your value, all of us who worked on this project pray that it can plant seeds of faith and restore confidence in yourself and your ability to let go and let the Savior manage your life. May *FORTY WEEKS ~ Letters From Prison* and the songs on Worth of Souls be effective tools for you whether you are the prodigal, the pilgrim, the doubter, the saint. Each of you is in our prayers.
Sincerely,

Paul Cardall, President of Stone Angel Music Inc.

Other Books by William M. Watson, SJ

Sacred Story:
An Ignatian Examen for the Third Millennium

Forty Weeks: An Ignatian Path to Christ
with Sacred Story Prayer (English and Spanish)

Inviting God into Your Life:
A Practical Guide for Prayer

Sacred Story Rosary:
An Ignatian Way to Pray the Mysteries (English and Spanish)

Sacred Story Affirmations

The Whole-Life Confession (English and Spanish)

My Sacred Story Missal

Understanding the Spiritual World

Sacred Story Press
1401 E Jefferson St, STE 405
Seattle, WA 98122

website: sacredstory.net

Dedicated to Our Lady of the Way

IMPRIMI POTEST
Scott R. Santarosa, S.J.

IMPRIMATUR
George V. Murry, S.J.
Bishop of Youngstown

Unless otherwise indicated, Scripture quotations are from the Holy Bible, New American Bible, revised edition © 2010, 1991, 1986, 1970 Confraternity of Christian Doctrine, Washington, D.C.

Cover photograph by William Watson, S.J.
St. Ignatius Answers Prisoner's Prayers, The Gesu: Rome, Italy
Jacket and Book Design: William Watson, SJ
General Editor: Betsy Stokes ~ Copy Editor: Eileen Meinert

Manufactured in the United States of America
ISBN-13:978-1983779671
ISBN-10:1983779679

DEDICATION

 I wish to express my heartfelt thanks to the person most responsible for making this book possible, Deacon Patrick B. Logsdon: 11/19/1948 ~ 11/3/2017. "Deacon Pat" introduced Richard R. Roman to my *Forty Weeks* program in 2013. Deacon Pat first met Ritchie when he was in his early twenties and has helped him as a caring friend and spiritual guide for many years. This book and my collaboration with Ritchie happened only because of the selfless work and dedication of Deacon Pat.

Deacon Pat ran Anthony House for thirty years, a transitional home on Long Island, New York. At Anthony House, Deacon Pat gave nine men at a time a bed, counseling, tough love and home-cooked meals. Many of these men served for decades in prison, were homeless or addicts, and due to Deacon Pat's dedication, were given that second or third chance they needed to find a new life. He knew it was dangerous work but it was also a faith mission he happily embraced. Deacon Pat's life was ended on November 3rd, 2017 by one of the men he served.

I dedicate this version of *Forty Weeks* to Deacon Pat Logsdon, and the many prison chaplains and inmates who work and live on life's margins. Deacon Pat, your life-long work of mercy will live on through this book which you inspired. You will continue to help thousands to find Christ's healing love and peace. Thank you for your life of faith and loving service.

Deacon Pat, please pray for us.

Fr. Bill Watson, S.J.

"The LORD looked down from the holy heights,
viewed the earth from heaven, To attend to the groaning of the
prisoners, to release those doomed to die."
Ps 102: 19-20

CONTENTS

Foreword

My Friend,

For thirty-four years I've worked with gang members in Los Angeles. The day will simply not come when I am more noble, have more courage or am closer to God than the thousands of men and women I've come to know through Homeboy Industries. For many years, people have sometimes accused me of wasting my time in walking with gang members and the incarcerated. The Prophet Jeremiah writes, "For in this place of which you say, it is a waste...there will be heard again, the voice of mirth and the voice of gladness...the voices of those who sing" (Jer 33: 10-11).

Recently I took two homies, Louie and Joe, brothers, out to eat. They are in their late 20's and Joe is the older brother by two years. It's a burger place, a cut above fast food, with menus and a waiter. The two brothers order burgers and suddenly, in unison, ask the waiter nervously: "It doesn't come with mayonnaise, does it?" The waiter assured them that if they didn't want mayonnaise, he'd not put it on their burgers.

"You're BOTH allergic to mayonnaise?" I ask, as the waiter retreats. They proceed to explain their aversion. They both grew up in a very chaotic, violent and extremely abusive household. I would not have survived a single day of their childhoods. They were taken from their parents and raised by an erratic grandmother. The hallmark of their brief time with her was that they were always hungry. Starving, in fact. Most days, the only food they had in the house was flour and mayonnaise. So the grandmother would make these horrific, hockey-puck-like biscuits of flour and mayonnaise. They were hard to stomach.

When the waiter arrives with the dinner, they again ask, "No mayonnaise, right?"

They tell me that when they were nine and seven, they'd go to the local church on "food pantry" day and would be given a box of canned goods that they would lug home. "It was mainly crap," Louie tells me. "You know, lima beans, peas, stuff people didn't want?" Then Joe adds, "but then there were the silver cans."

There were usually about five silver cans where the label had fallen off and the two young brothers would pull chairs up to the kitchen counter and one by one they'd open the silver cans. First, though, they'd say this prayer together, with folded hands and eyes closed: "Please be pineapple. Please be pineapple." Louie, as the older brother, would operate the can opener. "And it was almost always crap...stuff you didn't know what it was."

"But once, it was different," Louie says. They say their "Please be pineapple" prayer, he opens it and Louie, in the telling of the story says; "And the gates of heaven were opened." The tiny brothers turn and look at each other, tears making their way down their cheeks. They lock eyes and whisper in unison: "Applesauce." Their tears flow freely now. "Applesauce."

Two brothers, in this together, telling their story, finding their voices, and inhabiting life as a most sacred story, even in its deprivation and hunger. The tender glance of God and a renewed commitment to live more fully in each other's hearts.

The book you hold in your hands will awaken you to your own sacred story and you will begin to hear your voice...singing. This experience will come gradually as you engage the spiritual exercises in this book. You will retrieve memories and real pain and find a new way to see it all as God does...in mercy, forgiveness, and with unconditional love.

To you who take this path, presently incarcerated, these letters and the

2

process of the *Forty Weeks* will re-introduce you to yourself with God's own vision and heart. The spiritual exercises you will engage allow the tender glance of God to reach your heart so he can show you how to live your life as a sacred story. Along with this, comes the sure and certain knowledge of who you are in God's eyes: EXACTLY what God had in mind when God made you.

You will be heartened by Ritchie Roman's spiritual journey, as he finds "God in all things" in the unfolding layers of his story. His journey from tragedy to hope becomes yours as he surrenders to a new and spacious lens from which to view what he has endured in his life...and to see it all in a different way. The graciousness so evident in these letters reveals the unshakable goodness in each one of you who will accompany this text. And undeniably, it will reveal the "God who is always greater" as St. Ignatius says, who loves you without measure and without regret.

So surrender to the God who longs to love you without measure and without regret. This is the God whose joy has always been to love you...and to deliver anonymous cans of applesauce.

For in this place of which you say, it is a waste...
there will be heard again, the voice of mirth
and the voice of gladness...the voices of those who sing.

Find your own voice and story through the journey of this book. When you do, your story will be aligned to the affection of God for you and everything belongs in this glorious mosaic and nothing is a waste. For your story is magnificent and indeed sacred.

Fr. Greg Boyle, S.J

Introduction to The Letters

Dear Friend:

In August of 2016, I received a letter from a federal inmate seeking spiritual advice. His name is Richard Rafael Roman or just simply, Ritchie. He had been given a copy of *Forty Weeks* by a Catholic deacon friend of his: Patrick Logsdon. Their relationship went back to 1987 when Ritchie lived in Anthony House, a Catholic transitional home for addicts and former felons seeking a way back into society. The house was run by Deacon Pat and sponsored by the St. Vincent de Paul Society in the Diocese of Rockville Centre, NY.

Ritchie, in his early fifties when he first contacted me, was starting year nineteen of a twenty-five-year sentence for armed bank robbery. He was sent to prison in 1997. We corresponded for a month or so before I suggested he go through the *Forty Weeks* program a second time. My proposal was that if he would write me questions for each week of the program, I would send him advice. The covenant was that I wanted his permission to publish our correspondence in a version of *Forty Weeks* to be called *Letters from Prison*.

It was placed on my heart to help Ritchie, both from Deacon Pat's encouragement and description of Ritchie's faith journey, and Ritchie's own sincerity in asking me for guidance. But always seeking the Magis of St. Ignatius (the greater good), I was convinced that working together we could help many like you find the Lord of healing, hope, and peace through a special edition of *Forty Weeks*.

If the *Forty Weeks* spiritual program was helping Ritchie so much, how many more could be helped with the addition of his personal story and reflections, along with some of my own spiritual advice? Ritchie readily agreed and said I could publish all of his letters.

It seemed practical to have our back and forth correspondence specific to each week, placed at the end of the exercises for that week. This way, when you are doing the program, you can benefit each step of the way by Ritchie's own spiritual journey and some of my input: almost like listening to your own life through Ritchie's life.

This book is intended for those of you who find yourself in jail or prison and like Ritchie, want a spiritual resource that offers practical steps to build a relationship with Christ and a life of prayer and discernment. It is also for your friends and family and the many chaplains who serve you in prisons and jails everywhere.

In this introduction, let me share with you the initial correspondence I had with both Deacon Pat and Ritchie before Ritchie and I started the letters in the book. It tells the story of how this project came about. It might also help you overcome some of the fear you may experience embarking upon this journey to Christ through your own sacred story. And yes, you do have a story that is sacred and holy.

Before reading the initial correspondence, let me give you some helpful background information on Ritchie and the people that helped him begin his own sacred story.

Tuesday of Thanksgiving week of 2017, as editing work was being completed on this book, Ritchie called me from his Federal Prison. It was Ritchie, I knew, because of the "Unknown Caller" on the screen. Not able to answer the phone because I was driving, lost, and late for an appointment, we did not make contact till the next day.

When we did make contact, Ritchie told me that Deacon Pat had been murdered on the 3rd of the month. It was hard for me to process the news. At first, I was numb and then began to realize the full impact of Ritchie's loss and that of so many men who had been helped by Deacon Pat. In a later letter Ritchie described his experience of losing Deacon Pat:

"The brutal death of Deacon Pat has hit me hard. He has been my sole connection to the outside world for almost ten years. I relied on Pat for all my needs—spiritual guidance, emotional support, and religious education. He was my only source of financial support. I would not be at this stage in my walk with Christ without him. Right now I feel like I am floundering aimlessly."

Ritchie, by God's grace, has begun to find some peace and hope in the months after Deacon Pat's death. In the course of doing *Forty Weeks*, Ritchie transferred from a penitentiary in the South to one in the Mid-West where he was accepted for the Life Connections Program (LCP).[1] We have secured financial support for him so he can stay at penitentiary to complete LCP. He hopes to be able to do the Residential Drug Program once Life Connections is completed. We will also continue our correspondence and periodically publish the Letters to help you reading this find a path to peace and hope amidst life's many difficulties.

Ritchie's other close friend and confidant, the man Ritchie said "knew his whole life story," was Fr. Mychal Judge, OFM. Ritchie met Fr. Judge at an AA meeting and after hearing his testimony, asked Fr. Judge to be his sponsor. "I'd never had anyone in my life to whom I'd told everything. He knew my whole life and didn't judge. He knew a lot of people, but always found time for me."

Fr. Judge was a chaplain to the New York Fire Department. He lost his life from flying debris in the terrorist attacks on the World Trade Center at 9:59 AM on that fateful day of 9/11. He was in the North tower lobby of when the South Tower collapsed. Fr. Judge was designated as "Victim

0001," the first certified fatality of 9/11, because his was the first body to be recovered and taken to the medical examiner. Cause of death was blunt force trauma to the head.

Ritchie wrote about the experience of knowing and losing Deacon Pat and Fr. Judge: "Having one person only, and that person totally being there for you in dire times, they become etched in your heart and their memory will never diminish. At different times, both Pat and Mychal were that person. I think of both of them every day. Not only missing them, but knowing they are in heaven and I will see them again someday. And any good I am able to do in this world will be a direct result of knowing them. That's the truth."

We must take heart that God's love always finds us and always sends angels our way to help us. Some are spiritual beings, like the saints and angels. That is why I chose the book cover that represents St. Ignatius Loyola in heaven, answering the prayers of prisoners. And some of those angels will be friends in this life, Like Deacon Pat and Fr. Judge for Ritchie. You can trust that they watch out for you and by their prayers and intercession on your behalf, will ensure that you complete your own sacred story.

Dear friend, believe in your heart that no matter the tragedies visited upon you through no fault of your own, and those that through your own choice, have brought hurt to yourself and others, they can never separate you from the love and mercy of God in Christ Jesus. St. Paul, before his conversion, hunted down and participated in the murder of those who followed Jesus. Later, God's work of mercy in him made him the greatest Apostle of the Christian faith. In Romans Eight, St. Paul expresses this boundless mercy of Jesus Christ better than anyone. Get your bible and read the whole chapter but here are the final two verses, 38-39:

For I am convinced that neither death, nor life, nor angels, nor principalities, nor present things, nor future things, nor powers, nor height, nor depth, nor any other creature will be able to separate us from the love of God in Christ Jesus our Lord.

Like Ritchie on his journey of faith and healing, even with the death of both Deacon Pat and Fr. Mychal, always have hope that God will be with you and stand with you and support you, no matter what you have done or where you find yourself. I will be praying daily for you who use this path to discover the limitless mercy and love of God in Jesus Christ. He is our Divine Physician.

Dear friend, you are in my prayers.

Peace,

Fr. Bill Watson, S.J.
January 25, 2018
The Conversion of St. Paul

FORTY WEEKS ~ LETTERS FROM PRISON
MINISTRY FOR INMATES

To Inmates, Chaplains and Friends:

If you are an inmate and have a copy of *Forty Weeks Letters from Prison* and would like to have someone to correspond with you over the course of the program as I did with Ritchie, please write to us at the address below. We will work to find you a good spiritual guide and friend to help you with your questions.

To initiate the process, send us in two pages your life story and why you want to begin this walk with Jesus over the course of forty weeks. We will read what you say and work to find you a good spiritual guide and friend to correspond with you and help you along the way as I did with Ritchie.

If you are a prison chaplain or a friend who wants to participate in our letter writing program or help us with this project, please go to our website (https://sacredstory.net/forty-weeks/) and you will find a link to give us the information we need to get you involved.

FORTY WEEKS ~ Letters from Prison is collaborating with Paul Cardall and award winning songwriters and singers on an album titled, Worth of Souls. The record label, Stone Angel Music Inc. and Sacred Story Institute are still working to find a way to get this music to the incarcerated in prisons as *Letters from Prison* goes to press. In the meantime, we will provide a link for free downloads to interested prison chaplains and those who work with the incarcerated. Contact us at: https://sacredstory.net/forty-weeks/ and fill out the interest form under Letters from Prison -- Prison Ministry.

Sacred Story Institute
Letters from Prison Project
1401 E Jefferson, STE 405
Seattle, WA 98122
https://sacredstory.net/forty-weeks/

Preliminary Letters of Deacon Pat and Fr. Bill

Hello Father Bill,

I just read the Sacred Story Newsletter and saw your letter from Ritchie Roman. I am the one who sent him your books these past years. I have used your books with other prisoners and they have found them very helpful.

I have known Ritchie for many years (he was a resident in our program back in the 1980's) and the conversion he has gone through these past years is incredible. Any support or encouragement you can give him would be such a blessing. You have no idea what it would mean to him.

I have pages of his letters where he talks about his conversion and his deepening walk with Christ. You may want to encourage him to share more and put it in some newsletters. There are so many in prisons, in recovery, and in such an inner mess that I really feel this letter to you by Ritchie is Christ knocking on your door to reach out to people in this situation.

Thank you again for your work, God is using it to bless many.

Sincerely,

Deacon Patrick
Anthony House

ᛋ

Dear Patrick:

I was unaware you were in our newsletter database. Thank you for reaching out. I was going to write to you as Ritchie suggested to confirm that he was "legitimate." I only published part of his letter and did not want to reveal his full name or location.

Thank you for giving prisoners copies of Forty Weeks and my other books. I am moved that prisoners have found Christ through them. I gave my first cousin, a Redemptorist priest chaplain at the federal penitentiary here in Seattle, copies of Forty Weeks for the men's and women's libraries in hopes that some would find the Lord through them.

So my desire has been to reach this population of people on life's margins who need Christ's mercy in very real ways. Maybe if you send a phone number we can chat about some possibilities.

Blessings in your ministry and I look forward to hearing from you.

Peace,

Fr. Bill Watson, S.J.

෫

Dear Father Bill:

Yes, Ritchie is the real thing. I have some incredible letters from him over the years about his conversion process. In most prisons there is very little help in the spiritual life. His last prison just had Mass maybe once a month in Spanish. So that Forty Weeks and your Sacred Story Rosary I sent him offered some structure and guidance.

I really think that your approach in the Forty Weeks could find many who need the message. It is just finding the open doors especially for those in recovery and 12-step groups. I know many would find it a big help. Maybe some connection with the Matt Talbot retreats all over the country?

I would be happy to talk with you and share ideas, insights and thoughts. I have been running this home for prisoners, recovering, homeless for 32 years so I know the neighborhood.

About 16 years ago I had friends who were very involved in starting Centering Prayer in prisons. They started in Folsom prison and it spread. They made some good videos through the Centering Prayer Group, ltd.

But my concern (not to criticize CP) was that about 99% of the men cannot really handle silence as a positive experience. For so many of *them silence has been a source of punishment from an early age and awakens too many demons in them. They can handle silence in short periods but it is often a cause of restlessness.*

I feel the better approach is one that gives more content, helps them understand and integrate their human journey and provides tools that help them deal with their real life. Which is why I find Forty Weeks helpful for them because it is a good blend of spiritual principles, recovery insights, and human psychology.

Well enough on this - time to cook dinner and I would be happy to keep in touch!

pat

Anthony House

☙

Hello Patrick:

Thank you again for reaching out. I have attached the letter I sent to Ritchie and I hope he responds positively (see page xviii).

Maybe we can set up a time for a phone call next week. Let me know if you have some time and what works best.

My prayers for your important work.

Peace,

Fr. Bill

☙

Hello Fr. Bill,

Great to get your letter. Ritchie is bright and perceptive, but has little formal education which he is self-conscious about, so he may need a little extra encouragement and patience. The whole prison environment is set up to just cause chronic low-grade depression, especially as men get older. Also, on a practical note, Ritchie has no support on the outside. I help him with a few $ as I can, and will make sure he has enough for postage, etc.

I am not sure how much contact you have had with prisoners and the prison system, but a very good, short book to check out is A Saint on Death Row by Thomas Cahill. He uses "saint" in the spiritual and not religious sense. It is an excellent look into the prison life and a touching story of a young man's life.

Yes I would enjoy talking with you. I figure you are out west ? and I am Long Island so we just need to work out the time. About the only time not good for me is between 5pm to 7pm (eastern time) each day. But if you give me a heads up, we can work out almost any other time.

Just to give you some context about me. I am a deacon in the Rockville Centre Diocese, since 1990. I have been here at Anthony House since 1984. The focus of our program here is to help men (in recovery, homeless, coming from incarceration etc.) to get back to independent living.

I was a high school teacher, then worked with LA gang kids for a number of years after college. Then I spent a few years in a contemplative monastery, after that I lived with the Little Brothers (of Charles de Foucault) helping them run a shelter in the bowery of Manhattan and worked with Salvadorian refugees in San Antonio.

Then I ended up here; after a year or so they asked me to consider being sponsored as a deacon for this ministry. I am single, not sponsored by a parish for parish work but to run this ministry/outreach. I was approved and have been here since. So I am an "embedded" deacon, living at the house and have this ministry to befriend, accompany, and serve those who come here and those we reach out to in the neighborhood and community.

Over the years as more men were incarcerated, our outreach to prisoners increased. We usually have around 100 inmates writing and calling us. Many calls are for information on our program and for help when released, others just to keep in touch and have an outside *connection.*

Ritchie was here back in 1987 and we have had contact off and on, especially for the past 10 years or so.

Well if I keep writing, we won't have anything to talk about!

pat

> "...He who refreshes others will himself be refreshed."
> (Proverbs 11:25)

ᘓ

Hello Pat:

I am just back after Labor Day break. Thank you so much for this information and the story of your life's work and your important ministry. I am very moved by it and feel blessed by your work.

I remembered you and your apostolate at Mass yesterday on the Feast of the Birth of Mary.

I have you on my calendar to call you tomorrow, Wednesday, at about 5 PM your time (2 PM my time). Looking forward to it and let me know if Wednesday does not work and we can find another day.

Peace and prayers,

Fr. Bill

ᘓ

Dear Fr. Bill,

Thanks for the call and for the prayers, especially at holy mass. I am letting the ideas "percolate" and will see if the holy spirit pops up with something or opens any doors.

One point I forgot to mention is that you may want check out some deacons/formation programs? Maybe a presentation at some deacon retreats or their formation programs. Also, most of the dioceses out here require continuing education and Forty Weeks would fit right in for some credits.

I am not the man for deacon contacts. If you are single as a deacon, you never "fit in", if you are not involved in parish work. You really don't fit in and end up being an enigma that no one knows how you got to be a deacon!

Since Pope Francis, I have been blessed with all the affirmation I can handle that this is a valid but little understood way to live the diaconate. But there are thousands of deacons, in parishes, and chaplains in jails and prisons. I think many could really benefit from Forty Weeks in their own lives and could share it with those in their ministry.

Keep praying for all of us here!

pat

"...He who refreshes others will himself be refreshed."
(Proverbs 11:25)

ര

Hello Deacon Pat:

I did offer that Mass and will keep you in prayers. Yes, I do have plans for Deacons but that will be a year or two out. I will let you know when I hear from Ritchie. Prayers for your labors and may they be richly blessed.

Peace to you,

Fr. Bill

ര

Fr Bill,

I received a good letter from Ritchie today, he was very excited over your offer and told me he is "all in". He was very excited and mentioned a number of times how happy he feels and how good things are.

He has not had many happy days in his life. It made his day hearing from you so I know you will be hearing from him soon.

Please keep praying for all of us here. I am not getting younger and am running this place by myself 24/7. Hopefully we will find someone interested in this type of ministry.

If I can be of more help, just email me but looks like you and Ritchie are starting a journey and I do my best when I stay out of the way!

pat

"...He who refreshes others will himself be refreshed."

(Proverbs 11:25)

Deacon Patrick
Anthony House

 C3

Preliminary Letters of Richie and Fr. Bill

To Whom It May Concern,

My name is Richard Rafael Roman and I am a fifty-two-year-old Federal inmate currently residing at a U.S. Penitentiary. I've been incarcerated for nineteen years and I am scheduled for release in 2021.

Over the years I've become prolific at praying but something was lacking. God had already decided that my life here on earth was to become dedicated to prayer and service. I was stuck as to how to go about it.

A few years ago, my only friend in this world sent me a copy of Fr. Watson's Forty Weeks: An Ignatian Path to Christ with Sacred Story Prayer. It changed my life. The prayer structure was exactly what I needed; not to mention the many similarities between St. Ignatius' story and mine. I've learned that I am definitely not unique.

Forty Weeks was followed by Sacred Story Rosary and just recently, The Whole Life Confession. All of these books have been exceedingly enlightening and helpful. Without them I'd still be fighting the daily urge to give up. With them I've been able to accept God's grace and ward off the enemy of my authentic human nature. Fr. Bill's books have been a blessing. But believe me, it's still a battle, made a bit more difficult by being in here.

My friend who sent me these books is a Catholic Deacon and he runs a halfway house for alcoholic ex-convicts on Long Island. He is an awesome man. Unfortunately for me he is a very busy man and he readily admits he doesn't really have the time for meaningful correspondence with me. I'd mentioned in the past that I really would like to have someone to learn from and to share my spiritual/sacred story journey with. He suggested I pray about it and things will happen like they should.

I must admit that I hadn't mentioned that in my prayers in quite a while. Then last week, the day after concluding *The Whole Life Confession* during my evening 15-minute prayer session it occurred to me to write the Sacred Story Institute for some guidance.

I realize this is not an ordinary request. If you could possibly put me in contact with someone who would share his/her experience with me and help guide me along on my journey I'd appreciate it very much.

I have no ulterior motives for this request other than my desire to overcome all the obstacles to my discipleship and to become the man God created me to be. If necessary, I can furnish you with my friend, Deacon Pat's, contact information. I am sure he would vouch for my intentions.

Thank you very much for any help you can provide on this matter. God bless Fr. Bill Watson and the Sacred Story Institute.

Sincerely,

Richard Roman

ԱՇ

Dear Ritchie:

Thank you for your note. I can say it brought me consolation to know that someone in prison was brought closer to the Lord through Forty Weeks. I'd like to use your more familiar name, Ritchie.

Deacon Pat reached out to me to confirm that you are the "real deal" as he says, and that your journey to Christ has been remarkable. I published the section of your letter below on our sacredstory.net web newsletter today and left specific identifiers out to protect you. I have received quite a few responses that it has brought hope to many people, including Deacon Pat.

Deacon Pat said he has quite a few letters from you about your spiritual journey over the years. He believes your reaching out to me and my *publishing your letter is a sign that I should be reaching out to those in prison to offer them spiritual help.*

Perhaps you might be interested in helping with this project. Here is what I propose: I propose that you write me once a month about your spiritual journey—say two to three pages. It will help for me to have the knowledge of where you were before you met Christ and the process that led to your "conversion". If you can focus your questions and queries about your journey using the Forty Weeks program, that will be a big help.

I will send you a response back to those monthly letters with some spiritual advice. To help others, I would like to publish those in a new version of Forty Weeks as "Letters from Prison". It can be used as a spiritual tool for outreach to others who are incarcerated and for their relatives. Let's see if we can bring others to Christ with the Forty Weeks Program. This will give you a way to help others from prison. Perhaps this will make your time remaining more hopeful and give you a focus for what you can do after you leave prison in 2021.

I can leave out your full name and remove any things that might identify you if you like but I will leave that up to you.

I think this way I can help you and we can help many others who might need the spiritual guidance and consolation that a conversion like yours can inspire in people.

Let me know if you like this idea, Ritchie, and we can go from there.

I will offer Mass for you today and pray that the Lord Jesus hold you close.

Peace,

Fr. Bill Watson, S.J.

ᘛ

Dear Fr. Bill

Thank you very much for responding to my letter so quickly. I wasn't quite sure what to expect when I wrote but I was pleasantly surprised to hear from you personally. And your proposed "Letters from Prison" project definitely exceeded my expectations.

I am glad that Deacon Pat has come forward and "vouched" for me. He was working at Anthony House when I went through there thirty years ago. He's still there doing God's work. Although it was thirty years ago, I still have fond memories of my stay at the house.

Pat and I lost contact with each other and restarted our friendship when Pat looked me up and found me in prison nine years ago. And I sure am glad he did. Pat referring to me as the "real deal" is probably the best compliment I could possibly receive. It means a lot to me considering how I used to be.

Pat is very busy. He will readily admit that he doesn't have the time necessary to correspond with me on a regular basis. A couple of years ago I asked him if he would try to find someone who would be interested in corresponding with me regularly in order to share my journey and to have someone who could advise me when things get tough. Pat told me to just hold on, that things would work themselves out. Two years later I found your address in the back of The Whole-life Confession. What's funny is the address was also in the back of Forty Weeks which I've had for almost three years. Things obviously work out when and how they are supposed to.

I just wanted to get a letter out to you quickly to let you know that I am grateful for your interest and support. I cannot fully explain the emotional lift your response has given me. I have high hopes for this relationship and look forward to your spiritual advice.

Tonight, I will begin writing about where I was before I met Christ. I'm not sure how much detail is necessary, but I will pray and let Jesus guide me.

Feel free to publish anything you deem to be helpful or interesting to others. Edit at your discretion. You may use my full name and all other identifiers. Everything I share with you is fair game. I would be alright with you publishing my mailing address in case anyone wanted to contact and share with me personally. Obviously, that would be your decision.

The idea of having more of my time being used to talk about Christ and my Sacred Story has me feeling better than I have in a long time. Thank you very much, Fr. Bill.

You should be hearing again from me very soon.

Respectfully,

Ritchie

ॐ

Dear Fr. Bill,

I hope this letter finds you well. I am well, much better since having heard from you. Your letter, with the promise of guidance and advice, along with the proposed "Letters from prison" project has really boosted my outlook and has caused me, without realizing it right away, to recommit and double down on my Sacred Story Prayer practice. Again, thank you for your time and interest.

You had asked me to tell you a bit about my life prior to my "conversion". It is obvious from my return address that my life hasn't been going as I'd hoped. Actually, my life has never gone as I hoped.

I was adopted as a young child. I never felt I belonged to my adoptive family, nor did I have any feelings for my biological family with whom I had very little contact. I had behavioral issues and performed poorly in school.

My military service was less than satisfactory. During the thirteen years between the end of my military service and when I came to prison at the *age of 33 in 1997, I abused alcohol and drugs, worked fifteen different jobs, lived in New York (where I was born and raised), North Carolina, South Carolina, Florida, and California, was arrested five times for petty crimes.*

I went through dozens of "friends". I never really felt close to anyone. Being a selfish and self-centered person made it difficult to have any affection for others. I've never been in a romantic relationship, although I was quite promiscuous.

Over the years I have been an on again, off again member of Alcoholics Anonymous, with varying degrees of success. I'd received my First Holy Communion, attended six years of catechism, and was confirmed. I attended Mass only once or twice per year as an adult. I did not have a relationship with Christ. I barely acknowledged HIM.

During my short-lived career as a criminal and substance abuser I answered to no one. I had no friends and no relationship with God: only my narcissism, run amok.

I am doing time for numerous bank robberies. About nine years ago, after I'd already served ten years in prison, a man I'd known and lost contact with twenty years earlier, Deacon Pat, found me and wrote to me. His arrival back into my life was a gift from God: definitely part of His plan.

At the time I didn't have a friend in the world. I wasn't receiving mail and I had no one to call. Pat caught me at the right time. After a few letters he suggested I pray the rosary. At first my heart wasn't in it but I kept on. I tried other prayer, with the same results.

Then, in July 2013, I found myself in a precarious situation. Being housed in a high security Federal Penitentiary can sometimes lead to dangerous situations, to say the least. I found myself in such a situation, with what seemed to me at the time, only two possible outcomes. Neither one good. This was a life/death situation.

I spent all night silently praying: silently because I had a cellmate. Finally, at my wit's end, I prayed something like "If anyone doesn't deserve your mercy it is me. I know you did not create me for this. All I ask is that your will be done". The next day the other part of my situation was inexplicably transferred quickly out of my area of the institution. I haven't seen or heard from him since.

We've all prayed for situations to work out in our favor. Sometimes the results are exactly what we were hoping for. But this time it wasn't the result that changed my thinking.

I didn't say to myself "wow, prayer really works!" Instead, I was overcome with gratitude and the realization that God loves me. Despite me. That Jesus died on the cross for me. That it was time to start living the life God created me for.

I still didn't know what to do with my newfound realizations. I shared all of this with Pat and he sent me a copy of Forty Weeks. I had found what I was looking for! Right away some of the Sacred Story Affirmations jumped out at me and became part of my daily prayer practice:

Christ, who walked before me, shares my every burden.
Christ, who has walked before me, will help me resolve every crisis.
Christ, who has walked before me, knows my every hope.
Christ, who has walked before me, knows everything I suffer.
Christ, who walks before me, will always lead me home to safety.

Nothing I say or do in the course of the day eases my journey more than the above Affirmation.

Having been a sometimes member of A.A. for years, I've heard a lot of personal stories. None had come as close to my inner thoughts and feelings as Ignatius' story: gambling addict, sexually self-indulgent, arrogant, hot headed and insecure, narcissistic, psychological problems, and sinful "vices". Like Ignatius, I was obsessed with my vain fantasies.

I'd never heard anyone speak of their "narcissistic daydreams". I'd been totally consumed by them for thirty years. They literally ruled my life! Even today these self-centered daydreams find a way into my thoughts while I'm praying the rosary, my fifteen-minute Sacred Story Prayers, even my short prayer upon awakening.

The name I have chosen to use when praying and referring to the Lord is "God of Mercy and Compassion". He has shown me nothing but mercy and compassion since my heart was opened to Him.

Fr. Bill, I know this letter was all over the place and it may contain too much information. Since Forty Weeks and The Whole Life Confession, along with my weekly journal and written reconciliation, I've gotten in the habit of writing. After I hear back from you I will move on more to how things are now, my hopefulness and my difficulties.

Thank you and I hope to hear from you soon.

Respectfully,
Ritchie

ᘓ

Dear Ritchie:

Thank you for your latest letter that I received few days ago. The role of a "spiritual director" is primarily one of listening. You are doing the talking in your letters and I am listening. I will offer some points of reflection based on each of your letters. I am imagining you are sitting in my office offering these points about your life and spiritual journey. I would like you to imagine that you are also here in my office listening to my reply.

I will always focus on what I consider the most important elements from your letters for your own spiritual and human wellbeing. I will also try to help you see more clearly how God is working in your life and how the one St. Ignatius of Loyola calls the "enemy of human nature" is working in your life.

You said you were adopted and never felt like you belonged—either to your adoptive family or your biological family—that you never felt close to anyone. Not having the experience of security and love at a young age was bound to leave emotional and spiritual wounds in your heart. It is understandable why you had behavioral problems.

It is also understandable why you abused alcohol and drugs. A friend of mine, Dr. Gabor Mate, wrote a book called In the Realm of Hungry Ghosts—Close Encounters with Addiction. Gabor lives in Vancouver, British Colombia. He spent many years working at the Portland drop-in clinic in Vancouver where the worst drug abusers used to come for help. He writes:

"The question is never "Why the addiction?" but "Why the pain?". The research literature is unequivocal: most hard-core substance abusers come from abusive homes. The majority of my Skid Row patients suffered severe neglect and maltreatment early in life…. The autobiographical accounts and case files of the Portland residents tell stories of pain upon pain: rape, beatings, humiliation, rejection, abandonment, relentless character assassinations…. Not all addictions are rooted in abuse or trauma, but I do believe they can all be traced to painful experience. A hurt is at the center of all addictive behaviors. It is present in the gambler, the Internet addict, the compulsive shopper and the workaholic. The wound may not be as deep and the ache not as excruciating, and it may even be entirely hidden—but it is there as we'll see, the effects of early stress or adverse experiences directly shape both the psychology and the neurobiology of addiction in the brain." (pgs. 36, 38)

So, look at those early difficult years as possibly leading to the behavioral troubles and you not feeling like you belonged anywhere. Perhaps the loss of security and friendships was the reason you sought escape in alcohol and drugs. And you are correct, pain and the drugs make an individual much more self-focused and unable to reach out to others.

The plan of Satan from the start was to trick us into turning to ourselves and away from God. He knew it would devastate our hearts and make all relationships complicated and difficult. Satan knew the pain would work perfectly for his plan to destroy us, though Jesus would never let that happen.

Satan wanted you to believe that you had made a total mess of your life and you had not the slightest right to expect God's help. Go back and read the parable of the Prodigal Son to see how God responded to someone else who makes a complete mess of his life. Keep recalling too, how the God of Mercy rescued St. Ignatius from a messed-up life.

Look how God reached out to you, Ritchie! When you were at your lowest, Jesus sent Deacon Pat back into your life. He suggested you take the focus from yourself and place it on God when he asked you to pray the Rosary. You indicated praying the Rosary was not helpful, nor were other types of prayer.

Then you had your great crisis—your "life and death" situation as you describe it. You poured out your heart to God at night begging for help and telling God that you don't deserve His mercy. The way you describe this is much like what Peter said when he told Jesus: "Leave me Lord, for I am a sinful man." (Lk 5:8).

But then you made your most powerful surrender. You simply said: "Lord, your will be done," just like Jesus in Gethsemane. The very next day your "life and death" situation ended. You then knew in your heart not only that God is merciful, but that God loves you! You describe being filled with gratitude.

God has always been at your side, Ritchie—when you were given up for adoption, when you abused drugs and alcohol, and when you robbed banks and were sent to prison. And God's response to the sadness you feel in your life is: "I love you, Ritchie, and you are precious in my eyes. I died for you so that you would believe that I love you." Perhaps that is why you chose the name for God: "God of Mercy and Compassion"?

Ritchie, continue to believe not only that God loves you but also that he will use what you think of as the mess of your life and turn it into something beautiful. Continue to pray each day, "Lord, your will be done," and He will lead you to a future of hope.

It is very likely that one day you may be doing for others what Deacon Pat did for you—helping people turn to God when they feel they have made a complete mess of their lives and they no longer believe they deserve God's mercy.

Know you are in my prayers.

Peace,

Fr. Bill Watson, S.J.

PS: I thought you would like this prayer-poem from the 11th century.

We awaken in Christ's body
as Christ awakens our bodies,
and my poor hand is Christ, He enters
my foot, and is infinitely me.

I move my hand, and wonderfully
my hand becomes Christ, becomes all of Him
(for God is indivisibly
whole, seamless in His Godhead).

I move my foot, and at once
He appears like a flash of lightning.
Do my words seem blasphemous? —Then
open your heart to Him

and let yourself receive the one
who is opening to you so deeply.
For if we genuinely love Him,
we wake up inside Christ's body

where all our body, all over,
every most hidden part of it,
is realized in joy as Him
and He makes us, utterly, real,
and everything that is hurt, everything
that seemed to us dark, harsh, shameful,
maimed, ugly, irreparably
damaged, is in Him transformed
and recognized as whole, as lovely,
and radiant in His light,
we awaken as the Beloved
in every last part of our body.
(Symeon the New Theologian, 11th Century)

Dear Fr. Bill,

Upon receiving your reply to my most recent letter I went directly to the Book of Luke and the Parable of the Prodigal Son, as you suggested. I must admit that the parables are not exactly my strong suit. But knowing what to look for made sense of it for me.

The fact that, after a life steeped in narcissism, and being fooled by the enemy of my authentic human nature, God loves me just as much as one who has never strayed, brings tears to my eyes. I am blessed.

When I first opened to Week One of Forty Weeks I couldn't help but be immediately dismayed when I read, "First... this should be a place of quiet, free from technology – a place apart." There really is no such place here. I came very close to giving up right then and there. I knew this wasn't for me. This wouldn't work for me. There is no privacy in prison. There is never quiet.

Even without realizing at the time what force was behind my thoughts about giving up so soon, I continued reading and this Affirmation convinced me to go on:

I will not tire of asking God for help since God delights in my asking.
The urge to stop Sacred Story Practice always
comes before my greatest breakthroughs.

My first breakthrough was the realization that with God, everything is possible. I may not be able to strictly adhere to Sacred Story practice at all times, but God gives me the strength and desire to persevere.

I am almost always able to say my prayers upon waking and retiring, the exercises during the day, and my journals and reconciliations, with minimum interruption. My difficulty is in trying to complete my two fifteen minute daily Sacred Story prayer sessions.

I know it is suggested to sit in a comfortable place and position, a place of quiet. Often times that is possible, but not always. I can sit in the recreation yard and pray and I won't be interrupted. Very often I insert my earbuds, leave my Walkman turned off, and walk the track.

28

Usually, I am not interrupted and am able to pray the entire fifteen minutes while walking laps. But, as I am sure you are aware, even walking without interruption is still a distraction, taking valuable concentration and focus.

Any suggestions on how to overcome the constant noise and motion surrounding me in order to clear my mind and open my heart for my prayer sessions would be helpful.

Fr. Bill, when I do find a good, comfortable, quiet space and I am able to clear my mind of all the craziness surrounding me, my fifteen minute prayers are the highlights of my day: Creation, Presence, Memory, Mercy, and Eternity. Once I get going I don't want to stop. The fifteen minutes go by so quickly.

In addition to the Sacred Story prayer exercises, I also pray the Rosary twice daily. One of my rosary prayers is always the Mysteries which are generally prayed on that given day. But I also always pray the mysteries of sorrow each day. They have a special place in my heart. They are the mysteries that make me feel closest to my Savior. The Sacred Story Rosary has helped me come to appreciate the Rosary.

In a relatively short time I have gone from the ho-hum drudgery of praying the Rosary to not being able to get through the day without it. I've awakened in the middle of the night realizing I hadn't prayed the Rosary.

I live in a two-man cell so I just quietly lie in bed and pray while counting the Hail Mary's on my fingers. I often pray the Rosary prior to my fifteen-minute prayer sessions. It helps to get me focused and motivated for my Sacred Story Prayer.

I realize that everyone is different. No one's prayer life is exactly the same. God has made it clear to me that prayer is to be a huge part of my life. The Sacred Story prayer has provided the structure I've been searching for. I have a lot of work to do in order to maximize my efforts. I have a lot to learn.

Again, I thank you very much for your thoughtfulness and assistance in my journey. I look forward to your continued guidance.

Respectfully, Ritchie

Thank you for the 11th Century prayer-poem

∽

Dear Ritchie:

This will be a short letter as I want to propose a way to conduct our letter writing that will give more focus.

I would ask that you start Forty Weeks over again. I would like you to send me short letters of no more than 4-5 pages. I would like you to do four weeks at a time and send me reflections/questions for each of the four weeks: WEEK ONE, WEEK TWO, etc.

I will respond to the reflections/questions for each week. This will give more structure to your reflections and also give us something other inmates might find useful and possibly lead them to take the Forty Weeks journey.

Keep trying to find those quiet places in the penitentiary and keep up your habit of the Rosary and the daily Examen prayer. There is a saying that every saint has a past and every sinner has a future. I hope you find that consoling. I do!

You remain in my prayers, Ritchie.

Peace,

Fr. Bill Watson, S.J

FORTY WEEKS

Letters From Prison

There are very few who realize what God would
make of them if they abandoned themselves
entirely to His hands, and let themselves be formed
by His grace. A thick and shapeless tree trunk
would never believe that it could become a statue,
admired as a miracle of sculpture...and would
never consent to submit itself to the chisel of the
sculptor who, as St. Augustine says, sees by his
genius what he can make of it. Many people who,
we see, now scarcely live as Christians, do not
understand that they could become saints, if they
would let themselves be formed by the grace of
God, if they did not ruin His plans by resisting the
work which He wants to do.

St. Ignatius Loyola[2]

Introduction

St. Ignatius became a great spiritual guide by surrendering his heart to Christ under the guidance of the Church. He passed his wisdom along in his Spiritual Exercises and the methods of Examen (on which Forty Weeks is based), and in his letters and instructions. His spiritual disciplines invite a deep, personal relationship with Christ. It is Christ's forgiving and healing love that burns away the selfishness and hardheartedness of sin's legacy in one's history, transforming it into a sacred story, with fruit that endures to eternity.

Following Ignatius's wisdom, all you need to engage this spiritual journey is a generous heart and a willingness to be transformed by Christ's purifying forgiveness and mercy. It is the narrow path to holiness held out by the Church for millennia and the one followed by every saint in our history. The weekly lessons are not complicated. Pray for a generous heart, and ask Christ for His help every step of the way. Simple enough!

What Do We Mean by "Weeks?"

You may be engaging this prayer journey as an individual or as part of a group. If you are doing this by yourself, you may find it beneficial to discipline yourself to stick to a seven-day week for each chapter of Forty Weeks. St. Ignatius's spiritual wisdom for the four weeks of the Spiritual

Exercises was to allow one to move forward based on the fruit being experienced. In this framework, a "week" was measured by the spiritual profit being received, and not by hours and days. Use the time frame of spiritual fruit to measure your weeks if you so desire. Sometimes it may be helpful to repeat a week several times to fully internalize the lesson! Trust your heart.

If you are part of a group doing these spiritual disciplines, my best advice is to discipline yourself to stay together as a group. That is, keep a seven-day week structure for the whole forty weeks. You can mark places and weeks that you may want to revisit for additional reflection and spiritual profit. Great spiritual fruit is also gained by tracking your "weeks" with the community you belong to.

No matter which way you are doing Forty Weeks—solo or with a group—realize that the exercises are incremental, building on each other. Doing them slowly and in order will help you stay better focused and live in the present moment. Trust the structure, and do not read or practice the disciplines out of their natural order.

Listen to your heart, at all times, in the present moment. God is in the present moment. This way, the Sacred Story prayer will, by God's grace and your free submission, lead you to the deepest desires of your heart.

How and When to Engage Forty Weeks

St. Ignatius proposed fifteen minutes as the optimal time for his Examen prayer discipline. Twice daily was the recommendation for Jesuits. The laity who practiced the prayer were encouraged to do it at least once daily. As you begin this prayer journey, make a decision whether you want to pray once or twice daily. You can always adjust your commitment to either of the options, but setting a goal for your practice is important.

Our extensive experience has shown that those who have practiced the Sacred Story Examen method in Forty Weeks have found praying in the morning, at midday, or midafternoon to be the most sustainable over time. Those who set evening hours for their prayer were less faithful to the discipline. Use your judgment. Ignatius advised it be done at midday and after the evening meal. Everyone has different schedules and life rhythms.

You will receive further guidance on the structure and use of these fifteen-minute times of quiet as the lessons progress. For now, it is sufficient to choose the time(s) you intend to pray daily. You would do well also to select a primary location for your fifteen-minute prayer times. Let it be a place apart—a technology-free zone. If you are incarcerated, you might have difficulty finding quiet and a place apart. Fear not. Ask God for the best place to be and you will find it.

Ask God to strengthen your resolve and desire for entering these times of reflection. Your fidelity to Sacred Story depends less on you, and more on your decision to continually ask God to be faithful.

Many of the instructions are written in the personal "I." For example, "I am invited; I will now…". This wording is intended to affirm your role in opening to Christ. It also helps emphasize the relational dimension of faith and prayer.

Additional Resources for Your Spiritual Journey

If you are a chaplain or a pen-pal with a prisoner, know that there are lots of resources provided free online at sacredstory.net that you can download and print out and send to those you are helping along the way. There is a weekly series of supplemental resources we call "Encouragements and Wisdom" or "E&W." The E&W are important aids for deepening your understanding of the prayer materials. They are available when you register (at no cost) as a member at sacredstory.net.

Chaplains and pen-pals realize that once you begin the Forty Weeks program, you are not given prompts to consult the E&W, but please make a mental note to do this weekly to help those you are ministering to. They will be greatly blessed! Many of the additional questions you and they have are likely to be contained in this very helpful supplemental prayer resource.

A simple journal exercise is a discipline linked to the Forty Weeks Sacred Story prayer. Purchase a small spiral notebook at the commissary or have a friend mail you one for this purpose. Have it with you when you do your structured fifteen-minute prayer periods. There is a blank page at the end of each week and eight more at the back of the book for your notes. Feel free to use this book as your notebook if you so desire. A free logbook can also downloaded from the Members section of sacredstory.net.

If You Hit a Wall

If you reach a point in the forty-week prayer process where you think you can't continue, here is my advice: Jump to the last chapter, "Abide in Me," and read it. I placed this chapter at the end to encourage people to commit to a lifelong process of Sacred Story prayer. But sometimes, that encouragement is necessary to simply complete the process that will carry you for life. Just keep trying, and "Be not afraid!"

Part One
Listening to Your Story

"Come to me, all you who labor and are burdened, and I
will give you rest. Take my yoke upon you and learn
from me, for I am meek and humble of heart;
and you will find rest for your selves.
For my yoke is easy, and my burden light."

Mt 11:28–30

Entering Your Sacred Story

Sacred Story prayer, modeled on St. Ignatius's classic examination of conscience, is a proven path to spiritual growth. It is the narrow road but the one taken by many saints and ordinary laity in the Church's history. If you are ready to make Christ the center of your life, you will find no better daily spiritual prayer discipline. Divine love is an abiding relationship that God invites you to share daily. Listen to the wisdom below to help prepare you to enter this relationship with God before you begin Week 1. Here are some "rules of engagement":

✠ If you are looking for quick fixes to spiritual or psychological problems, you will soon lose heart. The full healing of your wounds, and the path to complete peace, only begins on this earth. You will achieve no final victory for what ails you this side of eternity. However, you will find the path to that final victory, and it is here that you will find peace.

✠ If you seek only external confirmation of religious or political biases, you will be frustrated. Surrendering fixed ideologies and a judgmental heart is required fare on your Forty Weeks journey.

✠ If you live principally by rules and laws, or if you avoid all rules and laws, you will be surprised. Those who live by laws alone will encounter the fierce Love that exceeds all laws. And those who reject laws will discover that Love has unambiguous boundaries of right and wrong.

✠ If you are being asked to do these spiritual exercises to fulfill someone else's plan, or for any sort of program requirement, kindly tell your sponsor, "No, thank you." Unless you engage Forty Weeks in complete freedom of heart, you will fail in the practice and undermine its purpose.

So, who should engage this prayer journey? St. Ignatius wanted people with generous hearts who were aware that they needed God's help.

✠ Jesus proclaimed that the sick needed a physician, not the well (Mk 2:17). We are all sick, and only those willing to see their spiritual ills will submit to the Divine Physician's healing embrace in these exercises. If you know you are ill and believe you cannot get better without God's help, welcome.

✠ Jesus calmed the storm that terrified His disciples (Mk 5:35–41). Engage Sacred Story prayer if you are distressed about the chaos in your life and believe God is calling you to a secure shore.

✠ Jesus can heal chronic illness, but He has come to forgive us our sins and open to us eternal life (Lk 5:17–26). Engage in these exercises if you want to experience Jesus's power to forgive your sins.

✠ Jesus encouraged John the Baptist and his followers not to take offense at Him when their faith in Christ brought them suffering and threats (Mt 5:2–6). Engage these exercises if the practice of your faith is causing you to suffer persecution for Christ's sake. Hold fast to belief in Him as the Son of God, and take no offense.

✠ Jesus invited the weary and the overburdened to find rest in Him (Mt 11:25–30). Engage these exercises if you are weary with your life and find yourself overburdened.

✠ Jesus invited the rich young man to surrender his possessions and follow Him (Mk 10:17–25). Engage these exercises if you are ready to let go of what is holding you down and willing to follow a new path.

✠ Jesus invited Zacchaeus to come down from his tree and follow Him home (Lk 19:1–10). Engage these exercises if your privilege, position, and places of honor have not brought you the peace, security, and hope they promised.

✠ Jesus invited the woman of Samaria to drink the living water that wells up to eternal life (Jn 4:4–42). Engage these exercises if you are ready to surrender the cynicism of failed love and relationships, ready to forgive, and ready to move forward with your life.

✠ Jesus chided the work-anxious Martha to allow Mary to sit at His feet (Lk 10:38–42). Engage with these exercises if you are ready to sit still awhile, each day, and listen to the Kingdom within.

✠ Jesus invited Peter to join Him in His work (Lk 5:10–11). Engage these exercises if you trust that your sins, addictions, and failures do not limit Jesus's desire to take your hand in discipleship as He writes your sacred story.

✠ Jesus demanded to know the names of the Gerasene's demons (Mk 5:1–20). Engage these exercises if you are weary of your spiritual, psychological, and material demons. Welcome these exercises if you are willing to name them, with Jesus by your side, and allow Him to exorcise and heal the spiritual and psychic darkness—the habits, sins, and addictions—that rob you of freedom and peace.

✠ God invited the Blessed Virgin Mary not to fear but to say yes and participate in the eternal plan of salvation (Lk 1:26–38). Engage these exercises if you are ready to let your heart be Christ's home and so labor with Him for universal reconciliation.

✠ Jesus invited His disciples to dine with Him (Jn 15:1–17). Enter

Sacred Story prayer if you desire unbounded love, joy, peace, and a share in Jesus's glory—and His sufferings.

✠ Jesus invited all those wishing to follow Him to deny themselves, pick up their cross daily, and follow Him (Lk 9:23). Engage these exercises if you can willingly allow Christ to reveal your narcissism and by His grace, transform your life into sacred story.

✠ Jesus invited His disciples to keep a vigilant heart, to reject carousing and drunkenness, and to avoid getting trapped in the anxieties of life, lest they be surprised on the day of the Son of Man (Lk 21:34–36). Engage these exercises if today is your day to hearken to the Son of Man and to return to God with all your heart.

℧

Many of us have never taken the time to listen to Jesus's story by reading, prayerfully, one of the four accounts left for us by His early followers. Before advancing to Week 1, we will read one of the four Gospels. Only read one of them, but read it reflectively and prayerfully in a place of restful solitude. This place can be at home or some other favorite place you love to be alone in peace and quiet. (Perhaps it will be your place of prayer for these next forty weeks.)

Which Gospel should you read? Matthew writes to convince the Jews that Jesus is indeed the promised Messiah, the Davidic King, foretold by the prophets. Mark's focus is to reveal Jesus as the true Son of God who suffered and died to achieve complete victory over sickness, sin, and death. Luke, the physician, writes to reveal Jesus as the promise and hope of the poor and the weak. And John reveals Jesus as the Logos, the Word of God, who preexisted creation with the Father as the One who would save us.

Read the Gospel that immediately speaks to your heart at this time in your life. Don't rush your reading; there is no hurry. You might read one chapter per day, or several, until you have read the entire Gospel. Relish the story of the One who holds you and all creation in being.

Jesus is real and wants to become part of your daily life. He wants a relationship with you. He waits to be your hope, your forgiveness, and your peace. Open your heart to Him as you read His sacred story.

ଓଃ

NOTES

Week I

FIRST
I will choose one or two times each day to set aside for a fifteen-minute space of contemplative rest and reflection. This should be a place of quiet, free of technology—a place apart.

SECOND
I will be specific about the time of day and the place (or places) where I can find these moments of reflective quiet. I will take a moment to ponder where these will be and see them in my imagination.

THIRD
I will take my fifteen-minute quiet moments this week to read through the lesson that follows and to meditate on the Sacred Story Affirmations.

Set your heart to the path you are to take. Trust it. The path leading to Christ in the Sacred Story practice has some simple rules that will help you immensely.

I will not read ahead.
I will awaken to the present moment.
I will take each day and each exercise as it comes.
I cannot do Sacred Story better by going faster.

CB

You will have a new prayer exercise for every week of this journey. The exercises for this first week offer discernment principles that will help you along your way. Listen to the exercise, and pay attention to your feelings. Engage the prayers and exercises of Sacred Story with your whole being—with your "mind in your heart." Be a thinking, reflective "feeler" and believer. Awaken!

Remember, you are a pilgrim (journeying alongside Ignatius himself) in this prayer journey. The Lord Jesus will reward you for your courage and your resolve. Christ promises to be faithful to you! He will help you every single step of the way, because He came, lived, and died so you might have abundant life and bear fruit that endures to eternity. Thank Him in advance for the great blessings and insights you will receive. Live a life of gratitude to God for all life's blessings and gifts.

CB

The "Sacred Story Affirmations" sketch most of the realities you will encounter in your spiritual journey with Sacred Story prayer. As your first spiritual disciplines of this process, take some days to reflectively contemplate these affirmations for your Sacred Story practice. Use your fifteen-minute prayer times for this purpose. Take as many days as you desire, and listen attentively to them. Do not limit the number of days or sessions you spend with them. Your heart, by its peacefulness, will lead you forward to the next exercise at the right time. Trust God's grace working in your heart to lead you.

As you listen to the affirmations, be attentive to all the persons, events, and issues in your life. Be especially attentive to the things that cause fear, stress, anxiety, anger, or grief. When these emotions surface, notice how and if they connect with the affirmation that you are contemplating. Always listen with your mind in your heart to the events, issues, and persons in your life story. Be curious. Listen to how or why these events, issues, and persons may be linked to the spiritual, emotional, and moral dimensions of your experiences. Again, pay particular attention to those that might stimulate grief, anxiety, stress, anger, and fear.

Sacred Story practice focuses attention on things that are both delightful and difficult to experience. But as St. Ignatius learned, focusing attention on the difficult things is very fruitful. These aspects of your life history have the potential to rob you of hope, joy, love, and freedom. You can experience deeper, lasting peace by letting difficulties arise and allowing the Divine Physician to heal you. We have nothing to fear with Christ by our side. Take as long as you desire to reflect on the affirmations of your sacred story

CB

SACRED STORY AFFIRMATIONS

My sacred story takes a lifetime to write.

Be not afraid! Fear comes from the enemy of my human nature.

The pathway to God's peace and healing runs
through my heart's brokenness, sin, fear, anger, and grief.

God resolves all my problems with time and patience.

&

I will have difficulties in this life.

There are just two ways to cope with my difficulties.
One leads to life; one to death. I will choose life.

&

"Impossible" is not a word in God's vocabulary.

Sacred Story practice leads to my freedom and authenticity,
but it does not always make me feel happy.

&

My life's greatest tragedies can be transformed
into my life's major blessings.

Times of peace and hope always give way
to times of difficulty and stress.

Times of difficulty and stress always give way
to times of peace and hope.

&

I will not tire of asking God for help,
since God delights in my asking.

The urge to stop Sacred Story practice
always comes before my greatest breakthroughs.

℘

God gives me insights,
not because I am better than others, but because I am loved.

The insights and graces I need to move forward
in life's journey unfold at the right time.

℘

My personal engagement with Sacred Story accomplishes,
through Christ, a work of eternal significance.

Inspirations can have a divine or a demonic source.
I pray for the grace to remember how to discern one from the other.

℘

Christ, who has walked before me, shares my every burden.

Christ, who has walked before me, will help me resolve every crisis.

Christ, who has walked before me, knows my every hope.

Christ, who has walked before me, knows everything I suffer.

Christ, who walks before me, will always lead me home to safety.

℘

I will strive to curb temptations to react to people and events.
I will ask myself what causes my anger and
irritation at people and events.

I will seek to identify the source of my anger and irritation.

I will give thanks for what angers and upsets me,
for identifying their source will help to set me free.

I will strive to listen, watch, and pray. Listen, watch, and pray.
I will listen, watch, and pray!

ॐ

Everyone has been mortally wounded spiritually, psychologically,
and physically by Original Sin and the loss of paradise.

Journeying with Christ to the roots of my sins
and addictions will help break their grip.

I will not waste time worrying about my sins and failures. I will use my
time wisely and ask God to help me understand
the source of my sins and failings.

I will trust that Christ came to heal all my wounds.

ॐ

I alone control Christ's ability to transform my life
into a sacred story. The process begins when I ask
for the grace to honestly name my sins and addictions.

The process continues when I invite Christ to illuminate my narcissism.

Only God's grace and mercy can write my sacred story.

ॐ

I will strive daily to pick up the cross, for it leads to my life.
The closer I get to holiness, the more I will see
and feel sin's disorder in my life
The more I experience sin's disorder,
the more tempted I will be to disbelieve my life as sacred story.

The way through the temptation is
to surrender my powerlessness to God.

౸

It is never too late to open my heart to Christ and
live my life as sacred story.

Christ, who is close to the brokenhearted, restores my lost innocence.

The path to my sacred story is
Creation, Presence, Memory, Mercy, and Eternity.

౸

Your heart is prepared, and you have awakened to the path you are to take. Trust it. Remember: Do not read ahead. Do not exercise ahead. Awaken to the present moment. Take each day and each exercise as it comes.

౦ช

એ

I am starting a Relationship that will carry me
for the rest of my life.

I will learn the fundamentals and strive
to open my heart to God.

I trust that God will lead me.
I believe that my sacred story will unfold in truth,
in powerlessness, and with my patience.

I believe that Jesus awaits me with His
grace, mercy, and forgiving love.

What do I need for this journey?
A generous heart,
the willingness to take fifteen minutes to pray daily,
and the humility to always ask God for help.

ଓ

Letters from Week One

Dear Fr. Bill,

Even before I received your last letter I had decided I needed to start Forty Weeks over again. I'd noticed that I sort of cherry-picked parts I thought important and ignored others. With no one to share the experience with while doing it the first time, I had no feedback or guidance.

Your offer to respond to my reflections/questions for each week is greatly appreciated. Please do not hesitate to point out my errors or misconceptions in this process. I look forward to, and I am grateful for your guidance.

I am sure that it is not an accident that the Sacred Story Affirmations are presented in Week One. I hadn't been conscious of how big a part fear, stress, anxiety, anger, and grief had in my life, especially during the last nineteen years I've been incarcerated. Many of the affirmations help ease my fear, anxiety, and anger – my most glaring daily issues.

I very often have no idea as to why I feel the way I do. Now, when I am angry, I pray to identify the source, and give thanks for what angers me. Doing so does help to set me free. I do strive to listen, watch and pray.

When I am feeling anxious, not only due to the usual situations of prison life, out of fear for my salvation, fear for what will become of me in this life, fear that I will never become the man God created me to be, I repeat over and over:

Christ, who has walked before me, shares my every burden.
Christ, who has walked before me, will help me resolve every crisis.
Christ, who has walked before me, knows my every hope.
Christ, who has walked before me, knows everything I suffer.

Christ, who walks before me, will always lead me home to safety.

Throughout these Forty Weeks I will be sure to refer back to the Affirmations as needed.

Respectfully,

Ritchie

Dear Ritchie:

I imagine you in your jail cell reading and praying over the meditations of Forty Weeks. You might want to consider it your monk's cell. Many saints of the past fled the city to be in isolation in order to find the Lord. You, of course, were forced into your situation by life's circumstances and your own past. But it is now the place where the Lord chooses to find you.

The Affirmations were placed in the front of Forty Weeks to attune your heart to some basic rules of spiritual discernment. I knew certain Affirmations would speak powerfully to the hearts of those on the journey. Fear, anger, and grief are part of the human condition since the tragedy of our fall depicted in the book of Genesis. But I know from friends who work as chaplains in prisons that anger is an especially pressing issue for many behind bars.

You seem to have begun a process of awakening, however, much as did St. Ignatius. When you say you often don't know why you feel the way you do, at least you are starting to give thanks for things like anger. God will awaken you to why you are feeling angry so you can find greater hope and peace. Anger's energy is broken when we thank God for our feelings and ask to understand them. In the end, most anger will have to be resolved by our forgiving others and ourselves for things that have happened to us.

It is natural to feel the threat of prison life. What you need not fear, however, is your salvation. Jesus has guaranteed it and wants you not to fear, but to trust him. Just keep repeating those five Affirmations that bring you hope. The Lord has guaranteed that you will become the man he knows you can be. It will happen through God's grace and mercy and not your own hard labors. Let Jesus work in your heart. That is all he asks of you.

You are in my prayers,

Fr. Bill

NOTES

Week 2

FIRST

I will choose a place of contemplative rest and reflection. It will be a place apart—a technology-free zone!

SECOND

I will make a decision on whether to take one or two fifteen-minute prayer breaks a day. Regularity is key to sustainable disciplines of any kind, and this is especially true of a prayer relationship with Christ.

THIRD

During my fifteen-minute quiet moments this week, I will slowly and thoughtfully read part 1 of St. Ignatius's conversion story. I will commit to read reflectively and take my time. I will ask the Spirit to inspire me to fully see and hear Ignatius's story, especially as it relates to my life.

I will pray for an open mind and heart.
I will not read ahead.
I will awaken to the present moment.
I will take each day and each exercise as it comes.
I cannot do Sacred Story better by going faster.

℅

This second week is related to the conversion story of St. Ignatius. Your prayer exercise for this week is to read and ponder the beginning of St. Ignatius's sacred story. Pay careful attention to what in Ignatius's experience touches your own unique history. Thank Christ in advance for the blessings and insights you will receive.

Read and ponder. You may be inspired to reflect on the affirmations from last week. Be attentive to any memories that might arise and the feelings that stir as you pray this week. St. Ignatius was very clear in his teachings that careful attention to your internal spiritual movements marks the beginning of discernment. This heart-focused attention attunes your radar to the voices of the spiritual world.

☙

Part 1: St. Ignatius and His Legacy

Until his thirtieth year, Ignatius Loyola was unconscious of the sacredness of his life. Instead, he was sincerely devoted to life's pleasures and vanities. He was a gambling addict, sexually self-indulgent, arrogant, hotheaded, and insecure. Ignatius's mother died when he was an infant, and his father died when he was sixteen.

By our contemporary measures, Ignatius's family was dysfunctional. Was this person a possible candidate for sainthood? It did not look promising. But God does not judge by human standards. It is God's nature to pursue all who have fallen asleep through sin, addiction, and selfishness. God judges the heart; with unbounded grace and patient mercy, God reaches into the ruins that sin makes of our lives and transforms them into sacred stories.

Ignatius, with all his narcissism, psychological problems, and sinful vices, was awakened by God's great love. A failed military campaign and a shattered leg forced him into a lengthy convalescence back at Loyola castle, his family home. Ignatius's time of recuperation provided an opportunity for Love to shine a light on much more serious and life-threatening wounds that were spiritual, emotional, and psychological in nature.

These wounds were supported by the evolution of a destructive, sinful narcissism. For thirty years, Ignatius's narcissism had rendered him unconscious to his true human nature and oblivious to his life as sacred story. The pleasures he indulged in and the power he wielded functioned like a narcotic to numb the pain of his hidden spiritual and psychological wounds. His sinful vices and self-indulgent pleasures had blinded him to the possibilities of a fruitful life guided by a well-formed conscience.

God's grace reached into the reality of Ignatius's life and awakened in him a desire for innocence. His long-buried aspirations for living authentically suddenly became his prime motivation. He noticed it first while convalescing at Loyola. He became aware of new desires and a different energy as he daydreamed while reading stories of Christ and the saints. Pondering the saints' lives, he imagined himself living in a similarly selfless way.

He compared these new daydreams to his usual vain, narcissistic ones. The old daydreams drew energy from a life of sin, addiction, and vice, while the daydreams of selfless generosity produced their own energy. Ignatius also noticed a significant difference between the feelings produced by the two sets of daydreams. The vain fantasies entertained him when he was thinking about them. But he noticed that when he set them aside, he felt empty and unsatisfied.

The new holy daydreams also entertained him when he was thinking about them. Yet when he set these aside, he remained content and felt an enduring calm and quiet joy. By paying close attention to the ultimate affective results of these two sets of daydreams and discerning their difference, Ignatius made a discovery that transformed his life and the history of Christian spirituality.

Ignatius's Awakening Mirrors His Unique Examen Prayer

Ignatius's Awakening Experience Mirrors →	His Examen Prayer
A GRACED EXPERIENCE OF GOD'S LOVE OPENED IGNATIUS TO ↓	GIVE THANKS FOR FAVORS RECEIVED ↓
A DISSATISFACTION WITH VAIN FANTASIES, WHICH LED TO SURRENDERING TO HOLY DAYDREAMS, CHARACTERIZED BY CONSOLATION, WHICH IN TURN ↓	PRAY FOR GRACE TO SEE CLEARLY ↓
CAUSED HIM TO REVIEW HIS LIFE AND ACTIONS, LEADING TO ↓	GIVE A DETAILED ACCOUNT OF CONSCIENCE: GENERAL AND PARTICULAR ↓
GRIEF WITH YEARNING FOR PENANCE AND REPENTANCE FOR HIS PAST SINS, CULMINATING IN ↓	ASK PARDON FOR ONE'S FAULTS ↓
IGNATIUS'S PASSION TO AMEND HIS LIFE AND A DESIRE TO LOVE GOD WHOLEHEARTEDLY.	RESOLVE AND AMEND TO SERVE GOD

Ignatius discovered that the new, selfless aspirations were influenced by divine inspirations. He further discovered that these inspirations reflected his true human nature and that the vain fantasies had deadened his conscience. His narcissistic daydreams led him away from enduring peace, because they masked his authentic human nature. The old daydreams were powerful, ego affirming, and familiar. He knew in his heart that living their fantasy was the path to self-destruction. On the one hand, he would be judged successful by the standards of the world—a world that measured success in terms of riches, honors, and pride. On the other hand, he would be judged a failure by the standards of the gospel—standards that advocated a life of spiritual poverty, humility and consequential service.

Ignatius was awakened to the emotional wisdom and spiritual truth of his new daydreams. He became aware of the significant damage that his old lifestyle had done both to himself and others. What had been awakened in him was the divine gift of conscience, and with it, Ignatius experienced profound regret and sorrow for having wasted so much of his life on self-indulgent pleasures and fantasies, seductions that could never bring him lasting peace and satisfaction. He began to understand that living in pleasure and fantasy destroyed his authentic human nature and silenced his deepest desires.

Divine inspiration led Ignatius to seek forgiveness for wasting his life and abusing his innocence. Grace enabled him to take responsibility for his sins against God and his authentic human nature. Divine inspiration provided Ignatius with the desire, energy, and courage to renounce the thoughts, words, and deeds of his sinful habits. Grace, received through the sacrament of Reconciliation, heightened Ignatius's consciousness and enabled him to imagine a new path for his life, and new ways to express his gifts and talents.

As usually happens when people respond to the grace of conversion, Ignatius's new aspirations confused and disconcerted many of his closest family members and friends. Nonetheless, he acted on these aspirations. Ignatius was now able to understand a path to God, a pattern of conversion that countless thousands would imitate.

A Menacing Fear Unmasked

After some months of living in the light of these new positive virtues, habits, and divine inspirations, Ignatius was suddenly gripped by terror and panic. How could he manage to live the rest of his life without the pleasures of the past? It was easy to live virtuously for some months, but for the rest of his life? This was a real crisis, because Ignatius began to wonder if this was an impossible goal.

Ignatius had two vital insights about this menacing fear. First, he realized it was a counter-inspiration prompted by the enemy of his true human nature. Second, he saw that the counter-inspiration tempted him to return to his old narcissistic vices and habits. Seduced by their powerful influence, Ignatius would abandon all hope for a life of virtue. In essence, Ignatius was tempted to surrender living the authentic life that had finally brought him peace. He sensed an evil source inspiring this menacing fear, and he challenged it head-on: "You pitiful thing! Can you even promise me one hour of life?"

A Decisive and Enduring Commitment to Remain Awake

Not knowing how he would endure, Ignatius dismissed the counter-inspiration and its evil author by recommitting to this new wakefulness for the remainder of his life. This was Ignatius's major insight: never trust the messages prompted by menacing fears! Counter them with a firm commitment to stay the course, to awaken and remain conscious.

This decisive, enduring commitment to persevere restored tranquility, and his fear abated. Ignatius had discovered, unmasked, and cofronted the deceiver. In this, Ignatius learned another lesson about speaking truth to power that would guide his new life and help shape his first set of foundational discernment principles.

Ignatius's Experiences Reveal His Discernment Principles

Ignatius's Experiences→	Discernment Principles
AN ENEMY VOICE EVOKED IGNATIUS'S FEAR OF A LIFELONG STRUGGLE WITH HIS SINFUL HABITS. ↓	THERE IS CONSCIOUS FEAR AND ANXIETY OVER SURRENDERING SINFUL AND ADDICTIVE HABITS. ↓
IGNATIUS REJECTED THE "ENEMY OF HUMAN NATURE" AND CONFRONTED THIS ENEMY'S FALSE PROMISES. ↓	ONE CONFRONTS THE THREATENING "VOICE" OF SIN AND ADDICTION WITH THE TRUTH THAT THEY BRING DEATH, NOT LIFE. ↓
PEACE WAS RESTORED AFTER IGNATIUS TRUTHFULLY NAMED SIN AND ADDICTION AS DEATH DEALING.	FINALLY, PEACE RETURNS AND ANXIETY DISSOLVES.

Ignatius had to face these same fears many, many more times. Eventually he knew they were false fears, inspirations of the enemy of his human nature. Most importantly, he gradually learned how to defuse them, and to defend against them. It is vital that we understand this lesson from Ignatius: anyone who changes his or her lifestyle through a divine awakening and who, by grace, consciously and consistently enters his or her sacred story will encounter the same menacing fears. You can be strongly tempted to fall asleep and slip back into old habits and vices. When you are faced with these menacing fears—when, not if—confidently recommit to the path of life, and to the Author of life. The fears, in time, will subside. The enemy of human nature will always be disarmed.

Our spirit, our body, and God's grace at work in us compose a holy trinity. God made us this way. All three parts working cooperatively are necessary for holiness and human growth. In the paradise depicted in Genesis, the perfect cooperation of this trinity of human nature rendered us immortal. By turning from the fullness of God's grace, our immortality was lost; the perfect balance of the divinely crafted trinity of human nature—body, spirit, and God's grace—shattered. Christ's incarnation and death opened the way to immortality once again.

Our Christian life is a labor of love. In order for God's love to heal us, we must do our part to open ourselves to His graces. This requires conscious and ongoing effort to abstain from sinful, addictive habits in thoughts, words, and deeds. There is a need to pray for God's grace, and first we must awaken to that grace.

With that same grace, we have the strength to resist and abstain from sinful, addictive attitudes and behaviors, both spiritual and material. God's grace infuses our spiritual disciplines, activating the trinity of our human nature. Grace helps us climb out of the spiritual, mental, physical, and emotional ruts of our bound self. In doing so, God graces us with a future of increased hope, holiness, and balance.

CB

I am starting a Relationship that will carry me
for the rest of my life.

All relationships require time and patience.
I will strive for patience and ask for God's help
when I don't understand a lesson.

I will learn the fundamentals and open my heart to God.

I trust that God will lead me.

I believe that my sacred story will unfold in truth,
in powerlessness, and with my patience.

I believe that Jesus awaits me with His
grace, mercy, and forgiving love.

EO

Letters from Week Two

Dear Fr. Bill:

I felt a connection with St. Ignatius from the very beginning of his own sacred story. Ignatius' parents died when he was young. Although I had adoptive parents, I felt no connection to them and, therefore, in my mind, I had no one to answer to and could conduct my "life of sin, addiction and vice" as I pleased. And I did live a life of sin, wrongly assuming that my self-destructive behavior was only affecting me.

Until reading Ignatius' sacred story, I honestly had <u>never</u> heard anyone describe their daydreams. I thought I was unique in that I spent an inordinate amount of time with negative daydreams. I didn't have the label "vain and narcissistic" but that's exactly what they were.

One would think that once I was incarcerated for what would turn out to be many years, I would have immediately started to work on becoming a better person, to maybe atone for the sinful life that got me to that point; but, no.

For the first fifteen years of my incarceration I spent hours and hours each day, sometimes all day, laying in my bunk in my cell daydreaming, glorifying the "good times" prior to getting locked up — drinking and abusing illegal drugs, aberrant and promiscuous sexual behavior, criminal behavior, self-indulgences of every variety, and just plain arrogance. And I was making plans to resume all of this, hopefully to a greater degree and with more success, upon my release.

I do still sometimes experience these daydreams, but I am now blessed that they have mostly been replaced with daydreams of positive, divinely inspired thoughts — about prayer, about service, about becoming a kind, caring disciple. I credit Divine inspiration for "the desires, energy, and courage to renounce the thoughts words and deeds" of my sinful habits. I often wonder if this is "an impossible goal", but I try to remember

Ignatius' second insight: "Never trust the messages prompted by menacing fears." They come from the enemy of human nature. I know that now, and that knowledge makes all the difference. I continue to pray for God's grace in order to abstain from "sinful habits in thoughts, words and deeds".

Respectfully, Ritchie

Dear Ritchie:

St. Ignatius was certainly shaped by his past life experiences, as are we all. One of St. Ignatius' modern biographers says this about him:

"This primordial bonding between Íñigo and his mother, or rather the nonexistence of such a bonding, suggests the absence of the protective, liberating, fostering maternal presence that would have given him early direction, basic confidence, and would have opened up new objectives for him. This absence of affective nurturing during his early years could have even resulted in retarded physical growth. Íñigo was a runt, hardly a representative of the Basques, who are considered the tallest of the Spanish people. The lack of nurturing by a mother engenders habits of depression later in life; it affects the way one reacts to and relates with others; it incites vague feelings of guilt. Again, we cite Rof Carballo, who has written extensively on the relationship between psychoanalysis and religion, on this particular point: "Deep within the recesses of his affectivity, every wandering adventurer is responding to the hidden and irresolvable need to compensate for the lack of that maternal nurturing, whose function is to provide the child with affective perimeters."[3]
So, wandering into paths of sin and vice, Ritchie, were made much easier because you did not feel you had people who cared for you or for whom you cared. And those first fifteen years in prison simply continued that wandering in your daydreams--thinking how you would continue the life of vice and pleasure and get even better at it. But realize that as you

were daydreaming, even daydreams you describe as negative, you were still trying to find a life of peace and hope in the only way you understood.

It was here that God decided to enter your life and help you find those holy daydreams that St. Ignatius discovered. Don't beat yourself up that you wasted fifteen years in prison not working on becoming a better man. Maybe you were not ready for God's loving touch and maybe you could not have accepted it any earlier. Never spend time regretting the past but realize that God can transform all bad things into glory if we let him. Nothing is wasted in God's economy of grace!

Give thanks instead that you have found the path to those holy daydreams. As they become more and more the substance of your dreams, realize that God is leading you to the true meaning of your manhood and your true identity as a child of God. He is the one who will continue to transform your "thoughts, words and deeds".

You are in my prayers,

Fr. Bill

NOTES

Week 3

FIRST

I will find a place each day where I can pull aside for a fifteen-minute space of contemplative rest and reflection, free from technology's distractions.

SECOND

I will review my decision on whether I will take one fifteen-minute prayer break or two fifteen-minute prayer breaks a day.

THIRD

During my fifteen-minute quiet prayer periods this week, I will gradually read through part 2 of St. Ignatius's conversion story. Reading reflectively, I will take my time. I am reading for spiritual insights about Ignatius's sacred story and my own. Prayerful reading, known in the Catholic Tradition as lectio divina (holy reading) is done slowly. Resisting the efficiency pressures of the modern age, I realize Sacred Story is not about going faster, but deeper.

I will not read ahead.
I will awaken to the present moment.
I will take each day and each exercise as it comes.
I cannot do Sacred Story better by going faster.

☙

Welcome to the third week of our pilgrimage. The exercises for this week continue with the conversion story of St. Ignatius. As you listen to St. Ignatius's history, reflect on your own. As you read, recall that Ignatius woke up to the fact that there were two plots in his daydreams: Plot "A" entailed the goals and fantasies rooted in his wounded heart and in following narcissistic dreams. Plot "B" entailed fantasies of a heart rooted in Christ and discovering healing and peace by following holy dreams. You are invited to search your own daydreams and fantasies for signs of these two plots. Consider your life as you listen to Ignatius's story. God used him to guide us. Each person has the same challenge of finding the narrow path that leads to our true human nature.

You have two options for how to pray with this week's text. Some like to read during the fifteen-minute periods, while others prefer to read the whole text on Sunday and then focus on smaller sections during the fifteen-minute prayer periods for the rest of the week. Do whatever is best for you. Your goal is to listen to Ignatius's story and be attentive to any issues that seem important to you. Listen to Ignatius's story, and pay attention to whatever stirs in you, be it hope and peace or anxiety and fear. Doing this sharpens your spiritual radar for things that make your heart say, "Pay attention!" Thank Christ in advance for the blessings and insights you will receive.

Part 2: A Journey to the Heart

Ignatius's decisive and enduring commitment to his conversion launched him directly into the center of his heart's brokenness and the pride masking those wounds. After leaving home, Ignatius traveled to Montserrat and spent three days reviewing his life. It was at this time that he made a general confession of all his past sinful deeds. This first life confession initiated an enduring habit of weekly confession and communion. In this written confession, Ignatius consciously detailed his sinful attitudes, behaviors, and passions: gambling addiction, sexual self-indulgence, arrogance, and violent outbursts of temper. It took all three days to write the story of his past life.

Yet he discovered that simply detailing and confessing his sinful habits and addictions did not disarm them. That would require going deeper, to their source in his heart and history. Only in these deepest recesses could he confront the pattern of spiritual and psychological dysfunction that was most responsible for eroding his freedom and distorting his authentic human nature.

It is this inward journey that fully awakened his conscience. It was only at this depth that he discovered his authentic human nature and regained the creativity of childlike innocence. We do well to understand the tipping point of Ignatius's life from his root vices and narcissism to his new life of wakefulness, light, peace, and hope. This is how his story unfolded.

Ignatius's new, pious habit of regular confession evolved into a destructive, obsessive, and compulsive torture. He confessed and reconfessed past sins multiple times, never feeling he had gotten to the bottom of his immoral deeds. This excruciating spiritual and psychological torment lasted for months. He was so anguished by his obsessive guilt that numerous times he wanted to commit suicide by throwing himself off the cliff where he prayed.

Well aware of the emotional damage caused by this obsessive confession habit, he still could not let it go. Instead he initiated new, harsher physical disciplines and spiritual regimens. His goal was to gain complete control and self-mastery over his immoral and dissolute past. He wanted to remember every detail of his past sins so he could be perfectly cleansed. But nothing worked!

Finally, exhausted and disgusted with his efforts, he realized he intensely despised the spiritual life he was living. Ignatius had an urgent and compelling desire to "stop it!" This thought alarmed Ignatius, and his spiritual radar went on high alert. Ignatius discerned that the inspiration came from another source, but what could it be? He discovered the inspiration's origin and author only by understanding where the inspiration was taking him. It occurred to him that the inspiration was leading him in the same direction as the menacing fear he had previously experienced. Inspired to abandon his newly awakened life, Ignatius was being tempted to abandon the peace, the service to others, and the virtuous life of his sacred story. But how had this counter-inspiration succeeded in gaining entry? Ignatius's decision to stop reconfessing his past sins reveals the enemy's strategy.

Surrendering Control to Embrace Powerlessness and Innocence

Ignatius's decision to stop his damaging confession habit appears inconsequential. But the choice was the most significant spiritual decision in his entire life. It was also the most difficult, because that one choice meant fully surrendering his life to God. It meant admitting his powerlessness over his sins and in humility allowing God, not himself, to be the source of his holiness.

Reflecting on the temptation to walk away from his new Christian life, Ignatius received an insight that the burdensome, destructive habit of reconfessing past sins was rooted in a pride to try and save himself. This pride forced him to his knees. On seeing this, he "awoke as if from a dream" and was given the grace to stop the habit.

Looking at his life spiritually and psychologically, it appears that behind the sexual misdeeds, addictive gambling, and violent temper, there was a controlling, narcissistic pride and a broken heart. Our narcissistic control is solidified by the searing spiritual and psychological pain of lost innocence—the pattern of sins we inherit from the Original Sin, along with those sins committed against us early in life and later those sins committed by us.

Our narcissism, if you will, godifies us, severely restricting our ability to respond to the true God. We fill the void of our wounded, broken hearts with self-centered strivings for attention, power, and control. Our narcissism is a false identity, an anti-story. It blinds us to our authentic human nature and the deepest desires of our heart. It blinds us to our sacred story.

Ignatius's first life confession at Montserrat documented the visible manifestations of this deep distortion in his human nature. The Divine Physician next led Ignatius to the source of those visible sins. It was his wounded human nature that fueled the controlling, narcissistic personality. The pattern of visible sins, vices, and addictions was only the tip of the iceberg.

It is vital to remember that Ignatius's weaning from the narcotics of aggression, addictions, and dissoluteness opened a portal to his broken heart—his wounded human nature—where he could fully confront his powerlessness and brokenness. It is here that he finally met Christ face to face. It is here, in accepting Christ's forgiveness, that healing love begins. It is here that Ignatius admitted his powerlessness to save himself and surrendered control of his life to God. This is the spiritual paradigm of powerlessness.

Ignatius's struggle with the obsessive habit of reconfessing past sins was the symbol of his hidden root sin of pride. Christ labored hard to meet Ignatius right where he was, in this harrowing place. Ignatius's frenzied, damaging re-confessing of past sins was only the latest manifestation of the same hidden narcissism that had distorted his first thirty years of life.

The same sin had been in full view on the battlefield at Pamplona, when Ignatius forced his will on the commander and all the other knights to engage a suicide mission against a far more numerous and well-armed militia. Ignatius's pride earned him a shattering defeat and a shattered leg. Fortunately, his defensive pride was shattered by God's grace awakening him "as if from a dream."

After his frightful struggle with scruples following his confession at Montserrat, Ignatius finally acknowledged his powerlessness and surrendered control of his life to God. God had waited all of Ignatius's life to transform his deepest desires into a sacred story whose legacy would endure to eternity. This surrender defines Ignatius's second set of foundational discernment principles

An outpouring of mystical grace flooded Ignatius at this point. More importantly, a humble and obedient spirit was beginning to emerge which enabled him to respond to the slightest movements of God's grace in his thoughts, words, and deeds. In this humility and docility, he discovered a life of service that changed the Church and the world. Later in life he reflected on this discovery:

There are very few who realize what God would make of them if they abandoned themselves entirely to His hands, and let themselves be formed by His grace. A thick and shapeless tree trunk would never believe that it could become a statue, admired as a miracle of sculpture...and would never consent to submit itself to the chisel of the sculptor who, as St. Augustine says, sees by his genius what he can make of it. Many people who, we see, now scarcely live as Christians, do not understand that they could become saints, if they would let themselves be formed by the grace of God, if they did not ruin His plans by resisting the work which He wants to do.

Ignatius's Experiences Reveal His Discernment Steps

Ignatius's Experiences	Discernment Steps
Ignatius's struggle with scruples hid his vainglory. ↓	THE INITIAL CONFRONTATION WITH ONE'S ROOT SIN ↓
Ignatius constantly reconfessed to seek salvation by willpower alone. ↓	THE EFFORT TO CONTROL ONE'S ROOT SIN ONLY BY PERSONAL EFFORT OR FORCE OF WILL ↓
Ignatius experienced suicidal impulses, disgust, and the desire to walk away from his newfound faith. ↓	DESPAIR AND DESIRE TO GIVE UP FAITH WHEN HUMAN EFFORT ALONE FAILS ↓
Ignatius traced the spirit of disgust to a demonic source. ↓	INSIGHT THAT DESIRE TO REJECT THE SPIRITUAL JOURNEY IS A TEMPTATION ↓
Ignatius abandoned his compulsive confessing of past sins.	THE ADMITTING OF POWERLESSNESS TO SAVE ONESELF AND THE SURRENDERING OF PRIDEFUL ACTIONS

The proud narcissist, the man who was master of his own universe, became a humble and obedient servant of the universe's true Master and Creator. To arrive at this point, Ignatius had to admit his powerlessness. He had to surrender control over his life and the distorted aspects of his human nature that had evolved over the years. He had to learn how to live out of his newly emerging authentic self, his true and free human nature, a nature that had been hidden behind his wounded heart. Because of this, Ignatius also had to learn how to dismantle the narcissism that had evolved over the first thirty years of his life. The counter-inspirer, the enemy of his human nature, had cleverly concealed his true human nature, and Ignatius had to begin life over again, this time allowing God to reveal to him his authentic self. This was why, after the resolution of this greatest of his life's crises, Ignatius experienced himself being taught by God. It was, he said, exactly like "a child is taught by a schoolmaster."

The Divine Inspirer and the Counter-inspirer

This harrowing crisis taught Ignatius a most vital lesson about counter-inspirations. The willpower and resolute commitment to live virtuously for the rest of his life could be manipulated and turned against him by means of subtle inspirations. What seemed like a holy, pious, and noble practice—a serious approach to confession—devolved into a damaging habit that made him loathe his spiritual life, and in frustration, inspired him to abandon it. He learned that the counter-inspirations of the enemy of his human nature could act like "an angel of light." These inspirations appear holy but when followed, they end in disaster, distancing one from God and from one's authentic self.

Ignatius gained clearer knowledge of the two spiritual forces that inspire and seek to guide the evolution of one's story. He gathered what he had learned from "speaking truth to power" (to the enemy of human nature) and what he had learned from surrendering control of his life to God into guidelines for discerning these different inspirations. For now, it is sufficient to say that the Divine Inspirer is the author of one's original innocence, that is, one's authentic and free human nature. The Divine Inspirer works gently in and through every situation, especially the misfortunes associated with the damaging spiritual and psychological ordeals of life.

It is the nature of the Holy Spirit to offer forgiveness and provide shelter from the enemy of human nature, whose sole purpose is to destroy innocence. The Divine Inspirer forgives sins, restores lost innocence, mends broken and wounded hearts, releases captives, sets the oppressed free, and illumines one's sacred story and true human nature (Lk 4:18).

The counter-inspirer also works through all the events of one's life and relationships. His work is evident in the distortions of spirit and mind, the deep wounding caused by the evolution of sin from the Original Sin and also sin inherited from one's family and culture. The counter-inspirer works to corrupt innocence and deform one's spiritual, emotional, physical, and psychological nature—one's true human nature. Jesus condemned the violation of the innocent and the childlike. No human being can escape the machinations this evil breeds in one's body, mind, and spirit. Since the Original Sin, this evolutionary force has infected every person and consequently, all of human history.

The counter-inspirer conceals our original wounds, counseling and guiding our steps to build a false identity, an anti-story, characteristically identified by a distorted ego and defended by narcissism. Our narcissistic pride rationalizes the habits, vices, addictions, and lifestyles that form our anti-story. The counter-inspirer renders us unconscious to our sacred story and to our true, divinely shaped human nature.

God led Ignatius through this distorted evolution back to the lost innocence of his true human nature. To get there, Ignatius had to confront his pattern of spiritual and psychological distortions born from by his narcissistic pride. It was a mighty castle that he had built on the shifting sands of a child's wounded innocence, on a child's lonely, broken heart. God provided Ignatius the inspiration and grace to allow that castle to crumble. The shattering of his powerful defenses and the unmasking of his prideful, narcissistic pattern proved to be the tipping point of Ignatius's entire conversion process.

Wakefulness, Holiness, and Heightened Consciousness

Ignatius's conversion from his anti-story and his full awakening to his sacred story was not a single event but rather a gradual process. His full evolution from a vain egomaniac to a saint took the rest of his life. This is evident in his Autobiography. In three linked narratives recounting personal near-death experiences, Ignatius reveals his growth in holiness, a process that evolved over a long, twenty-eight-year period.

In the first account, he is filled with fear of judgment, because he understands that pride is still a strong temptation for him. In the second account, he is no longer afraid of death, but instead, he is filled with sorrow for his delayed response to God. In the third account, grace floods his heart, and he is filled with an intense devotion and desire for eternal union with God. These three episodes mirror the three classical stages of mystical growth: purgation, illumination, and union. The three episodes also convey the reality of Ignatius's patience with the process of his spiritual growth:

A Lifelong Commitment to Christ in the Church

It took Ignatius the remainder of his life to develop into the saint we know today. His was a gradual, steady evolution from a sinful narcissist in control of his own life to an innocent, obedient servant of God. He discovered and embraced the power and energy of living in the holy trinity of his authentic human nature—spirit, body, and God's grace, working in unison. Growth in holiness requires desire, patience, and daily effort to awaken to our authentic human nature. It takes time for grace to penetrate the influence of our anti-story so that our sacred story can more fully emerge. There are no shortcuts to holiness, not even for saints.

Ignatius' Three Near-Death Experiences Mirror the Classic Process of Spiritual Growth

Ignatius's 3 Near-Death Experiences →	Universal Principle →	Mystical Path
(1) 1522 Ignatius, justifying himself, anxiously recoiled and focused on his sinfulness. ↓	PANIC OVER ONE'S SALVATION DUE TO WEAKNESS AND SINFULNESS →	PURGATION ↓
(2) 1532 Ignatius, no longer fearful, regretted not having responded sooner to God's graces. ↓	SADNESS AT SLOWNESS OF ONE'S RESPONSE TO GOD'S LOVE AND INVITATION TO INTIMACY →	ILLUMINATION ↓
(3) 1550 Ignatius felt intense joy at the thought of dying and being with God. →	AN ARDENT, ALL-EMBRACING LOVE OF GOD AND DESIRE FOR COMPLETE UNION WITH THE TRINITY →	UNION

If you desire to surrender your anti-story and open to your sacred story, grace will awaken you, like Ignatius, to places in your heart's memories you might not wish to visit. The awakening will begin like Ignatius's. It starts with an honest identification of the visible manifestations of those spiritual and psychological distortions in the particulars of your human nature. These distortions disclose your lost innocence and a heart broken by the Original Fall and the cumulative sins of your family, clan, and culture.

Ignatius started this process with his life confession. He truthfully identified the habits, addictions, sins, and compulsions characteristic of his lost innocence and broken heart. Open yourself to the graces of God that will illumine the distinctive narcissistic elements fueling your sinful, compulsive behaviors. Ignatius needed much grace to overcome his defenses and unlock this hidden truth about his life. Everyone who embraces the invitation to walk this path can confidently rely on the same grace to navigate this vital part of the process.

Finally awakening to your sacred story will take you to the places in your heart where your innocence is wounded, your true human nature is distorted, and your heart is broken. Awakening to your sacred story will reveal the outlines of your anti-story. You will need to honestly evaluate the narcissistic pattern in your own life, identifying the pleasures, powers, and habits that act as narcotics, blocking the pain of your broken heart and lost innocence.

This pattern that masks your authentic self and your true human nature is the pattern of your false self. It is the deceit of the anti-story that hides the radiance of your authentic human nature and the sacredness of your life story. This was Ignatius's experience. By divine inspiration, he discovered his false-self masquerading as a pious, conscientious penitent.

Once he reached this point, Ignatius awakened, "as if from a dream," to his sacred story. By so doing, he was graced to unite mind and spirit, action and contemplation, the eternal in the present moment, and so to see the Divine Presence in all people and in all creation. His new consciousness of God so energized him that he could daily enter the stream of his sacred story, enabling him to reengage life's duties and obligations with a serene heart and with clarity of purpose. He courageously allowed God to write his sacred story over the remainder of his life—hourly, daily, weekly, monthly, yearly.

The vitality of Ignatius's personal relationship with God—in Father, Son, and Spirit—was possible through the grace and gratitude he experienced in the constant encounter with his personal sinfulness and disordered passions. These graced encounters always brought illumination, insight, energy, and hope, never discouragement, fear, or despair.

A proud, dissolute, insecure narcissist finally found serenity and security in God's full love, acceptance, mercy, and forgiveness. Interestingly enough, this happened in and through Ignatius's powerlessness and weaknesses, and perhaps even because of them!

That which so marred his early life became the very source of his strength and sanctity. Ignatius discovered, like St. Paul, that in his weaknesses and sin, he was strong in Christ (2 Cor 12:10). It will be the same for you.

ભ

I am starting a Relationship that will carry me for
the rest of my life.

All relationships require time and patience.
I will strive for patience and ask for God's help
when I don't understand a lesson.

I will learn the fundamentals and open my heart to God.

I trust that God will lead me.

I believe that my sacred story will unfold in truth,
in powerlessness, and with my patience.

I believe that Jesus awaits me
with His grace, mercy, and forgiving love.

ଚ

Letters from Week Three

Dear Fr. Bill:

My conversion, if that's the proper term, occurred over three years ago. It's when I finally realized that God loves me, despite, or because of, how I'd lived my life up until then. My main obstacle, the thing I could not get past and that was dragging my spiritual growth to a standstill, was the fact that my thoughts, words and deeds were not changing despite my recent awakening. I was convinced that this was due to a lack of faith. I prayed as much as possible, begging God for the faith needed to go on. I just assumed if I really had faith, then there is no way I could possibly still be holding on to my old thoughts, words and deeds.

I felt like St. Paul in Romans 7:15. I asked God for the same faith as Abraham and Noah, and Mary and Matthew. And the faith of the believers I'd known throughout my life. My praying for faith on a daily basis was incessant and probably, irrational. The lack of results caused me to almost give up completely. I was miserable and I thought, quite possibly, beyond redemption. Then, a couple of years ago when I began Forty Weeks for the first time, I read in chapter three about Ignatius' "destructive, obsessive torture" pertaining to his confessions. A light went on and I realized the similarities of our situations.

The burden of feeling as if I didn't have the faith necessary to become the man God created me to be was lifted. It occurred to me instantly, "If I don't have faith, then to whom and why am I praying"? I do have the faith and God will show it to me in His time. In the meantime, I knew I needed to keep going. And, like Ignatius' decision to stop his "damaging confession habit", my decision to stop beating myself up for my supposed "lack of faith" may seem inconsequential, but like for Ignatius, it was a decision that marked the turning point in my journey.

I now know that the counter-inspirer was behind my being convinced of my lack of faith. I now have to look to where my thoughts, words, and deeds are leading me in order to discern their origins. I used to think I was my anti-story, that I was just evil or crazy or both, and that I could never change. The last paragraph of Chapter Three means a lot to me. "A proud, dissolute narcissist finally found serenity and security in God's full love, acceptance, mercy and forgiveness." "That which marred his early life became the very source of his strength and sanctity. Ignatius discovered, like St. Paul, that in his weaknesses and sin, he was strong in Christ" (2 COR 12:10).

Knowing and accepting that I am forgiven and loved by Him is the source of the strength I need to move forward. Very often my gratitude and enthusiasm are fleeting. Sometimes I doubt my desire and daily commitment. My feelings of insecurity and doubt are shorter and occur less often as I move forward in Forty Weeks.

Respectfully,

Ritchie

Dear Ritchie:

Your discoveries in Week Three of Forty Weeks are very important and should be ones that you hold onto for the rest of your life. They provide a key insight into how the "enemy of human nature" is working on your heart and in your mind to drag you away from a faith in God.

Your opening to God three years ago, what you describe as your conversion, gave you a conviction for the first time that you were loved. You experienced God's love in spite of your weaknesses and sinfulness. It is true for all of us. Even Pope Francis said he felt great compassion for people in prison because he felt he had done things in his own life that might have merited his incarceration but was spared.

Knowing our weaknesses and that we really have nothing to offer God but our brokenness, is what makes Jesus desire to be with us. We can't save ourselves and he promises to do the saving for us. That is why he was born, lived, and died for us. We sing our Christmas carols because of what they promise. Ritchie, remember the words of "O, Holy Night":

> O holy night! The stars are brightly shining,
> It is the night of our dear Savior's birth.
> Long lay the world in sin and error pining,
> Till He appeared and the soul felt its worth.
> A thrill of hope, the weary world rejoices,
> For yonder breaks a new and glorious morn.
> Fall on your knees! O hear the angel voices!
> O night divine, O night when Christ was born;
> O night divine, O night, O night Divine.

The Prayer Over the Offerings for the Mass on Friday of the Third Week of Advent is very beautiful in this regard, too, Ritchie. It says: Be pleased, O Lord, with our humble prayers and offerings, and, since we have no merits to plead our cause come, we pray, to our rescue with the protection of your mercy.

Ritchie, what you discovered is that your enemy wanted you to lose faith in God because your life was not immediately transformed when you had your "conversion". So, you tried everything you could to get better and nothing seemed to work. Your enemy's goal was to get you to try ever harder to be better and to constantly look at how often you failed to change.

You are correct; it was much like St. Ignatius trying to save himself by his habit of re-confessing his past sins and getting more and more anxious and desolate that he could not get it right. The enemy's goal in both cases is to get you to lose hope in yourself and God.

Finally Ritchie, don't look to how you fall short by doubting and not feeling as committed as you think you should be. Pay attention instead to your desire to be transformed. God is the one who has given you the desire and the fact that you have been given this desire is a sign that God will bring it about!

God will achieve what you can't on your own. "We have no merits to plead our cause so come, we pray, to our rescue with the protection of your mercy!"

You are in my prayers. Please keep me in yours.

Peace,

Fr. Bill

NOTES

Week 4

FIRST

I will review my faithfulness to my daily fifteen-minute time(s) of contemplative rest and reflection. If my commitment has wavered, it may be helpful to write down the specific location and the time(s) of day. I ask God for the grace to recommit to this practice, which is the most important dimension of Sacred Story prayer. I will resist the temptation to judge myself harshly when I fail to live up to the ideal. Each day, I will do my best to be faithful to the commitment I have made.

SECOND

I will purchase a small spiral notebook (if I have not already done so) should I need more space for my journaling than is provided in the NOTES section at the end of each week. It will be needed later. However, you may find the Notes pages at the end of each week sufficient for your short daily journal entries.

THIRD

During my fifteen-minute quiet moments this week, I will read through part 3 of St. Ignatius's conversion story. It is spiritual reading. I will read and reread reflectively and take my time. I will invite God to be my companion as I read. I will ask the Lord to help me listen with my heart and be attentive to what moves me spiritually. I will use the process that works best for me. If I can better reflect on the material during my fifteen-minute prayer periods by reading it all first on Sunday, then I use that method. It may be helpful to highlight the sections of the readings that created hope and/or anxiety, and bring those sections to reflection and prayer.

I will not read ahead.
I will awaken to the present moment.
I will take each day and each exercise as it comes.
I cannot do Sacred Story better by going faster.

℅

Welcome to the fourth week of our pilgrimage together. The exercises for the fourth week move from the conversion story of St. Ignatius to your own story. You are invited to make a commitment to join with St. Ignatius, and all the holy women and men in the Church, to give your life to Christ for this great work of reconciliation.

Listen to the call and pay attention to whatever stirs in you, be it hope and peace or anxiety and fear. Doing this sharpens your spiritual radar for things that prompt your heart to say, "Pay attention!" Thank Christ in advance for the blessings and insights you will receive.

Part 3: The Call to Universal Reconciliation

As with Ignatius, God extends to us an invitation to awaken to the pattern of spiritual, emotional, and psychological dysfunction that has formed our anti-story. God invites us to awaken to our lives as sacred story and to produce fruit that endures to eternity. The awakening and growth will reveal where our freedom is compromised and how we close our hearts to our authentic human nature.

Christ compassionately shows us how our selfishness and pride have corrupted our creativity, robbing us of the joy of innocence. God's invitation is gentle. God's awakening is merciful. Rest assured that God's passion is to pursue us, rescue us, heal us, and bring us back to our original innocence. God's passion is personal. God's passion is love. God's passion is Christ Jesus.

God's intention is to gradually heal and transform our thoughts, words, and deeds. For every thought, word, and deed influences our history in the direction of an anti-story or a sacred story. Every thought, word, and deed—for good or ill—touches all people in my life, the entire world, and all of creation, shaping history's final chapter.

The effects of sin and narcissism—as well as the effects of virtue and selflessness—have individual, social, physical, spiritual, and ecological ramifications that reach to the ends of creation. For everything and everyone is one in Love—one in Christ Jesus—through whom and for whom everything was made (Rom 11:36).

Every thought, word, or deed, no matter how discreet, has positive or negative significance in the interconnected web of life that God has fashioned through Christ. It is Christ's being—His Sacred Story—that links each of our individual sacred stories. It is in Christ that the entire cosmos is joined together. God in Christ has made us responsible for and dependent upon each other and upon the earth that sustains us.

The Christ of the cosmos—through whom and for whom everything was made—became man and confronted, absorbed, and defused all the destructive force of evil's evolutionary anti-history running through human nature and the created cosmos. Christ reconciles in Himself everything in the heavens and on the earth to bring peace to all by the blood of His cross. His Sacred Story redeems and renews every chapter in our history, individual and collective.

Christ Jesus passionately awaits our participation to join His work of universal reconciliation. Our willingness to accept the path of conversion entails truthfully identifying our sins, dysfunction, and addictions. It entails experiencing and admitting our powerlessness to save ourselves. It requires the patience of a lifetime while Christ writes our sacred story.

My participation in Christ's work of reconciliation is the only worthy vocation and the only labor that produces fruit enduring to eternity. My accepting the invitation unlocks the very mystery of life.

When I accept the invitation, Christ promises to share His universal glory. Accepting the invitation to intentionally enter my sacred story has momentous consequences.

Now Is the Time to Wake from Sleep

Our time on this earth is so very brief. Since the time of Christ's birth, life, death, and resurrection, our story can only be measured and valued in light of His eternal mission of Reconciliation. Intentionally entering my sacred story will, over time, enable me to know God more intimately and serve God more generously. Like Ignatius, I am called to awaken from sleep—to awaken to wholeness and holiness. I was created and infused with the gift to awaken to a life that reverences the God who, in Christ and the Holy Spirit, is present in all creation: every person and everything.

Awakening to my sacred story, as Ignatius did, calls for courage, in the cleansing of the spirit and psyche that it initiates. The process requires discipline in the face of temptation and monotony. It requires consciously asking, even begging if necessary, for God's graces. It requires time and patience, deliberately choosing each day to be faithful to time and space for God. Awakening requires the patience of a lifetime. Embraced and trusted, the journey is rich with blessings beyond our wildest expectations. Encountering Christ daily in sacred story forever changes life, relationships, the earth, and eternity.

What is needed for the journey will be provided each day. In your journey through the memories and experiences past and present, you are promised the power and mercy of the Love that maintains and guides the entire cosmos. It is this Love that waits to transform your sins, addictions, angers, fears, grief, guilt and shame. It is this Love that restores your broken heart into a vessel of forgiveness, light, and peace. The more embedded and impenetrable the web of darkness, compulsion, sin, and addiction in your life, the more strategic and magnificent is God's grace in breaking its grip, for nothing is impossible with God (Lk 1:37).

On this journey, you will gain personal and real knowledge of sin and mercy, creation and eternity. You will come to know, experientially, our gracious God, present in Christ's Body in the Church, in the sacraments, in yourself, in others, and in all creation. Some of your insights will come in a flash; others will unfold over weeks, months, or years. From now on, the whole process of your life is about waking from sleep (Eph 5:14; Rom 13:11), bending to the real, to the authentic, to your true human nature, living and working for fruit that endures to eternity.

Your Sacred History

Your life (and each person's life) is inextricably interwoven with and integrated into Christ's Sacred Story in ways both mysterious and sublime. It is mysterious, because the ways of this world are not the ways of the Kingdom. What is deemed valuable and successful in this present age is in fact foolish and useless in the spiritual life. It is sublime, because the most private sufferings offered to God, the faintest cries for mercy and forgiveness, and the simplest acts of care, kindness, or generosity done for one's enemy, God's beloved poor, and His magnificent creation, are written in gold in the Book of the Lamb. These are the thoughts, words, and deeds that will endure to eternity.

There are no shortcuts to the story's unfolding. Conversion is lifelong but measurable when I intentionally, daily, consistently, and faithfully enter my sacred story. My story begins where Ignatius's began, in the grace of the call to conversion. My conversion will begin to take shape when I accept that call and follow the pattern of Ignatius's own conversion. I will discover things that disquiet, create shame and confusion, and unlock hidden angers, fears, and grief. I will encounter a heart broken, and innocence and paradise lost.

But most important, in all of this, I will be held, sheltered, and guided by the only thing necessary, Christ's love. I will be given strength to speak truth to power. I will be given grace to see and honestly name those sins, habits, and addictions that bring death—spiritual, physical, psychological—and not life. Then, as I surrender to my powerlessness in favor of God's power, the Divine Physician will rewrite my life as sacred story.

Surrendering control of my life to the care of the Divine Physician by admitting my powerlessness to save myself will enable me to be vulnerable, creative, innocent, and humble. Once my heart is open, the Spirit of God will continue to write my sacred story. My lifetime of patience will bear fruit that endures to eternity. My pilgrim journey, like Ignatius's, follows the proven and time-tested mystical path to wholeness and holiness. There are no shortcuts. Christ Jesus Himself has traveled the path. He will guarantee my journey's safe passage and carry my burdens, failures, shame, broken heart, and confusion.

I will hold in my heart the humble example of Jesus washing my feet. He endured humiliations, torture, and a disgraceful death so that I can find hope and healing for everything in my life that needs healing, forgiveness, and redemption. From the beginning of time His Sacred Story is mystically imprinted into the souls of His chosen people and the Church. Through the pattern of His Story, I, the Church, and all people can have their history rewritten as sacred story.

I will intentionally enter my life narrative for fifteen-minute intervals once or twice each day. My story, linked to Christ's Sacred Story and to all people and to all creation, runs from my birth in all my thoughts, words, and deeds to shape my destiny here and in the hereafter. Sacred Story prayer will help me attune to Creation, Presence, Memory, Mercy, and Eternity. When I encounter the fears, stresses, angers, temptations, failures, addictions, and sins in my day, I can briefly attune to Creation, Presence, Memory, Mercy, and Eternity and ask for the grace to see my whole story. By so doing, I invite the Divine Physician to heal me and awaken my heart to its true human nature.

Christ extends the invitation: His love, at the heart of the universe, awaits my response. I pray for the courage and generosity to enter with Christ into my sacred story.

ɔʒ

I am starting a Relationship that will carry me
for the rest of my life.

All relationships require time and patience.
I will strive for patience and ask for God's help
when I don't understand a lesson.

I will learn the fundamentals and open my heart to God.
I trust that God will lead me.

I believe that my sacred story will unfold in truth,
in powerlessness, and with my patience.

I believe that Jesus awaits me with
His grace, mercy, and forgiving love.

ꝏ

Letters from Week Four

Dear Fr. Bill,

Every thought, word and deed means something. Nothing is insignificant. We are either moving toward our anti-story or our Sacred Story. That, for me, is something I can easily grasp. Chapter Four states that "intentionally entering my Sacred Story will, over time, enable me to know God more intimately and serve God more generously". Fr. Bill, that is all I want or need.

Since that day three years ago when I realized God truly does love me, all I've wanted is to be able to feel His love for me, somehow express, in a meaningful way, my love and gratitude to Him for His mercy and compassion, and to serve Him in whatever capacity He desires.

The problem for me has been getting to that point. In theory it is simple, but when there is an enemy wanting me to stay where I am or go back to where I'd been for almost fifty years, it is difficult. But Chapter Four shows me that, beginning with begging for God's graces and accepting the call to conversion, I will be guided by Christ's love along the same path he travelled, to "wholeness and holiness".

Fr. Bill, at fifty-two years of age, in my nineteenth year of incarceration, with no material possessions or family or close friends, I am at the point where I always wanted to be but didn't know it. I know that Forty Weeks is much more than identifying and being inspired by St. Ignatius' story. I am aware that the real work begins now and I look forward to it.

Again, I want to thank you for taking the time to guide me through these Forty Weeks.

Respectfully,

Ritchie

Dear Ritchie:

Your reflections on Week Four continue to show the deep desire God has placed in your heart to follow Jesus. Once you realize there are only two directions you can go in life—towards God or away from God—you have come to the profound realization that, like St. Ignatius, you want to serve the Lord of Life!

The negative daydreams you wrote about in your reflections for Week Two have more and more lost their power over you. When you experience them in the future, and you will until the day you pass from this earth, simply say what St. Ignatius said to his vain, lustful, and narcissistic fantasies: "You poor creature, can you promise me even one hour of life?" When we consciously name these daydreams and false hopes and dead-end lifestyles, we become more mentally and emotionally committed to taking the path of light and life.

And Ritchie, you have discovered also in your reflections for Week Four the important Ignatian practice of "begging and asking God for the graces" you need. St. Ignatius emphasizes this important practice all through the Spiritual Exercises. I am sure he got the idea from Jesus in the Gospels when he says in Matthew 7:7-11:

Ask and it will be given to you; seek and you will find; knock and the door will be opened to you.
For everyone who asks, receives; and the one who seeks, finds; and to the one who knocks, the door will be opened.
Which one of you would hand his son a stone when he asks for a loaf of bread, or a snake when he asks for a fish?

If you then, who are wicked, know how to give good gifts to your children, how much more will your heavenly Father give good things to those who ask him.

Peace, Fr. Bill

Dear Fr. Bill,

I very much appreciate your comments and insights regarding my experience with Weeks One through Four of Forty Weeks. I am grateful for this opportunity.

I've heard many stories over the years about people being able to keep the faith and even grow spiritually under horrendous conditions – POWs, victims of abuse, hostages, the homeless and addicted, etc. Because of this I am hesitant to share the difficulties I experience here in prison where, quite frankly, I don't have it half as bad as some others who aren't incarcerated. That said, there are some things that impede my "spiritual program": finding quiet places for my two fifteen-minute Sacred Story Prayer sessions; two Rosary sessions; journal entries and, composing these letters to you.

Trying to keep any kind of set schedule is difficult due to the fact that no two days are the same around here. Violence, or even the possibility of violence, can disrupt my best laid plans. And even though I do, like you suggested, consider my cell my "monk's cell", I do have a cellmate, which sometimes interferes. My housing unit consists of 128 men and there is always a lot going on and everyone needs to be alert. The one thing I do know for sure is none of these obstacles are insurmountable.

I pray regularly for God's grace to overcome all obstacles to my discipleship. I am happy to be able to say that since starting Forty Weeks, time has been found for all of my rosaries, Sacred Story prayer sessions, and other requirements related to Forty Weeks. And, as of Nov. 27th, the First Sunday of Advent, I have been using a book titled "Sacred Reading", the 2017 Guide to Daily Prayer by Douglas Leonard. The format, including a daily Gospel reading, is very simple and helpful. I am very much enjoying this addition to my daily prayers.

Thank you for your insights concerning my lack of relationship with my birth mother. Through my twice daily rosaries I am attempting to learn how to come to the Mother of God to ask for her prayers and intercession, and also, guidance like a son would come to his mother for, something I've never experienced. The idea that Mary loves me like a mother would love her son is very reassuring.

Respectfully,

Ritchie

Dear Ritchie:

For my Christmas Eve homily, I read part of your letters. My point was that Christ was born into our world to save us from sin and death and that you had discovered this great gift in prison. Everyone at the Mass was very moved. I think they realized, better than they had before, the true gift Christ came to give us and the real meaning of Christmas.

In hearing of your experience of being saved by Jesus, one of the people there said to me: "Everyone in the room felt the spirit of love. Thank You!" So, you see how your experience of God is already reaching others?

Peace,

Fr. Bill

NOTES

Week 5

FIRST

I select my fifteen-minute quiet time(s) for the week ahead. I visualize where I will go each day and at what time(s). I ask God for the grace to make those appointments throughout the week, in a technology-free zone.

SECOND

From this point forward, I will bring my notebook to my prayer sessions for the remainder of the forty weeks.

THIRD

My fifteen-minute prayer times this week consist of two exercises:

1. I ask for the inspiration to discover the name of God that speaks directly to my heart. It can take two or more days to discover the name that unlocks my heart to God's love and mercy. If God does not inspire me in the first two days, I will set this exercise aside and move to the second exercise. But I will continue to ask for the inspiration for the rest of the week to find the name. I will thank God in advance, because God will give me the inspiration I need to reveal the name that speaks to my heart. I will thank God in advance for this important grace.

2. For the remainder of the week, I listen to the three parts of Ignatius's conversion story in light of my own story. A simple spiritual reflection

associated with this exercise is described below.

I will not read ahead.
I will awaken to the present moment.
I will take each day and each exercise as it comes.
I cannot do Sacred Story better by going faster.
I will ask God to help me.

℘

Take a moment to ask God for this grace: "Lord, open me to the knowledge of my own heart." The heart is where the important work of prayer takes place. The mind reveals facts. The heart reveals the truth of my being. The heart is how Scripture describes the most important aspects of the human condition. Here are a few examples:

✠ The heart reveals the state of corruption caused by sin (Gen 6:5; Jer 17:9–10; Mt 15:9).[4]

✠ The heart is where the process of conversion and forgiveness takes place (Ez 36:26; Mt 18:35; Rom 2:29).

✠ The heart is the point of convergence, where self-condemnation comes face-to-face with hope in God's power (1 Jn 3:19–20).

✠ The heart's purity enables one to see God (Mt 5:8).

✠ The heart is the locus of compassion (Lk 7:13).

✠ The heart is the custodian of memory and contemplation (Lk 1:29; 2:19, 51).

✠ The heart is the vessel holding the secrets that illuminate the true meaning of life (Mt 6:21; Lk 24:32; Ps 85:9).

✠ The heart is defined as the center of human consciousness and action, wherein God discerns the rightness or wrongness of my thoughts, words, and deeds. The heart is the center from which each person will stand before God and render the ultimate account of their thoughts, words, and deeds (Heb 4:12–13).

✠ The heart perceives love as the ultimate end, gift, and purpose of being (1 Cor 13).

✠ The testimony of Christ in Scripture speaks to the heart's desire for innocence, based on the weariness of life, and the burdens it carries, resulting from corruption (Mt 11:28–30.).

✠ Christ also promises to respond to the heart searching for Him and gives the conviction that He can be found by those who seek Him (Lk 11:9–11).

Seek knowledge of the heart, and ask God for the grace to open a pathway to your heart. Seek also knowledge of God's heart, present in Christ's Sacred Heart. This grace will help to unite your heart to the heart of Christ. "Lord, open me to the knowledge of my own heart."

For the first two days of fifteen-minute prayer periods this week:

Once you are settled in your place of prayer, ask for God's inspiration for this time. Then ask, in words from your heart, to be inspired to discover or remember the most intimate and/or meaningful name for God the Father, Son, and Spirit that you have used in prayer.

The name will resonate deeply in your heart and reflect God's relationship to you and your personal relationship with God. The following may be helpful:

Father, Loving Father, Almighty Father, Our Father, Father God, Loving Creator, Creator God, God of Love, My God, Holy God, Father of the Poor, God of All Mercy, God of All Compassion, Father of Jesus, Lord Jesus Christ, Lord Jesus, Christ Jesus, Dear Jesus, Adorable Jesus, Adorable Christ, Good Jesus, Jesus, Merciful Savior, Jesus My Savior, Son

of God, Dearest Lord, My Lord, My Lord and My God, Sacred Heart of
Jesus, Lamb of God, Good Shepherd, Crucified Savior, Holy Spirit, Spirit
of Jesus, Spirit of the Lord, Loving Spirit, Holy Spirit of God,
Love of God, Divine Spirit, Creator Spirit, Creator God

Ask for the grace to discover the name for God that touches your heart
most intimately. You will know the right name, because it has the power
to unlock your trust and your love and to stir your affections.

Write the name for God in your notebook when you discover it. From
this point forward, use this name when you address God. God delights
when you speak directly from your heart.[5]

For the remainder of the fifteen-minute prayer periods this week:

Review Ignatius's story and your own. Use this question as the focus for
the exercise: "Like Ignatius, have I discovered the one area of my life
that convinces me, beyond any doubt, that I cannot save myself and
must rely on God to save me?"

Recall parts 1 and 2 of St. Ignatius's narrative. In your prayer times,
review the sections of his story that resonate with your own story. In
these prayer periods, recall those parts of his story that moved your
heart in one of two ways:

1. "What spontaneously evoked anxiety in me as I listened to
   Ignatius's story?" I will reflect on why this anxiety was
   provoked. In my notebook, I will record what evoked my anxiety
   and why.

2. "As I listened to Ignatius's conversion story, what inspired or
   gave me hope about my life?" I will reflect on why I was inspired
   or hopeful. In my notebook, I will record what inspired me and
   why.

For the last fifteen-minute prayer period at week's end:

Using my notebook jottings, I will sift through the entries and ask for the grace to identify the one issue or idea that caused me the most anxiety. I will record this in my notebook. Then I will write down why I felt the anxiety. I may not know why something causes anxiety, so if it is not clear yet, I will not be anxious about that. Instead, I will invite God into this unknown area: "Lord, why did this make me anxious?"

In my notebook I will also record what I discovered that offered me the most hope or inspiration and why. If I don't know, I will invite God to reveal this to me: "Lord, why did this cause me to have hope?"

I will be brief and specific in my notebook entries. My reflection plus my writing exercises ought not to extend beyond the allotted time of fifteen-minutes that encompasses my prayer period.[6]

છ

I am starting a Relationship that will carry me
for the rest of my life.

All relationships require time and patience.
I will strive for patience and ask for God's help
when I don't understand a lesson.

I will learn the fundamentals and open my heart to God.

I trust that God will lead me.
I believe that my sacred story will unfold in truth,
in powerlessness, and with my patience.

I believe that Jesus awaits me with His grace, mercy, and forgiving
love.

છ

Letters from Week Five

Dear Fr. Bill,

It did not take long for me to discover the most meaningful name for God the Father, Son and Spirit that I will always use in prayers—God of Mercy and Compassion. Although my life has not so far turned out the way I had hoped or expected, the realization that it could be a lot worse—and that the only reason it hasn't been worse is because of God's intervention— made my choice easy.

More than three years ago, for the first time in my life, I threw myself down at God's feet and begged for his help. His love saved my life. I thank Him every day for allowing me to acknowledge that it was His mercy and compassion for this unworthy sinner that saved my life and opened the door to eternal life. Mercy and compassion remind me that I have an obligation to show that to others also.

St. Ignatius' story evoked much more inspiration and hope than anxiety. When reading that at times Ignatius felt that living a virtuous life forever was an impossible goal and that he considered quitting, even suicide, caused me anxiety at first, but then the fact that he got past it gave me hope. His narcissistic daydreams being replaced with selfless, generous daydreams gave me the hope that mine would also. His ability to stop his incessant confessing made me realize that I needed to truly surrender, that I cannot fix anything, particularly the insecurity I experience for feeling as if I do not have the faith necessary to change.

Respectfully,

Ritchie

Dear Ritchie:

In Native American culture, one's spirit name is more important than one's given name. Individuals are asked to pray to discover their spirit name which signifies more about their true personality and mission in life. I also believe that the God who knew us before we were born (Isaiah 49: 1) has placed a unique name for God in each of our hearts that unlocks them so we can personally feel that we are loved, cherished, and saved by Jesus Christ. I am grateful that God has given you the grace to know his name as God of Mercy and Compassion. Use that name often and allow God's love to touch you in the depths of your being where you need the most healing, hope, and peace.

Many people see the heroic pictures of saints or read about all the incredible things they accomplished, and say: "I don't think I could ever be holy like that". As you have heard before, "every saint has a past and every sinner a future". It is important to recognize the two major experiences you had reading about Saint Ignatius. The first one was anxiety when you heard about his narcissism and his desire to end his life.

That suicidal inspiration was rooted in his pride that he could not save himself. You most likely felt anxious because you, like most of us, share those same anxieties at various times in the course of life. But the more important thing to hold onto is the hope you felt when Ignatius surrendered to God and let him take over when Ignatius failed.

You don't have the faith necessary to change but God will give you that faith. It is his work, not ours. We just have to keep saying: "I can't do it! Please help me!" This prayer will always be heard, Ritchie.

Peace to you,

Fr. Bill

NOTES

Week 6

FIRST
I will plan my fifteen-minute quiet time(s) for the week ahead. I will visualize where I will go each day and at what time(s). I will ask God for the grace to help me keep those appointments throughout the week. I will seek a technology-free zone—a place apart.

SECOND
I will have my notebook at hand for each prayer period.

THIRD
The prayer exercise for this week is composed of two parts. I will take half of the week's prayer periods for the first part and the other half of my prayer periods for the second part:

Once settled in prayer, I will ask God to reveal to me the most important persons, life events, and/or issues that generate gratitude, hope, and love in me.

Then I will ask God to reveal to me the most important persons, life events, and/or issues that evoke anger, fear, or grief in me.

I will not read ahead.
I will awaken to the present moment.
I will take each day and each exercise as it comes.

I cannot do Sacred Story better by going faster.
I will ask God to help me.

This week, I will say this affirmation aloud once daily:
I ask God to reveal to me the most important people,
life events, and/or issues in my story up to this point.

⊂ℨ

Each of us has persons, issues, and life events that shape our life story, our history. We are conscious of some of these pieces, while others are buried deep in our memory. We seek grace to understand those things that, in negative and positive ways, most strongly shape our thoughts, actions, feelings, and beliefs linked to God, the world, and ourselves. These persons, life events, and issues are often linked to the spiritual plotlines in our life story, leading toward or away from God.

This week, we seek God's grace to awaken to our affective memories. That is, we want to recall persons, life events, and issues and feel the emotional weight—the heart value—they have in our history. Because these significant elements often evade our conscious awareness, we need to rely on grace to reveal them.

Naturally, I seek insight into the closest, most intimate circle of people and events in my life story—my parents, family, friends, and important events. I will be attentive to the feeling these memories evoke.

For one life event, I might feel fear (something that has the power to generate the anxiety I know as fear). For another life event, my predominant feeling might be anger (something that hurt me or a loved one). For one person, I might feel mostly love (someone who has cared deeply for me). For another person, I might feel anger (someone who hurt me in some way). For one issue, my predominant feeling might be grief (the loss of a loved one, or a missed opportunity that grieves my heart). For another issue, my experience might be gratitude or hope (an issue that has positively transformed my life for the better).

Pray that God enlighten your mind and heart to know each person, issue, or life event and the single predominant feeling (fear, anger, or grief; gratitude, hope, or love) each inspires.

For your prayer periods this week, sit apart in your quiet place. Find a comfortable position that permits you to be alert. Breathe deeply for a few minutes, mindful that God's love sustains your very life. Next, using the personal name for God you identified last week, ask God to enlighten your memory and imagination so that the most significant people, issues, and life events come into your mind and heart.

As you become aware of each, pause briefly to write down the name of the person or the issue or life event that comes to memory. Next to each of these, write a single word for the most predominant feeling that arises in your heart. A word of caution here: do not succumb to the temptation to analyze or judge the feelings as they arise.

For the first half of the week, use the first chart to ask God to inspire you to remember the elements (person, issue, or life event) that generate gratitude, hope, or love. Pray that those elements most important to your history come into your mind and heart.

For the second half of the week, use the next chart to ask God to inspire you to remember the people, issues, or life events that generate fear, anger, or grief. Pray that those elements most important to your history come into your mind and heart.

TEN PARTS OF MY LIFE HISTORY THAT GENERATE GRATITUDE, HOPE, OR LOVE

Persons / Life Events / Issues	*Gratitude / Hope / Love*
1.	1.
2.	2.
3.	3.
4.	4.
5.	5.
6.	6.
7.	7.
8.	8.
9.	9.
10.	10.

TEN PARTS OF MY LIFE HISTORY THAT GENERATE
FEAR, ANGER, OR GRIEF

Persons / Life Events / Issues	*Fear / Anger / Grief*
1.	1.
2.	2.
3.	3.
4.	4.
5.	5.
6.	6.
7.	7.
8.	8.
9.	9.
10.	10.

ଓ

I am starting a Relationship that will carry me
for the rest of my life.

All relationships require time and patience.
I will strive for patience and ask for God's help
when I don't understand a lesson.

I will learn the fundamentals and open my heart to God.

I trust that God will lead me.

I believe that my sacred story will unfold in truth,
in powerlessness, and with my patience.

I believe that Jesus awaits me with His grace,
mercy, and forgiving love.

ଅ

Letters from Week Six

Dear Fr. Bill,

During Week Six we were asked to chart the persons/life and events/issues that caused us Gratitude/Hope/Love and Fear/Anger/Grief. But we were warned not to "succumb to the temptation to analyze or judge the feelings as they arise". Much easier said than done! As I was studying my journal entries for this week I was surprised at some of the things that came up during my prayer periods: some people and events I'd forgotten about or hadn't thought about for some time. Apparently, most of my life has consisted of gratitude and anger, with very little in between. Without analyzing too much, I can say, unfortunately, that my gratitude was for people and things that fed my narcissistic life, and my anger was for people and events which stood in the way of pursuing my narcissistic, self-indulgent life. What an eye opener.

Respectfully,

Ritchie

Dear Ritchie:

Yes, I know how hard it is not to judge feelings when they arise, especially if strong or positive negative emotions surface. Many of us can develop an emotional editing tool that keeps us from acknowledging our strong feelings. I keep repeating to people doing the program that the goal for the Forty Weeks program is to become conscious of all that holds us back from finding freedom in Christ Jesus. That you discovered your gratitude and anger were narcissistically focused is a breakthrough for your growing freedom. You may be in prison physically but your spirit is being released a little more each day from its life-long prison. Psalm 38 is a good one for your reflection this week.

A psalm of David for remembrance:

LORD, do not punish me in your anger;
in your wrath do not chastise me!
Your arrows have sunk deep in me;
your hand has come down upon me.
There is no wholesomeness in my flesh because of your anger;
there is no health in my bones because of my sin.
My iniquities overwhelm me,
a burden too heavy for me.
Foul and festering are my sores
because of my folly.
I am stooped and deeply bowed;
every day I go about mourning.
My loins burn with fever;
there is no wholesomeness in my flesh.
I am numb and utterly crushed;
I wail with anguish of heart.
My Lord, my deepest yearning is before you;
my groaning is not hidden from you.
My heart shudders, my strength forsakes me;
the very light of my eyes has failed.

Friends and companions shun my disease;
my neighbors stand far off.
Those who seek my life lay snares for me;
they seek my misfortune, they speak of ruin;
they plot treachery every day.
But I am like the deaf, hearing nothing,
like the mute, I do not open my mouth,
I am even like someone who does not hear,
who has no answer ready.

LORD, it is for you that I wait;
O Lord, my God, you respond.
For I have said that they would gloat over me,
exult over me if I stumble.
I am very near to falling;
my wounds are with me always.
I acknowledge my guilt
and grieve over my sin.
My enemies live and grow strong,
those who hate me grow numerous fraudulently,
Repaying me evil for good,
accusing me for pursuing good.
Do not forsake me, O LORD;
my God, be not far from me!
Come quickly to help me,
my Lord and my salvation!

Peace to you,

Fr. Bill

NOTES

Week 7

FIRST

I will review my fifteen-minute quiet time(s) for the week ahead and visualize where I will go each day and at what time(s). I will ask God for the grace to keep those times sacred. I will have my notebook at hand for each prayer period. I will always use my personal name for God.

SECOND

During my fifteen-minute quiet prayer this seventh week, there are two prayer exercises. I will take the first half of the week's prayer periods for the first exercise and the second half of my prayer periods for the second exercise.

THIRD

1. I will ask God for the grace to identify how the Ten Commandments fit into my life as a gift to bring awareness, healing, balance, and God's peace.
2. I will ask God for the grace to identify the deepest hope of my heart for my life and my future.

I will not read ahead.
I will awaken to the present moment.
I will take each day and each exercise as it comes.
I cannot do Sacred Story better by going faster.
I will ask God to help me.

This week, I will say this affirmation aloud once daily:
The Ten Commandments are a profound gift from God
to the chosen people and to all humankind.

℘

Read 1 and 2 before starting your prayer sessions this week:

1. For the first half of the week:
Use the Decalogue Examination of Conscience to better understand your life story and the gift of healing and balance that God desires for you. Pray that your imagination be graced so that the most important issues in the Commandments, those that illuminate your history (your story), will come into your mind and heart. Pray to "see" what you have never seen before. Pray to see your life as God sees your life.

The Commandments were given to the Chosen People in a Covenant that was sealed with a blood sacrifice. The Church reflects that the power of the animal sacrifice sealing the Covenant receives its power from Christ's blood, which it foreshadows. The Commandments, as gift, are a foundation for God's work to repair our broken human nature, to forgive us, and to reopen the way to eternity: the work of Christ's death and resurrection. It is no wonder then that laws enshrining the Commandments' truths have transformed stories of violence and injustice to stories of civility and justice for countless millions of people in the last three millennia.

For this exercise, we are reflecting on the Commandments to enhance our understanding of their richness and wisdom. The exercise will help to clarify how each Decree carries its own responsibilities and boundaries. These Decrees revealed by God remind us of the truth about God, humanity, and oneself. They are a gift to guide our way home so our thoughts, words and deeds bring life, not death.

Before concluding your prayer period, use your notebook to record where in your life you have missed the mark in living the decree you reflected on. Be specific, honest, and courageous. Ask for the grace of integrity and openness to embrace the truth of your own experience.

This may be a helpful format to follow as you reflect on each decree: Identify the decree (and the sub-themes in the decree) as mild, moderate, or strong, depending on the challenge this specific decree presents to you. For example, you may write "6th—moderate, especially regarding [issue]" or "4th—mild regarding [person]" or "7th/10th—strong regarding [event]." Use codes if you prefer to safeguard confidentiality and augment honesty.

Note: The purpose of this exercise is to simply identify your challenges with the Commandments. With Christ by your side, watch with curiosity and detachment, without self-blame. God sees beyond any patterns of sin and failure you have, or think you have. God knows you for whom you are. God loves you. God is the Divine Physician who desires to help you honestly see your life as it is so He can bring forgiveness, healing, freedom and peace.

2. For the second half of the week:
Pray for the grace to remember the books, stories, songs, events, movies, and art that have the power to bring you to tears. The shortest phrase in Scripture is "Jesus wept" (Jan 11:35). Pray to remember the turn of phrase, the lyric, the dialogue, the word spoken to you, the melody, and the image that has touched your heart so profoundly that your only response is to weep. What causes us to weep holds significance in our history and informs our story. Pray to remember and feel what moves you to tears.

The Gospels record that Jesus wept twice. He wept over Jerusalem, for failing to recognize that the time of its deliverance was at hand (Lk 19: 41–44). And He wept over the death of His good friend Lazarus: "See how he loved him," the people said (Jn 11:33–6). Both instances reveal Jesus's deep longing for humanity's reconciliation and peace. It is Christ's desire to bring freedom from death's grip, that death which resulted from humanity's disobedience. Jesus's weeping expresses the deepest longings of His heart. His tears reveal His mission in life, a mission He received from the Father, for those He loves.

Tears reveal the deepest longings of our hearts, too. They are a window to the heart and soul. Ask God for the grace to remember and understand what brings you to tears, what breaks your heart or expresses your heart's longings for healing and peace.

Use your fifteen-minute prayers in the second half of the week to recall what causes you to weep, that is, what brings you to tears and expresses the deepest longings of your heart. Do not spend more than fifteen minutes for each of your prayer periods. For your prayer, sit apart in a quiet place. Find a comfortable position that permits you to be alert. Breathe deeply for a few minutes, mindful that God's love sustains your very life.

Next, using the personal name for God you identified, ask God to enlighten your memory and imagination so that you can remember and understand what brings you to tears, and why. How is your life mission—your story—revealed in your tears? What stories, movies, books, songs move you to tears, and what can God help you understand about your life from them?

Before your prayer period ends, write down what caused your tears and why it caused your tears (if it is clear). Reflect further on what this might possibly reveal to you about your story. Do your tears reveal your deepest longings and God's desire to bring you hope and peace?

THE DECALOGUE EXAMINATION OF CONSCIENCE[7]

First Decree: I am the Lord your God, you shall have no strange gods before me.

Is God the center of my life? Have I displaced God with my career, work, concern for wealth and pleasure? Does the worship and honor of God take shape in my weekly religious practices? Do I pray often? Do I turn to God for forgiveness often? Have I resorted to relying on superstition, the occult, or astrology in place of asking for God's assistance?

Second Decree: You shall not take the name of the Lord your God in vain.

Do I casually take God's name in vain? Do I have a habit of swearing in jest or in anger? Do I use God's name to damn other people? Do I nurse hatred of God in my heart? Do I harbor anger toward God for the difficult things in my life or in the world? Do I reverence God in my heart?

Third Decree: Remember to keep holy the Sabbath day.

Do I make every effort to prepare myself for the Sunday liturgy? Do I make every effort to attend the Sunday liturgy? Do I allow social or sporting events to displace or limit my attendance at the Sunday liturgy? Do I limit unnecessary servile work on Sunday? Is Sunday a true day of spiritual rest and refreshment?

Fourth Decree: Honor your Father and Mother.

Do I give proper reverence to my mom and dad for the gift of life? Do I thank them? Do I spend time with them? Do I strive to forgive the shortcomings of my parents? Do I hold anger or grudges against them in my heart? Do I try to respond to them with love and charity? Do I attend to them in their sufferings and weaknesses? Am I patient with their infirmity as they age?

Fifth Decree: You shall not kill.

Have I ever killed someone or participated in actions that have led to other's death? Do I strive to overcome the prejudices I have against individuals or groups? Do I resist acting on my prejudices so as not to harm persons with my words or deeds? Do I act with cruelty toward others? Do I risk my life or the lives of others by using illegal drugs? Do I risk my life or the lives of others by driving recklessly or intoxicated? Do I strive in words and deeds to promote the value of life from conception to natural death? Have I ever helped someone terminate a pregnancy or end his/her own life? Do I strive to do everything I can to uphold the value of each person? Do I harbor satisfaction in my heart at the death of those people whom I consider evil? Do I vote for politicians/civil servants because of their positions to protect and promote abortion, euthanasia, capital punishment or preemptive war? Do I mourn the loss of all human life, no matter the cause of death?

Sixth Decree: You shall not commit adultery.
Ninth Decree: You shall not covet your neighbor's spouse.

Do I protect my covenant relationship with my spouse and uphold its sacredness? Do I strive daily to support my spouse? Do I turn to other persons for emotional support to make my spouse envious? Do I denigrate my spouse by comparing her/him to others? Do I speak harshly about my spouse behind his/her back to gain the affections of others? Do I uphold the sacredness of my covenant commitment by never seeking the sexual attention of those to whom I may be attracted? Do I uphold my covenant by never engaging in any sexual activity with someone other than my spouse? Do I use pornography to arouse my sexual appetites or to avoid intimacy with my spouse? Do I denigrate the spiritual integrity of persons by focusing on their physical beauty or appearance? Do I protect my covenant relationship by not purposely fantasizing about sexual relations with someone other than my spouse? Do I hold sacred the gift of sexuality for marriage? Do I strive to cultivate purity of heart as a sign of God's own single-heartedness? Do I reverence sexual intercourse first and foremost as the gift most akin to God's creative energies, a gift of love to create a human life destined for an eternity with God? Do I casually inhibit God's presence in this divine gift with drugs or medical procedures when there is no legitimate reason?

Seventh Decree: You shall not steal.
Tenth Decree: You shall not covet your neighbor's goods.

Do I cheat on papers and exams to steal a better grade? Do I take things that do not belong to me? Do I keep things I have borrowed? Am I honest in my investments, taxes, and all my financial dealings? Do I use legal loopholes in tax laws or business practices to harvest financial rewards that ultimately hurt the less fortunate? Am I honest and truthful in my business dealings, even if it means I may lose profits or customers? Do I vandalize or harm property or goods that do not belong to me? Do I envy those who have more than I do? Do I let concern for wealth and comfort take center place in my life? Do I live lavishly because I have the resources to do so? Do I spend money on luxury goods I do not need? Do I live with envy of those who have more than I do? Do I respect the limited resources of the earth as a divine inheritance to benefit all people? Do I give a percentage of my earned income to the poor? Do I strive to live so as to minimize waste and protect the environment? Do I examine my investment patterns to discern if companies I own, or in which I have stock, are treating their employees justly and are protecting the environment in their practices? Do I ever put the drive for profits ahead of the welfare of persons or the environment?

Eighth Decree: You shall not bear false witness against your neighbor.

Do I uphold the honor of other people's reputations? Do I avoid spreading gossip and avoid seeking gossip from others? Do I share information about people with third parties, even if it is true, when that information threatens the person's reputation? Do I avoid spreading lies or rumors about other people? Do I challenge people who gossip and spread damaging information about others? Do I avoid and denounce TV, radio, magazines, and newspapers that employ the tactics of personality destruction and malicious gossip to sell news and generate profits? Do I tell others what they ought to do instead of getting my own house in order?

 CB

I am starting a Relationship that will carry me
for the rest of my life.

All relationships require time and patience.
I will strive for patience and ask for God's help
when I don't understand a lesson.

I will learn the fundamentals and open my heart to God.

I trust that God will lead me.

I believe that my sacred story will unfold in truth,
in powerlessness, and with my patience.

I believe that Jesus awaits me with
His grace, mercy, and forgiving love.

ᏽᎣ

Letters from Week Seven

Dear Fr. Bill,

Week Seven has been the most painful, demanding, and hopeful week of Forty Weeks so far. I spent an entire week of prayer sessions on the first part alone. At first glance the Decrees, the Ten Commandments, appeared to be just the basic rules we learned in Catechism when I was kid. Plain and simple do's and don'ts. But the sub-themes cause me to seriously reflect on how I've lived my life. Once again we've been asked to do something very difficult – to "simply identify your challenges with the Commandments" and "without self-blame".

That was pretty hard. I definitely needed to use codes in my journal as suggested. After a few days of beating myself up terribly for the horrible person I was for the majority of my life, I was able to see the words on the pages of Week Seven more clearly. God already knew all of this. "God sees beyond any patterns of sin and failure" I have! God loves me and living the commandments will "guide our way home so our thoughts, words and deeds bring life, not death".

I didn't think the second part of Week Seven was going to bring any significant insight. Sure, I've cried plenty in my life. I usually chalked it up to getting caught in the moment: a moment of weakness, maybe. I'd never given my tears much thought. I've lost a few people I'd considered close to me. Very few. I just did not have close friendships or relatives. It is not how I lived my life.

But even then, if I'm being totally honest, even then some of those tears were for me and how those losses would affect me. I <u>do not</u> enjoy admitting this. Everything was about me. Most of my tears were over things I've witnessed that were lacking in my life – sibling affection, parent/child affection, grieving over a loss, acts of pure kindness. Things I knew nothing about but had unknowingly been longing for.

Today the image of Christ on the cross, Christ with his crown of thorns brings me to tears. The pain and suffering Jesus endured in carrying out His Father's will for us is what brings me to tears. When I was a kid and we'd attend Good Friday service we'd sing "Were you there when they nailed Him to the tree?". I would tear up but never gave it any meaningful thought until now. I felt it.

Of the two rosaries I pray daily, the first is always the assigned mysteries for that day, but the second is always the sorrowful mysteries. They just mean so much to me. I can feel it and it gives me more gratitude than anything else I do.

I ask God every day to open my eyes, ears, heart, and mind to what I need in order to move forward to becoming the man He created me to be. Week Seven has been enlightening, demanding, painful and hopeful. My gratitude for being forgiven gives me such a desire to move forward, to see what God has in store for me.

Respectfully,

Ritchie

Dear Ritchie:

It sounds like Week Seven was a good one for you—difficult and hopeful—that is a good combination. You are continuing to "wake up" and notice your life for what it has been, and what it can become. It is good you caught yourself in the process of beating yourself up. That is what Satan wants us to do so we lose hope in ourselves and God.

Remember what Jesus has done for us from this line in the Book of Revelation 12:10— "Then I heard a loud voice in heaven say: Now have salvation and power come, and the kingdom of our God and the authority of his Anointed. For the accuser of our brothers is cast out, who accuses them before our God day and night". Satan is the one who urges us to act selfishly and then accuses us in our hearts when we do a *double whammy! But Christ has cast out the accuser and we should too. We are to keep our eyes on Christ and what he has done out of love for us.*

And this is where your tears come in to the story. You weep, and have since you were young, over the sufferings of Christ. This is both for what he suffered and how his suffering touches on your own suffering. But it is also tears of hope and joy that Jesus loved you so much that <u>he died for you</u>!

So in spite of all the things you lacked regarding family love, the one who is LOVE wanted you to know at a very young age, your value in his eyes. The Son of God died out of love for Ritchie Roman. Say that sentence to Jesus when you look at the crucifix, Ritchie. "Jesus Christ, Son of the Living God, you suffered and died for me because you love me so much."

You are in my prayers. Keep me in yours.

Peace,

Fr. Bill

NOTES

Week 8

FIRST

I will select my fifteen-minute quiet time(s) for the week ahead and visualize where I will go each day and at what time(s). I will ask God for the grace to keep those times sacred throughout the week, in a technology-free zone. I will always use my personal name for God.

SECOND

I will have my notebook on hand for each prayer period.

THIRD

My fifteen-minute quiet prayer this week consists of two prayer exercises. I will take the first half of the week's prayer periods for the first exercise and the second half for the second exercise. If I find it more beneficial, I can combine the two with the alternate exercise.

First Spiritual Exercise: I will ask God for the grace to become aware of any habitual vices that obstruct my quest for holiness and interfere with the freedom God desires for me.

Second Spiritual Exercise: I will ask God for the grace to become aware of any addictions I possess that are eroding my quest for holiness and the freedom God desires for me.

Alternate Spiritual Exercise: I will ask God for the grace to see the connections between any habitual vices that erode my freedom and their link with addictive behaviors in my life story.

I will awaken to the present moment.
I will take each day and each exercise as it comes.
I cannot do Sacred Story better by going faster.
I will ask God to help me.
I will awaken to my spiritual nature and to the inspirations that inspire faith, hope, and love.
I will awaken to the inspirations that inspire cynicism, impatience, and lusts. I will wake up!

This week, I will say this affirmation aloud once daily:
I believe that understanding the source of my vices and addictions can lead to greater joy, authenticity, and holiness.

ℭӠ

Read 1, 2, and 3 before starting any prayer sessions this week:

The two powerful spiritual diagnostics for this week's lesson offer you the potential for great enlightenment. Vices and addictions reveal valuable information about our life stories. If we seek medical advice for pain, the doctor asks us where we hurt. Christ, the Divine Physician, sees our vices and addictions as manifestations of where we are hurting and our unsuccessful attempts to anesthetize our hurt. The Gospel calls them "sinful," because they manifest habits that erode our true human nature and our faith, hope, and love. The doctor calls them destructive, because they ruin our lives and relationships.

If you can honestly identify addictions and vices in your life story, you are on a path to freedom. If you prayed to Christ, the Divine Physician, to wake up to the connections between them in your life story, you should rejoice. Because your healing, leading to interior freedom, can now begin. Christ came to save sinners, not the righteous, and Sacred Story is about allowing Christ to help us identify where we need His healing graces. This is the great gift He wants to give to us. Be not afraid. Christ knows you are working with him to wake up.

Pray with words from your heart that will enable you to see what you have not seen before and to see connections between aspects of your life story. A word of caution: resist the temptation to be judgmental, anxiously plan corrective therapies, or get lost in fear. If you find yourself slipping into any of these, gently stop the exercise, and refocus your heart. These two exercises, like all the others, are to be approached with a compassionate, honest eye. It may be helpful to recall that you are reflecting on these components of your life narrative with the Divine Physician by your side. The goal is simply to wake up! Watch and pray!

1.For the first half of the week:
Pay attention to the vices (pride, gluttony, lust, sloth, envy, avarice, anger). They are sometimes called capital sins (from caput, the Latin word for head) because they are root habits or vices that lead to many other problems. All of us are subject to vices, which have the ability to hook us mildly, moderately, or strongly.

Simply identify your capital sins/vices. Ask Christ, the Divine Physician, to help you understand their source and context in your life history. Ask for the grace of deeper understanding, and then with Christ, observe your life with compassionate curiosity, and with objectivity. God sees beyond any vices you have, or think you have. God knows you for whom you are and loves you. Jesus, the Divine Physician, watches compassionately and carries the burden for all your vices. He desires that you gain greater understanding and freedom. He has great compassion and patience for those seeking His help and healing.

At the end of each prayer period, mark down in your notebook all the capital vices that trap you and to which you are susceptible. Be brief in your writing, but specific. List how intensely (mildly, moderately or strongly) they ensnare you. For example: Gluttony—moderately when I'm anxious.

2. For the second part of the week:
Pay attention to your addictions. Ignatius had addictions to gambling and possibly to sex. Everyone has addictions (whether mild, moderate, or strong) to one or more things. Our addictions reveal valuable diagnostic information that is worth bringing to the Divine Physician.

Do not exceed your fifteen-minute limit for each prayer period. For your prayer, sit apart in a quiet place. Find a comfortable position that permits you to be alert. Breathe deeply for a few minutes, mindful that God's love sustains your very life. Next, using the personal name for God you identified, ask God to enlighten your memory and imagination so that you can see any addictions you have in the context of your life story.

Before completing your prayer period, record any addictions that surfaced. Be brief and specific. Identify each addiction by name and frequency: Seldom, Often, or Constantly. For example, you may write:
      Television—S   Exercise—O   Gambling—C

3. Alternatively:
You can combine the above spiritual diagnostics into a single prayer exercise. Here is how you might do it: For your first two prayer exercises of the week, pray for the grace to honestly recognize the vices and addictions that erode your freedom and compromise your true self. Write them out in your notebook as indicated above, listing the vices as mild, moderate, or strong and the addictions as seldom, often, or constantly.

Begin the rest of the prayer sessions in the standard manner. During your prayer session, review what you wrote in your notebook, and ask Christ, the Divine Physician, in very personal words, to help you discover the connections between the vices and addictions. For example, you may notice that when you are angry, you might move toward one or another addictive behavior. When you are envious, you might be drawn to other addictive behaviors, and so on for the other vices.

Recall that the grace you are asking for is the inspiration to understand the vices and addictions in and of themselves, and more importantly, to identify the connections between them as they manifest in your life story. When, through grace, you begin to wake up to the links between the thoughts, words, and deeds of your life story, then growth in holiness and authenticity can occur.

Before the end of each prayer period, record any discoveries you make between the vices and addictions that God reveals to you. Thank God for the courage to honestly see yourself as you are. Thank God for the grace to wake up to live in greater freedom.

THE SEVEN CAPITAL VICES

Pride

Pride is an unrestrained and improper appreciation of our own worth. This is listed first because it is widely considered the most serious of the seven sins. Pride—narcissism—was the foundation of Adam and Eve's sin that made them fall for the serpent's temptation to "be like gods." Adam and Eve displaced God, the Creator, as the arbiter of truth and goodness. They, who were creatures, made themselves gods, the final judges of truth and goodness. Their action led to the loss of paradise and to a world of sickness and death. Pride often leads to the committing of other capital sins. Pride is manifest as vanity and narcissism about one's appearance, intelligence, status, wealth, connections, power, successes and all the other things that one uses to stand apart from others and from God.

Greed

Greed is also known as avarice or covetousness. It is the immoderate desire for earthly goods and power. It is a sin of excess. The object of one's greed need not be evil. The problem lies in the way a person regards or desires an object, making it a god and investing it with inappropriate value. Greed can inspire such sinful actions as hoarding, theft, fraud, tax evasion, environmental waste, or unethical business practices.

Gluttony

Gluttony comes from the Latin word meaning to gulp down or swallow. It is the sin of overindulgence and usually refers to overconsumption of food and drink. Gluttony can be eating too soon, too expensively, or too much. St. Alphonsus Liguori explained that feeling pleasure in eating is not wrong. Because food tastes good, we are delighted by this gift. It is not right, however, to eat with pleasure as the only motive and to forget food's function in sustaining vitality and health.

Lust

The sin of lust refers to corrupted desires of a sexual nature. Sexuality is a gift from God and pure in itself. However, lust refers to the impure thoughts and actions that misuse that gift. Lust deviates from God's law and sexuality's sacred purpose of allowing woman and man to participate in God's creative nature. Indulging in the sin of lust can include, but is not limited to, fornication, adultery, bestiality, rape, masturbation, pornography, and incest.

Sloth

Sloth is often described simply as the sin of laziness. However, while this is part of sloth's character, its true face is spiritual laziness. The sin of sloth means being lazy and lax about living the Faith and practicing virtue. Paraphrasing the Catholic Encyclopedia, we could say that sloth means aversion to labor or exertion. St. Thomas calls it sadness in the face of some spiritual good that one has to achieve. In other words, a slothful person is bothered by the effort to sustain one's friendship with God. In this sense, sloth is directly opposed to charity.

Envy

The sin of envy or jealousy is more than just someone wanting what others have. Sinful envy leads one to emotions or feelings of upset at another's good fortune or blessings. The law of love naturally leads one to rejoice in the good luck of one's neighbor. Envy opposes such love. Envy is named among the capital sins because of the other sins to which it leads.

Anger

Anger or wrath may be described as excessive and powerful feelings of hatred and resentment. These feelings can manifest as a passionate denial of truths expressed by others. Anger can also manifest in the form of denying truths about one's own life and impatience with the procedure of law. Anger is manifest, too, in the desire to seek revenge outside of the workings of the justice system. Anger, in essence, is wishing to do evil or harm to others. The transgressions born of vengeance are among the most serious, including assault, murder, and in extreme cases, genocide and other crimes against humanity. Anger is the only sin not necessarily associated with selfishness or self-interest, although one can be angry for selfish reasons, such as jealousy.

CB

A Short Primer on Addiction

The word addiction is used in many contexts. Common usage of the term has evolved to include psychological dependence. In this context, the term goes beyond drug addiction and substance abuse problems. It also refers to behaviors that are not generally recognized by the medical community as addictive problems, such as compulsive overeating or hoarding.

When the term addiction is applied to compulsions that are not substance-related, such as problem gambling and computer addiction, it describes a recurring compulsion one engages in despite the activity's harmful consequences to one's individual physical, mental, social, or spiritual health.[8]

Other forms of addiction could be habitual defrauding or tax evasion, money addictions, work addiction, exercise addiction, habitual overeating, habitual shopping, sex addiction, computer addiction, email addiction, video game addiction, pornography addiction, television addiction, and social media addiction.

Gabor Maté sums up addiction's profile: "Addiction is any repeated behavior, substance-related or not, in which a person feels compelled to persist, regardless of its negative impact on his life and the lives of others." According to Maté, addiction can be identified by the following four traits:

> 1. compulsive engagement with a behavior or a preoccupation with it,
>
> 2. impaired control over the behavior,
>
> 3. persistence or relapse despite evidence of harm, and
>
> 4. dissatisfaction, irritability, or intense craving when the object—be it a drug, activity, or other goal—is not immediately available.

03

I am starting a Relationship that will carry me
for the rest of my life.

All relationships require time and patience.
I will strive for patience and ask for God's help
when I don't understand a lesson.

I will learn the fundamentals and open my heart to God.

I trust that God will lead me.

I believe that my sacred story will unfold in truth,
in powerlessness, and with my patience.

I believe that Jesus awaits me with
His grace, mercy, and forgiving love.

80

Letters from Week Eight

Dear Fr. Bill,

I can already see the progression of growth in my spiritual life and I almost cannot believe it. By the time I began the Week Eight exercises I'd already become able to not beat myself up over the things I am learning about myself. Asking for God's grace seems to be the key. The connections between God's Commandments, the Seven Capital Vices, and Addictions are quite evident. Constantly being aware that God knows all of this already and that I am forgiven makes this much easier. I realize this for my present and future life, the life God wants me to live.

The Seven Vices and the addictions they spawned <u>were</u> my life, period. Pride could be the title, with chapters of Greed, Gluttony, Lust, Sloth, Envy and Anger. With no one close enough to me for me to feel obligated to explain myself or even to fake being a responsible, caring person, I was able to do as I wanted and suffer whatever consequences ensued. An "improper appreciation of our worth" is an understatement as far as my life is concerned. My persona was built on lies and my brutal judgements of others were based on those lies.

I wanted money and things so I robbed and stole. My need for instant gratification and self-indulgence led to alcoholism, drug addiction, and probably, sex addiction. Envy – I didn't want anyone to have more than me or anything I couldn't have. "Wishing to do evil or harm to others" fits for all who had more than me, all who knew that deep down I was a fake, phony fraud who was afraid but had no idea what I was afraid of.

My anger was focused on whoever might doubt any part of my narcissistic façade. The part of addiction which really hits home is "persistence or relapse despite harm". Fr. Bill, I didn't care about the harm because I thought I was only harming myself and I was just a composite of sins—not a full person—no redeeming qualities—godless. What was there to harm?

Obviously, I know better now. God has a plan for me. I've no idea what it is, but I'm ready. I do know that all of the things I spent my life doing and trying to acquire by any means are exactly the things God is telling me I'll no longer want or need in the future. Amen to that!

Respectfully,

Ritchie

Dear Ritchie:

You express very clearly the life of vice and addiction that was your identity for so many years. You detail it with brutal honesty and a forthright spirit. The reason you were able to live this life was because you had no sense of your worth as a person. You were wounded and afraid, plain and simple!

The fact that you can speak so freely about all those years you lived like that is a clear sign that you have moved beyond them and are closer than ever to your life as sacred story. In your heart you know that God has a plan for you. You don't know what but you profess to be "ready".

You can think of 1 Samuel 3:10: "Speak Lord, for your servant is listening". You will know in time what to do and how you can serve. For now, you are serving Him by going through the Forty Weeks program and writing your reflections. All shall be revealed.

Please know that I keep you in my prayers, and I know in my heart that God does love you and has a beautiful plan for your life, Ritchie.

Peace,

Fr. Bill Watson, SJ

NOTES

Week 9

FIRST

I will select my fifteen-minute quiet times for the week ahead and visualize where I will go each day and at what times. I will ask God for the grace to keep those times sacred throughout the week. I will have my notebook at hand and spend no more than fifteen minutes in each formal prayer session. I will always use my personal name for God.

SECOND

My fifteen-minute quiet prayer this ninth week consists of six simple prayer exercises, one each for Monday through Saturday. I can use my Sunday prayer time to read over the prayer exercises and set my heart for the week ahead. If I am doing two prayer sessions a day, I have the option to engage each exercise twice.

THIRD

I will begin each fifteen-minute prayer period by sitting in a comfortable position. Speaking God's name, and with personal words from my heart, I ask to be open to my own heart and life story as I enter the short time of prayer. If I focus better by breathing deeply and saying God's name with each inhale and exhale, then I will do so. I will pray with personal words from my heart to see what I have not seen before, and to see connections among aspects of my life story. I am invited to watch these components of my life narrative with the Divine Physician by my side. Christ invites me to wake up in my life.

I will awaken to the present moment.
I will take each day and each exercise as it comes.
I cannot do Sacred Story better by going faster.
I will ask God to help me.
I will awaken to my spiritual nature
and to the inspirations that inspire
faith, hope, and love.
I will awaken to the inspirations
that inspire cynicism, impatience and lusts.
I will wake up!

This week, I will say this affirmation aloud once daily:
I believe every thought, word, and deed of mine
carries a force that can change me, others, and history.

ଔ

The six spiritual diagnostic exercises for this week's lesson offer you the potential for more enlightenment. Spend your fifteen-minute sessions this week listening to your heart. Ask God for the grace to discern the key elements in your life story linked to the following: gratitude; relationships; spiritual, social, and financial values; and people you need to forgive or whose forgiveness you need to accept. Take one day for each of the six spiritual diagnostics. Deciphering these can help you see the two plot-lines (like Ignatius's prideful, self-centered story and his spiritual, selfless story) in your life history more clearly. Be sure to ask for God's assistance to "see" each of these six elements. Use the personal name for God to ask for this grace for each day's prayer.

Monday
GRATITUDE

I ask God for the grace to remember the one experience, event, or person for which I am most grateful. It could be a kindness someone showed me. It could be a loving gesture from a parent, friend, husband, wife, or child. It could be something that did not happen to me—some danger or threat, sickness or accident that was avoided or minimized. It could be some significant event in my life that moved me in a new direction. It could be a spiritual experience that opened me to a deeper hope and joy in my life. What comes to mind? I will pray for the grace to recall the feelings I felt at the time of the event and take note of the reasons why. I pray to see connections in my responses to other prayer exercises as they occur. Before I finish my prayer, I will write my memory and why it inspires gratitude, in one sentence.

Example: At first, I thought having a brother with Down's Syndrome would be a great burden to our family, but it brought our family together in a way we had never been before, teaching us the true meaning of life and love.

Tuesday
RELATIONAL GOAL

I ask God for the grace to identify the most important relational goal I can imagine for my life story. It could be with God, my spouse, my children, my family, or a close friend. This is the one relational goal that if I accomplished it, I would believe that my life was fulfilled. I will look for connections in my responses to other prayer exercises as they occur to me. Before I finish my prayer, I will write my relationship goal and why it would define my relational success, in one sentence.

Example: My family situation growing up was less than ideal, and I have always wanted to achieve success in life by working hard to be a great husband and father.

Wednesday
SPIRITUAL GOAL

I ask God for the grace to understand my most hoped-for spiritual goal for my life story. It could be with God, my spouse, my children, my family, or a close friend. It is the one spiritual goal that if I accomplished it, I would believe that my life was fulfilled. I will look for connections in my responses to other prayer exercises as they occur to me. Before I finish my prayer, I will write my spiritual goal and why it would define

144

spiritual success for me, in one sentence.

Example: I know I can be lazy and a bit self-centered, and so success in my spiritual life would be to pray daily and always try to do something for someone I see who needs help.

Thursday
SOCIAL GOAL

I ask God for the grace to understand my most hoped-for goal that represents the positive social impact of my life story. It is the one social goal that if I accomplished it, or helped accomplish it, I would believe my life was fulfilled. I will look for connections in my responses to other prayer exercises as they occur to me. Before I finish my prayer, I will write my social goal in one sentence and why it would define social success for me and the world.

Example: I want to be known for making a difference in the world by standing up for those in society who are the most powerless and forgotten and to be fearless in doing so.

Friday
FINANCIAL GOAL

I ask God for the grace to understand my most hoped-for financial or economic goal or ambition for my life story. It is the one financial goal that if I accomplished it, or helped accomplish it, I would believe my life was fulfilled. I will look for connections in my responses to other prayer exercises as they occur to me. Before I finish my prayer, I will write my financial goal in one sentence and why it would define financial success for me.

Example: When I was younger, making lots of money seemed important, but now, I hope I can work to live and not live to work, and hopefully teach my children the same values.

Saturday
FORGIVENESS

I ask God for the grace to understand the one person who would be most grateful to receive my forgiveness. I also ask God for the grace to understand the one person whose forgiveness I would be most grateful to receive. Before finishing my prayer, I will write two short sentences below, one for each person, describing why gratitude would be present in each instance of forgiveness.

Example: It has been hard for me to forgive my parents for divorcing, and success in this area would be to ask God for the grace to not hold on to anger but to forgive them as Jesus forgave on the cross.

ଔ

I am starting a Relationship that will carry me
for the rest of my life.

All relationships require time and patience.
I will strive for patience and ask for God's help
when I don't understand a lesson.

I will learn the fundamentals and open my heart to God.

I trust that God will lead me.

I believe that my sacred story will unfold in truth,
in powerlessness, and with my patience.

I believe that Jesus awaits me with His grace, mercy, and forgiving
love.

ଇ

Letters from Week Nine

Dear Fr. Bill,

For Week Nine we are asked to write one short phrase at the end of each prayer session pertaining to each spiritual exercise. I assume I should include those phrases and expound on them.

GRATITUDE

Every time I hear the word "gratitude", no matter what the context, the same thing always comes to mind – July 2013; "God loves me". It was a very trying time for me, prison and violence related, when it seemed to me God was not responding to my pleas. Out of frustration I just gave up and said "your will be done". It was the beginning of my present journey, one I hope to live forever. I shared this experience with you before. The overwhelming sense that God loves me came from my surrender. Although I've experienced gratitude toward others, and in various situations, this will always be number one as long as I live.

RELATIONAL GOAL

"Without God I am nothing." There is only one relational goal that if accomplished would fulfill my life – that is a relationship with God. Without it nothing matters. I didn't have a relationship with God for most of my life – and my life was nothing, less than nothing! I recently read somewhere that the difference between nothing and something is God. I truly believe that the reason I have no spouse, children, other family or close friends in my life is because my relationship with my God of Mercy and Compassion is meant to be all encompassing – my entire being. And I feel blessed for being made aware of this. I am honored to be in this position. I hope and pray every day to eventually come close to fulfilling the plan He has for me.

SPIRITUAL GOAL

"Consequential Service." I do not claim that God speaks directly to me

but during my prayer periods and times of quiet contemplation I get very strong feelings like "wow, that's right," or I realize things that I've always known or believed, but somehow wasn't conscious of. Recently the idea of "consequential service" —your words—just keeps growing and growing in me to the point that I am realizing that everything does happen for a reason. Most of the things of this world have been taken from me by one means or another, leaving me with what I know is to be my life – prayer and service. What form this takes remains to be seen.

SOCIETAL GOAL

As a man who is blessed to be forgiven, I have an obligation to live by example – to treat everyone with respect, to not judge and to spread the word that there is hope for all of us, not matter our circumstances. If I can be saved everyone can.

FINANCIAL GOAL

"No dependents, no responsibilities, no worries." God has been quite thorough in eliminating all distractions from my discipleship. Although (being a) mendicant would not be prudent in this day and age, I've recently come across a term suitable as a fitting lifestyle for me – "Joyous, Downward Mobility." Matthew Chapter 6: "Therefore I tell you, do not worry about your life, what you will eat or what you will drink, or about your body, what you will wear...." I've spent enough of my life chasing material things and instant gratification. I would like to think I have the faith to know my needs will be met.

FORGIVENESS GOAL

Knowing that everything that has transpired in my life was necessary to get me where I am today makes things very simple for me. I am forgiven; therefore, I must forgive. This is for both of my mothers, long deceased. My biological mother, on whom I have at times blamed every problem I've ever experienced, deserves forgiveness. We all make mistakes and like most of us, she did what she felt she needed to do at the time. And my adoptive mother, to whom I acted in the most unkind and cruelest manner imaginable, I hope she has forgiven me.

Respectfully, Ritchie

Dear Ritchie:

You have learned the most important lesson about love—forgiveness. In this season of Lent, we will hear again Jesus' last words from the cross: "Father forgive them, for they know not what they do." I am sure that both your mothers, long deceased as they are, feel your spiritual awakening and with joy and hope, pray for you and love you. I am sure that Jesus would allow them this mercy of knowing your forgiveness too. Take comfort in this. Jesus loves you and because of His kindness and tenderness toward you He lets their love for you from beyond this life reach your heart.

Do you feel the same need to forgive your two fathers or was that relationship different than for your mothers? See if this surfaces in your prayers.

For your reflection on Gratitude, I think the capacity to have relationships with others is connected to our having a real relationship with God. Perhaps God is giving you the experience of being loved and anchoring your heart in Him as the basis for some future human relationship(s). And those relationships might be in your helping others in need who don't feel loved so they have the confidence to reach out to God as you did in July of 2013. Being loved by God and desiring so close a relationship with Him will lead and guide you to what is next.

Stay anchored in Him and He will lead you and give shape to that desire at the right time.

Your current and future mission seems to be in these few short phrases you write with respect to your societal goal. Ponder these words and let the Lord open you to where they will lead. It will most likely be what you describe as "Consequential Service' in your Spiritual Goal.

Peace, Fr. Bill

NOTES

Week 10

FIRST

I will select my fifteen-minute quiet times for the week ahead and visualize where I will go each day and at what times. I will continue to ask God for the grace to keep those times sacred. I will have my notebook at hand, and I will spend no more than fifteen minutes in each formal prayer session. I will always use my personal name for God.

SECOND

My fifteen-minute quiet prayer this tenth week is composed of simple prayer exercises for Monday through Saturday to help me find links in my life story. I may use my Sunday prayer time to read over the prayer exercises and diagnostic charts so I can set my heart for the week. If I am doing two prayer sessions a day, I will have more reflection time.

THIRD

I will begin each fifteen-minute prayer period by sitting in a comfortable position. I will speak God's name, and with personal words from my heart, I ask to be open to my own heart and life story. I will ask for the grace to see connections between aspects of my life story. I am invited to watch these components of my life narrative with the Divine Physician by my side. Christ invites me not to be afraid but to wake up in my life—my spiritual life. I will watch and pray with Christ.

I will awaken to the present moment.

I will take each day and each exercise as it comes.
I cannot do Sacred Story better by going faster.

I will ask God to help me.

I will awaken to my spiritual nature
and to the inspirations that inspire faith, hope, and love.

I will awaken to the inspirations
that inspire cynicism, impatience, and lusts.
I will wake up!

This week, I will say this affirmation aloud once daily:
I affirm that everything that has happened to me
and everything I have experienced in my entire life
is present in my memory.

ॐ

Read this page and the next before starting any prayer sessions this week.

Whether you have or have not done the exercises for weeks 6 through 9, you can still do this week's exercises. If you wrote notes for the past weeks, refer to them. If not, take this exercise as a stand-alone piece, and sometime later, go back and do the weeks you passed.

For week 10, there are five diagnostic charts to contemplate. These charts are designed to help you pray for graced insights from God to better understand your life history. The five diagnostic charts are as follows:

1. List of the vices and Commandments

2. Chart for listing key elements in your life story

3. Chart with four elements in your life story where you can pray for

insights to see links or connections

4. Chart that shows the progressive levels of sin's impact on Ignatius's spiritual and material being, and the way that originating sins and wounds lead to core sin, and finally to the fruit of these sins (those that are most visible or manifest in his story), and

5. the same chart as above, repeated with blank spaces for you to fill in your own unique experiences

The data from your life diagnostic charts will be helpful to you throughout the year. You are only in the beginning period of attempting, with God's grace, to see your sin history more clearly. Your goal is to better understand how to listen to your sacred story.

Remember, Christ watches with you with love, patience, compassion, and infinite mercy. Be not afraid! What follows are suggestions for how best to use the fifteen-minute prayer sessions in this tenth week of Sacred Story prayer.

INSTRUCTIONS FOR EACH DAY'S PRAYER PERIOD

Sunday: I contemplate briefly the list of vices and Commandments and all the diagnostic charts and ask God for the grace of openness to see both the trees (unique elements of my life history) and the forest (the unique elements that when combined, form a single life story).

Monday: I fill in the first diagnostic chart with at least one element for each of the statements provided.

Tuesday: I fill in the second diagnostic chart, with the goal to write at least three of the five things requested in each category.

Wednesday: I contemplate the diagnostic chart I filled in on Tuesday, praying to see if there are any obvious links among Commandments, vices, addictions, persons, and/or events. I draw lines linking those connections that are clear to me.

Thursday: I contemplate the diagnostic chart of how sin impacted the life of St. Ignatius and try to see the links in his original (root), core (trunk), and manifest (fruit) sins.

Friday: I contemplate the elements from the diagnostic charts I filled in earlier in the week and pray for the grace to see more clearly how sin has impacted me at the roots, trunk, and fruit of my life. For each of the blank spaces on the last chart, I write those elements (at least one each) that I believe are present in my life as original sins (root), core sins (trunk), and manifest sins (fruit).

Saturday: I contemplate the charts I filled in this week and ask for God's grace to see any connections that will aid me in my Sacred Story journey. I ask for God's grace to be open this entire forty-week journey so I can begin to see my life story in its entirety.

LISTS OF VICES AND COMMANDMENTS

VICES

PRIDE   ENVY   GLUTTONY   LUST   SLOTH   GREED   ANGER

COMMANDMENTS

First   I am the Lord your God; you shall have no strange gods before Me.

Second   You shall not take the name of the Lord your God in vain.

Third   Remember to keep holy the Sabbath day.

Fourth   Honor your father and mother.

Fifth   You shall not kill.

Sixth   You shall not commit adultery.
Ninth   You shall not covet your neighbor's spouse.

Seventh   You shall not steal.
Tenth   You shall not covet your neighbor's goods.

Eighth   You shall not bear false witness against your neighbor.

LOOKING FOR LINKS IN MY STORY

Monday: I fill in the first diagnostic chart with at least one element for each of the statements provided.

A COMMANDMENT THAT CHALLENGES ME	
VICES THAT ENSNARE ME	
ADDICTIONS I LIVE WITH	
PERSONS/EVENTS THAT GENERATE FEAR, ANGER, OR GRIEF	
PERSONS/EVENTS THAT GENERATE FAITH, HOPE, OR LOVE	
STORYLINES IN BOOKS/ MOVIES THAT ALWAYS BRING ME TO TEARS	
WHAT ALWAYS MAKES ME ANGRY	
WHAT ALWAYS MAKES ME GRATEFUL	
WHAT ALWAYS INSPIRES FEAR IN ME	
MY ULTIMATE FAITH GOAL	
THE AREA OF MY LIFE MOST OUT OF CONTROL	

LOOKING FOR LINKS IN MY STORY

Tuesday: I fill in the second diagnostic chart, with the goal to write at least three of the five things requested in each category.

FIVE COMMANDMENTS I AM MOST CHALLENGED IN LIVING	FIVE VICES THAT ENSNARE ME	FIVE ADDICTIONS I LIVE WITH	FIVE PERSONS/EVENTS THAT CAUSE FEAR, ANGER, OR GRIEF

Wednesday: I contemplate this chart praying to see any obvious links among Commandments, vices, addictions, persons and/or events. I draw lines linking those connections that become clear to me.

Thursday: I contemplate the diagnostic chart of how sin impacted the life of St. Ignatius and try to see the links in his original (root), core (trunk), and manifest (fruit) sins.

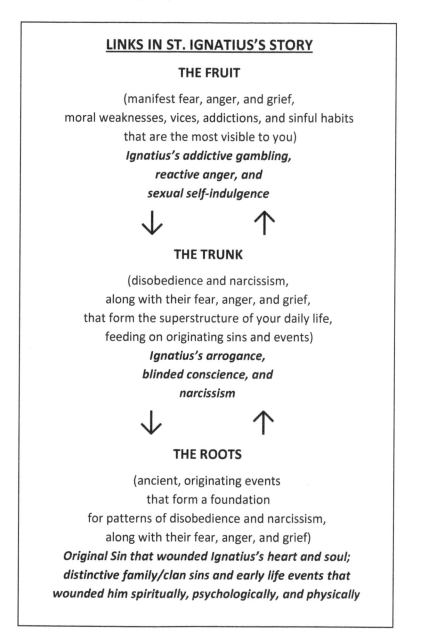

LINKS IN ST. IGNATIUS'S STORY

THE FRUIT

(manifest fear, anger, and grief,
moral weaknesses, vices, addictions, and sinful habits
that are the most visible to you)
Ignatius's addictive gambling,
reactive anger, and
sexual self-indulgence

↓   ↑

THE TRUNK

(disobedience and narcissism,
along with their fear, anger, and grief,
that form the superstructure of your daily life,
feeding on originating sins and events)
Ignatius's arrogance,
blinded conscience, and
narcissism

↓   ↑

THE ROOTS

(ancient, originating events
that form a foundation
for patterns of disobedience and narcissism,
along with their fear, anger, and grief)
Original Sin that wounded Ignatius's heart and soul;
distinctive family/clan sins and early life events that
wounded him spiritually, psychologically, and physically

Friday: I contemplate the elements from the diagnostic charts I filled in earlier in the week and pray for the grace to see more clearly how sin has impacted me at the roots, trunk, and fruit of my life.

For each of the blank spaces on the chart below, I write those **elements** (at least one each) that I believe are present in my life as original sins (root), core sins (trunk), and manifest sins (fruit).

MY MANIFEST SINS—THE FRUIT FROM MY TREE

↓   ↑

MY CORE SINS—THE TRUNK OF MY TREE

↓   ↑

MY ORIGINAL SINS—THE ROOTS OF MY TREE

CB

I am starting a Relationship that will carry me
for the rest of my life.

All relationships require time and patience.
I will strive for patience and ask for God's help
when I don't understand a lesson.

I will learn the fundamentals and open my heart to God.

I trust that God will lead me.

I believe that my sacred story will unfold in truth,
in powerlessness, and with my patience.

I believe that Jesus awaits me with His grace, mercy,
and forgiving love.

EO

Letters from Week Ten

Dear Fr. Bill,

Week Ten clearly put into perspective and linked the Commandments which challenged me the most, my vices, addictions, and the causes of my fear, anger and grief. I have to tell you Fr. Bill, that until now I considered any adult or later-in-life-behavior, sin or feelings occurring as a result of family sin or other early life-events to be nothing more than psychobabble. The root/trunk/fruit chart is pretty much irrefutable. I am definitely not looking for someone or something to blame my life on. Knowledge and the desire and ability to change are what I am searching for.

Roots: not knowing my biological parents, being ashamed of my adoptive parents and the fact that I was adopted. The sense of abandonment and being unwanted would rule the majority of my life.

Trunk: as a result, I decided to go it alone. I did as I wished with no one to answer to. No fear of repercussions, lack of conscience (or, blinded conscience) gave me an undeserved arrogance which manifested in these fruits:

Fruits: narcissism, hate, anger, fear, greed, uncontrollable sexual desires, the need for instant gratification, etc.

Obviously, I felt worthless from the beginning of my life and spent the next forty-plus years proving that I was right. The good thing is that that part of my life is over. Or, more to the point, the old Ritchie is dead and the new Ritchie is emerging in Christ.

Respectfully,

Ritchie

Dear Ritchie:

All the fruits you mention are attempts to fill up that hole of abandonment in your heart—of not feeling loved or loveable. It took a long time to figure that out but God has a plan for each of us and works with our lives as they are.

I may have mentioned this earlier but it is worth repeating. The main result of the Original Sin in the human heart is the feeling of abandonment. It is what Jesus had to experience on the Cross for all of us to a degree unimaginable.

Anytime you feel abandoned now or in the future, look to the Cross of Jesus who suffered the ultimate abandonment of not feeling his Father's love. Look at him on the Cross and know he did that so your own abandonment, and that of your mother's and father's and everyone else, could be healed.

You are in my prayers,

Fr. Bill

NOTES

Week 11

FIRST

I will select my fifteen-minute quiet time(s) for the week ahead and once again visualize where I will go each day and at what time(s). I will ask God for the grace to keep those times sacred. I will have my notebook at hand for each prayer period for this week. I will spend no more than fifteen minutes in each formal prayer session. I will always use my personal name for God.

SECOND

My fifteen-minute quiet prayer this eleventh week is a simple prayer exercise for Sunday through Saturday. I will write a letter to Christ Jesus asking for His help and healing for my life story. The letter is my confession of faith in Him who comes to heal me and forgive me. The letter is also a snapshot of my whole life. It is my opportunity to tell Christ where I have been wounded by sin and life's difficulties, how I struggle for wholeness, and why I need Jesus's help and forgiveness. I will ask Jesus to be my Savior.

THIRD

My prayer sessions this week only can be longer than fifteen minutes, because I am writing a letter. Nevertheless, I still begin each prayer period by sitting in a comfortable position. I will use my favorite name for Jesus specifically (such as Christ Jesus, Lord and Savior, Redeemer, etc.) for this week's personal prayer, because Christ is the Person of the Trinity who won my freedom from sin and death. This week, He is the one to whom I am speaking.

I will awaken to the present moment.
I will take each day and each exercise as it comes.
I cannot do Sacred Story better by going faster.
I will ask God to help me.
I will awaken to my spiritual nature and
to the inspirations that inspire faith, hope, and love.
I will awaken to the inspirations that
inspire cynicism, impatience, and lusts. I will wake up!

This week, I will say this affirmation aloud once daily:
Lord Jesus Christ, you experience great joy when I allow you to forgive my weakness and sinfulness, because you lived, died, and rose again so that I might have new life in you.

ℭ

A LETTER TO CHRIST JESUS

You may be wondering how you will make use of the prayer exercises from the past few weeks. This will become clearer as your journey continues. Have faith that your efforts will be spiritually fruitful. You are not expected to see the complete picture in everything you have done so far. We have been on a treasure hunt of sorts, pulling together many diverse elements of our life story. The process of piecing the parts together will happen throughout the rest of your life—both by your careful attention and by the grace of God. So, have patience and trust. As time goes on, everything you have done up to this point will take on greater meaning for you (if you follow the lessons in order and ask for God's help).

For this week's exercise, to prepare your whole-life confession, you can refer to some of what you wrote in the previous weeks.

What do we mean by whole-life confession? A whole-life confession is different from a confession of your whole life. It is not helpful, nor is it required, to twice confess sins and faults you have already confessed. The opportunity of a whole-life confession is to look at connections and patterns of sin and failure across your whole life—what we have been working on these past weeks. You are invited to ask for God's help to see a holistic picture of your life—your story—with Christ as your Divine Physician and healer.

Think of this confession as your report to Christ—based on your spiritual diagnosis—after these weeks of prayerful reflection. You can confess current issues and past issues that have been overlooked. As you do this, you are telling Christ the chronic patterns of sin and weaknesses that your prayer and reflection, with the help of God's grace, has awakened in you. And importantly, you are telling Him how these issues are linked to your life story—your history.

Consider this reflection from Pope St. John Paul II:

> It must be recalled that...this reconciliation with God leads, as it were, to other reconciliations, which repair the other breaches caused by sin. The forgiven penitent is reconciled with himself in his inmost being, where he regains his innermost truth. He is reconciled with his brethren whom he has in some way offended and wounded. He is reconciled with the Church. He is reconciled with all creation.[9]

As you look at your life story with Christ, the Divine Physician, address Him directly, and acknowledge why you need Him as your Savior. This could be the very first time you have reviewed your life, seen clearly why you cannot save yourself, and directly asked Jesus to be your Savior. What a profound grace to know why you cannot save yourself and to ask Christ for this tremendous gift! A profound grace, indeed!

Look at this from Christ's perspective, too. There is no greater gift you give to Christ than your sinfulness and weaknesses as you ask for His healing love, mercy, and forgiveness. By doing so, you take seriously the gift of His life, passion, death, and resurrection. You are telling Jesus you need His cross to be healed. You are thanking Jesus for suffering and dying for you so you can be renewed in Him. This is the real focus of the Christian life! Jesus really loves you and wants to hear what you have to say to Him. He waits with compassion and great longing to hear your story. He waits to carry your burdens and to offer you His forgiveness.

> The Pharisees and their scribes complained to his disciples, saying, "Why do you eat and drink with tax collectors and sinners?" Jesus said to them in reply, "Those who are healthy do not need a physician, but the sick do. I have not come to call the righteous to repentance but sinners." (Lk 5:30–32)

With Jesus as your Divine Physician, a whole-life confession makes perfect sense. He understands you and everything about your life. He has an intense desire to hear your life story and wants to respond as your Savior. Your letter is a statement of your need and a confession of your sins and patterns of sin, as well as a request for forgiveness, healing, and hope. What follows are a few guidelines to help you prepare for this simple, holy, and graced letter:

One picture is worth a thousand words. Your life is a picture, a story. Write a letter to Christ that is no more than 1,000 words. If typed, it would be about three and a half pages, double-spaced. But you do not have to write that much. I repeat: write no more than 1,000 words.

Use personal words that are heartfelt. Early on, you identified the name for God that touches your heart. This week, if you haven't already, find the name for Christ specifically that speaks to your heart. Perhaps it is

Christ Jesus, Lord and Savior, or My Lord. You are speaking to the One who won your victory and who came into the world to save you. This week, we want to speak directly to Christ Jesus. Speak to Jesus in the first person: "Please forgive…; I remember…; I suffered…; Please heal me…." Write the confessional story—your history—directly from your heart to the heart of Jesus.

Strive for honesty. Strive earnestly for courage and honesty in your letter. The letter is for you and you only, unless you choose to share it in sacramental Confession (Reconciliation). You need not impress anyone. What is significant is your courage and honesty. Be honest too, about the forgiveness you need to extend to others. Write from your heart.

You are not climbing Mount Everest. Please, pray for the grace not to turn this simple, graced letter/confession opportunity into a huge, exhausting task. You are not climbing a mountain. You are having a conversation with Christ about your life. Hear Him say this to you:

> Come to me, all you who labor and are burdened, and I will give
> you rest. Take my yoke upon you and learn from me, for I am
> meek and humble of heart; and you will find rest for your
> selves. For my yoke is easy and my burden light. (Mt 11:28–29)

Pray for Patience and Compassion. Awakening to your life story will take the rest of your life. It takes a lifetime for Christ's work of healing and forgiveness to embrace your heart and soul. There is no finish line or ultimate enlightenment you can reach on this earth. You will always need healing at deeper levels. You will constantly grow in love and enlightenment, selflessness and humility, until the day you pass from this earth. You will not be finished until the day the Divine Physician sits you down at His eternal banquet.

> But as for the seed that fell on rich soil, they are the ones who,
> when they have heard the word, embrace it with a generous

and good heart, and bear fruit through perseverance. (Lk 8:15)

Set the scene in your heart's imagination. Here is how you might set your heart's imagination as you write: imagine you have been given the opportunity to be alone with Christ when He is walking from one town to another. You will have fifteen minutes with Him…alone. See the road and the other followers walking up ahead of you and the Lord. No one else can hear you. Write your letter as if you are speaking to Christ in this setting. He knows why you want to speak with Him and is ready to hear you. Before you begin talking about your life, He looks you in the eyes and says, "Soon, I will be lifted up on my cross. I am doing this for you so that you can find forgiveness, healing, and hope for the sins, weaknesses, and suffering you experience in your life. As I conquer all death and sin—as I breathe my last breath—I will hold you and your life story in my heart. You will find victory and eternal life in me and one day be with me in paradise."

> Then Jesus said, "Father, forgive them, they know not what they do." Then he said, "Jesus, remember me when you come into your kingdom." He replied to him, "Amen, I say to you, today you will be with me in Paradise." (Lk 23:34, 42–43)

What follows is a template for how you might structure your heartfelt conversation/letter/confession to Christ Jesus, the Divine Physician:

✠ "Dear Jesus, I am so grateful for all the gifts you have given to me." Spend some time writing from your heart why you are grateful. Use Jesus's name often as you write, and give very particular examples of why you are grateful.

✠ "Lord, I am profoundly aware of how some of my past experiences [life history, family, friends, work, school, neighbors] are linked to areas of unfreedom in my life and how these experiences have created embarrassing and/or discouraging habits and rooted patterns of sinfulness." Spend some time looking back over your life, and offer particular examples that capture the links and patterns of sins, addictions, vices, and Commandments where you are challenged and desire spiritual growth. If you cannot discern patterns yet, simply speak about these areas individually. If there are central people in your life story who are linked to these destructive patterns, mention them to Christ. If you are confused about some of the things you do, tell Jesus what they are, and then ask for His help to better understand why you do what you do. From your heart, ask Christ's grace to gain greater freedom from these sins, patterns of sin, habits, and vices.

✠ "But Lord, there is one central pattern of sin that causes me the most embarrassment, shame, confusion, and discouragement." Spend some time being very specific in your conversation with Jesus about this pattern of sin in your life and why it is so difficult for you. Tell Jesus the particular circumstances when you seem to fall under its spell the most and the circumstances that surround your failures. Tell Jesus how you feel when you fail. If there are specific incidents of this pattern of failure that you have not confessed, tell them to the Lord, and ask for His healing and forgiveness.

✠ "Lord Jesus, I have come to realize that I cannot save myself, and I ask for your compassion. I ask that you be my Savior. Rescue me and be with me all the rest of my days." Spend some time speaking with Jesus, in very particular words, about why you have come to realize you cannot save yourself and why you need His grace—why you need Him to be your Savior. Tell Him in very clear words why you know (because of x, y, and z) that you cannot save yourself. Tell Him about any persons you cannot forgive and what they did to you. Tell Him why it is difficult for you to forgive them. Tell Jesus that with His grace, you can desire to forgive them and in time, be able to forgive them. Ask for that grace. Ask the Lord to keep His attention on the core issues in your life (name them) that constantly trip you up, and pray that you never tire in seeking His forgiveness and that you never lose hope in yourself or in Him. Ask the Lord to be your Savior.

✠ "Lord Jesus, I thank you that you have given me the courage to face any fears I had and to trust you with my life in this healing sacrament of your redeeming love." Close your letter/conversation/ confession with very personal words from your heart, thanking Jesus that He has heard your prayer and that He will always be your Savior. With heartfelt words, thank Jesus that He understands your life, and ask that He continue to walk with you, give you grace, and be with you till the end of your days. Ask Jesus for the grace to serve Him more each day with everything you think, say, and do. Ask for the grace to work for fruit that will endure to eternity.

✠ "Thank you Jesus for being my Savior." Close your heartfelt letter by thanking Jesus for being your Savior. Ask for His continued grace as He writes your sacred story.

CB

I am starting a Relationship that will carry me
for the rest of my life.

All relationships require time and patience.
I will strive for patience and ask for God's help
when I don't understand a lesson.

I will learn the fundamentals and open my heart to God.

I trust that God will lead me.

I believe that my sacred story will unfold in truth,
in powerlessness, and with my patience.

I believe that Jesus awaits me with His grace, mercy,
and forgiving love.

SO

Letters from Week Eleven

Dear Fr. Bill,

I now realize that the past ten weeks were leading to this moment. Everything makes sense now. I see the links, trends and patterns. Although I am forgiven for the sins I've confessed in the past, I need to tell my Savior that I get it – that I know how I got to where I was, that I don't not want to go back there, and that I give myself to Him unconditionally, to do with as he pleases.

I spent most of Week Eleven praying for the right words for my letter to my Savior. I asked for the honesty and willingness necessary for my Whole-Life Confession. I took your advice and imagined walking alone with my Lord Jesus. Not only was this helpful, I also began dreaming this. As I began writing my letter, I felt totally confident and at ease.

Respectfully,

Ritchie

Dear Ritchie:

Please know that you will find the words to speak to Christ Jesus from your heart. He will also give you the honesty and help you remember what is most important to say. The confidence and ease you experience is something St. Ignatius would call Spiritual Consolation. Trust Him!

Peace,

Fr. Bill

NOTES

Week 12

FIRST

I will select my fifteen-minute quiet time(s) for the week ahead and visualize where I will go each day and at what time(s). I continue to ask God for the grace to keep my times of prayer sacred and to seek a place that is technology-free. I will bring my notebook to each prayer period and commit to spending no more than fifteen minutes in each formal prayer session. I will always use my personal name for God.

SECOND

My fifteen-minute quiet prayer this twelfth week consists of one simple prayer exercise for Sunday through Saturday.

THIRD

I will keep working on my letter, or if it is complete, I will reflect on what I have written during my prayer times. I will read and reflect with Christ as my companion and stay with my letter to Christ Jesus, asking for His help and healing for my life story.

I will awaken to the present moment.

I will take each day and each exercise as it comes.

I cannot do Sacred Story better by going faster.

I will ask God to help me.

I will awaken to my spiritual nature and to

the inspirations that inspire faith, hope, and love.

I will awaken to the inspirations that
inspire cynicism, impatience, and lusts. I will wake up!
Be not afraid!

I will not make any decisions that bend into my fears and my anxieties.
They are founded on bad information and will not lead to my peace.

This week, I will say this affirmation aloud once daily:
Lord Jesus Christ, I affirm you will always transform my sin and
weakness into grace and blessings! I will not be afraid!

Ⳡ

Your letter to Jesus may or may not be complete. Use your fifteen-minute prayer times this week to continue the reflection and writing process, or if complete, reflect and pray with the letter. Bring your notebook to your prayer sessions. After each session, write one sentence for what brings you the most hope as you read your letter and one sentence for what causes you the most discouragement as you read your letter.

If you have resolved to bring your letter to confession, make an appointment with a priest for sacramental Reconciliation. Consciously commit to scheduling the appointment for some time in the next two weeks. If the priest you seek for confession is not familiar with the Forty Weeks method, explain to him what it is. Let him know that you would like to read to Christ your confession in this letter form. Tell him that you have spent twelve weeks preparing it, and thank him for letting you go to confession in this manner.

☙

I am starting a Relationship that will carry me
for the rest of my life.

All relationships require time and patience.
I will strive for patience and ask for God's help
when I don't understand a lesson.

I will learn the fundamentals and open my heart to God.

I trust that God will lead me.

I believe that my sacred story will unfold in truth,
in powerlessness, and with my patience.
I believe that Jesus awaits me with His grace, mercy,
and forgiving love.

❧

Letters from Week Twelve

Dear Fr. Bill,

I completed writing my Whole-Life Confession this week. There was no downside. It was a totally uplifting experience. Surely, I have regrets and wish things had been different. The fact that I had abandoned my Lord Jesus for so long and He hadn't abandoned me made me so very grateful. I went to the recreation yard on a cold, miserable morning instead of going to breakfast. I was the only one on the yard. I found a corner spot, sat down and read my letter to my Savior.

I appreciate your offer of hearing my Whole-Life Confession. This is a new institution, one-third full, with an inexperienced Chaplain Staff – no Catholic priest on staff. We had a volunteer priest come in to celebrate Mass last week for the first time in months. Forty-five minutes, in and out. Definitely not enough time to explain and have him hear my Whole-Life Confession.

Making plans, getting approval, and you getting in here to hear my confession are not feasible, especially since I can be transferred at any time. I know it is suggested to have my confession heard within two weeks, but maybe we can coordinate it when I get to my next institution.

I know this is going to sound beyond out of the ordinary, but would it be OK to send you my Letter/Confession by mail and have you respond? I realize it would not be an actual confession, but I would like for you to see/hear it.

I received the copy you made of Weeks Five through Eight for me. I really appreciate that and all of your guidance through Forty Weeks.

Respectfully,

Ritchie

Dear Ritchie:

It was a consolation to hear that your letter to Jesus was a blessing and one that was peaceful and hopeful. I liked that you skipped breakfast and even on a cold and miserable day, went to the yard to open your heart to the Lord Jesus.

Yes, you can send me your Letter/Confession and I will respond to it by letter back to you. Perhaps it will be possible for me to hear it in person when/if you get transferred for the Life Connections program. I keep that in my prayers. In light of your letter to Jesus, Ritchie, I will leave you with St. Ignatius' Suscipe prayer (Take Lord, Receive)

Take Lord, and receive all my liberty, my memory, my understanding, and my entire will, all that I have and possess. Thou hast given all to me. To Thee, O lord, I return it. All is Thine, dispose of it wholly according to Thy will. Give me Thy love and thy grace, for this is sufficient for me. Amen

Peace,

Fr. Bill Watson, S.J.

NOTES

Week 13

FIRST

I will select my fifteen-minute quiet times for the week ahead and visualize where I will go each day and at what times. I will petition the Lord for the grace to keep sacred my times of prayer and strive to pray in a place that is technology-free, a place apart. I will bring my notebook to each prayer period and commit to spending no more than fifteen minutes in each formal prayer session. I will always use my personal name for God.

SECOND

For this week's fifteen-minute prayer sessions, I have one simple prayer exercise for Sunday through Saturday.

THIRD

I continue to stay with my letter to Christ Jesus asking for His help, insight, patience, grace, and healing for my life story. I will either keep writing or speaking to Christ, or sit with my letter in prayer. The letter is a snapshot of my whole life, and it is of supreme spiritual worth to be present to Christ with my life story. So, I will either continue writing or pray over what I have written and confessed.

I will awaken to the present moment.
I will take each day and each exercise as it comes.

I cannot do Sacred Story better by going faster.

I will ask God to help me.

I will awaken to my spiritual nature
and to the inspirations that inspire faith, hope, and love.
I will awaken to the inspirations that inspire cynicism,
impatience, and lusts. I will wake up!
Be not afraid!
I will not make any decisions
that bend to my fears and my anxieties. They are founded
on bad information and will not lead to my peace.

This week, I will say this affirmation aloud once daily:
Lord Jesus Christ, I believe you came into the world, born of Mary,
so that I may have life and have it abundantly.

℘

We are a people of faith who live in the light of the Cross of Christ, the light of the Resurrection of Christ, and the light of the Second Coming of Christ. We are His sisters and brothers. We live because we are loved by God.

During these days, as you reflect on your whole-life confession, remember that confession includes grateful praise along with admission of sins and faults. Remember that Christ, the Divine Physician, came so that you can triumph through your failings and weaknesses, by His healing and forgiving grace, to produce fruit that endures to eternity. St. Ignatius once marveled that he did not think, in the entire history of the Church, there was ever someone who sinned as much as he did, who was also given so many graces. "Where sin increased, grace overflowed all the more" (Rom 5:20).

If you have not yet made your confession, you have time both to write a letter and to go to confession this week. These weeks of prayer are about developing a deeper relationship with God in Christ. Do not surrender to your anxiety or perfectionism that may suggest that you have not done enough of the prayer sessions to make a confession or write a letter. If you feel you are behind, do what you can to keep moving forward.

If you have made your confession, use your fifteen-minute prayer periods this week to be with Christ and the letter you wrote to Him. Bring your notebook to your prayer sessions. After each session, write one sentence for what brings you the most hope as you read your letter, and one sentence for what causes you the most discouragement as you read your letter. Linger over the words and phrases that brought you hope and peace. Remember the experience of your confession, and allow its graces to penetrate deeply into your heart.

CB

I am starting a Relationship that will carry me
for the rest of my life.

All relationships require time and patience.
I will strive for patience and ask for God's help
when I don't understand a lesson.

I will learn the fundamentals and open my heart to God.

I trust that God will lead me.

I believe that my sacred story will unfold in truth,
in powerlessness, and with my patience.

I believe that Jesus awaits me with His grace, mercy,
and forgiving love.

BO

Letters from Week Thirteen

Dear Fr. Bill,

I wanted to let you know that one of the local priests who comes in to celebrate Mass was willing to take the time to hear my Whole-Life Confession. I went ahead and had the priest read the relevant chapter of Forty Weeks and we proceeded from there. It was a positive experience and I am so glad I was able to do it.

I spent another week reading it aloud to my Savior Jesus Christ and sitting alone in silence with it in an attempt to fully understand and appreciate what is taking place. I've concluded that this is the real beginning of my life, a fresh start. Not only am I forgiven for the dissolute life I've lived, but I now fully understand why and how I became that person.

I've let go of old anger and resentments, forgiven those who needed to be forgiven, prayed for forgiveness from those I've hurt, and asked for the grace to become the man I was created to be. Jesus Christ died on the cross for me, not so I can continue to live a wasted, sinful life, but so I can become a loving, caring disciple and spend eternity with Him.

I know exactly what Ignatius meant when he thought no one in the history of the Church had sinned as much and received as many graces as he did. Society had deemed me irredeemable, not fit to walk the streets.

I wasn't a decent person who had some issues with sin. I was a full-time intense sinner. My entire being was based on and in, sin. My old life was extreme, and through prayer, meditation and forgiveness, my Lord has instilled in me the need and desire to live new life just as intensely and extreme.

Here is my Whole-Life Confession

Jesus Christ, my Lord and Savior,

I come to you as a new man, a new man in Christ. In the summer of 2013 I came to you as a fearful, hurting child with nowhere else to turn. You saved me. You touched me with your love and as a result I have the need, desire, and strength, through your grace, to become the man I was created to be. Jesus, with you I can do this. Without you I am nothing, without hope. You are my Savior. I now have hope for eternal life and someone to turn to as I try to make it through this earthly life. For this I am grateful beyond words.

Lord Jesus, through your grace I am forgiven. You know all the thoughts, words, and deeds of my past. I am still amazed that my early life—being given up by my birth mother, living in foster care, and eventually being adopted by people who did not have my best interests at heart, and the abuse that followed, had such an impact on how I would go on to live my life.

The sense of embarrassment I experienced at being a foster child would ensure that I never again let anyone know enough about me that I could ever again be embarrassed. My feelings of abandonment and lack of love made me determined to never feel that way again. Once again, my fears manifested in not letting others close to me. I became filled with hate--for both my birth mother and adopted mother, who I blamed for my plight, and also for those who seemed to have "perfect lives", filled with love, family, and friends.

My success in not allowing myself to get close to people, to not letting others know me meant that I was on my own. With no one to answer to I was able to do whatever I wanted whenever I wanted. If there were consequences, I would bear them without complaint. This allowed my sense of abandonment and embarrassment to turn into jealousy, anger, hate, greed, arrogance and all types of instant gratification and self-indulgences, including drug and alcohol abuse, gambling, sexual deviancy and promiscuity, the use and abuse of others, and the breaking of the law to obtain what I wanted.

Lord, as you know, there were times when I exhibited absolutely no redeeming qualities whatsoever. I was totally godless. I encountered good, honest people and I sucked all the good out of them. People would then become hesitant to go out on a limb for others due to how I treated them. I ruined people's lives. Wretched man that I am, I am blessed for being forgiven. I am so grateful that through your grace I am forgiven and I do not have to live that way any longer.

My Lord, as My Savior you have guaranteed that I no longer have to live that sorry, narcissistic life. Even though I know you've blessed me with the ability to overcome all of these obstacles, and to continue finding myself fighting the urge to quit: to cut and run; to admit defeat like I have so many times before. Lord, I've failed at everything I've ever attempted. I've never finished anything good. I've never done anything that anyone would look at and say that they were proud of me.

Not until I answered your knock on my heart's door. And even still today I sometimes wonder how long I can be obedient to you. Quitting on you would immediately send me back to that horrible place.

All of my habits, addictions, vices, and sins would be back. All hope would be lost. So, if there is one thing I could ask for, it would be for the ability to persevere, to keep my eyes on the prize. Jesus, being my personal Savior is the difference between my old life and my new life—the difference between success, failure, life, and death. I never thought I could do it on my own. I always knew I needed you. I just didn't care before. I had no desire to give up my ways. I knew what was best for me. And even during those few short periods when I contemplated asking you for help, my sense of ultimate failure would dissuade me.

Lord, you've accepted me as I am but I am sure you do not want me to remain as I am. I am far from the man I was created to be, but with you all things are possible. I am forgiven by you, and because of that I have been able to forgive, in my heart, all persons who have harmed me. There is no longer hate in my heart and I ask you to continue to allow me to grow in your love.

Lord, just like when, in the Garden of Gethsemane you asked that your Father's will be done, I continue to ask the same. My life is yours. Without you I am hopeless and helpless. Without a constant, conscious relationship with you I would quickly revert to my old narcissistic lifestyle. You love me. I owe you everything. I have one goal in this earthly life--to become the man I was created to be in order to serve you and to bring glory and honor upon your name. I pray that despite myself and my flirtations with the enemy, that through your grace, I can do this.

Thank you, Lord, for allowing this unworthy sinner to experience your love, mercy, and grace. Thank You, Lord.

Your grateful servant,

Ritchie

Dear Ritchie:

So much of our "life of sin and suffering" goes back to early things that set us on a wrong path. Realize that Jesus was with you when you were given up for adoption and when you suffered intense embarrassment from being a foster child. You felt unloved and were ashamed that no one "wanted you."

Covering for that shame had led you to seek relief from your pain in all sorts of things that may have helped block the embarrassment, but made you more withdrawn and feeing even more unloved and unlovable. Jesus was with you in all of this, loving you and knowing one day that you would feel his love.

One of the great consolations of our Christian, Catholic faith is that we understand that Jesus loved us even when we are sinners. St. Paul in Romans tells us:

> "Indeed, only with difficulty does one die for a just person, though perhaps for a good person one might even find courage to die. But God proves his love for us in that while we were still sinners Christ died for us. How much more then, since we are now justified by his blood, will we be saved through him from the wrath. Indeed, if, while we were enemies, we were reconciled to God through the death of his Son, how much more, once reconciled, will we be saved by his life. Not only that, but we also boast of God through our Lord Jesus Christ, through whom we have now received reconciliation." (Romans 5:8-11)

So Ritchie, relish the feelings and convictions that you now feel your life beginning anew in your reconciliations from a past that was in your experience, "dissolute." But know that your life had infinite value to Jesus even when you were at your worst. He died for you at your worst so you could become your best. You have always been loved by Jesus, always, always, and always will be, no matter what! Let that sink in to your heart and give you even greater hope.

St. Ignatius had his moment of God saying "I love you" early in his career and it was in light of his sins and awakening to God's desires for him to be the man he was destined to be. Ignatius lived the rest of his life shaped by that experience. So, hold on to yours. It was God's way of putting you on course by letting you know you are loved and your life has value and meaning.

Peace,

Fr. Bill

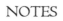

NOTES

Part Two
Learning Sacred Story Prayer

"It was not you who chose me, but I who chose you and
appointed you to go and bear fruit that will remain,
so that whatever you ask the
Father in my name he may give you.
This I command you: love one another."

Jn 15:16–17

WEEK 14

FIRST

As I begin part 2 in Forty Weeks, I consciously determine if it is beneficial to change the number of times I pray daily. I will ask for patience to start each day with renewed commitment, even if I miss a day's prayer. If I am using a notebook separate from the Forty Weeks "Notes" pages, I will bring it to each prayer period. I will begin this week, in my notebook or on the "Notes" pages, a habit of simple daily journaling.[10] At the end of each day, I will mark one event that increased my faith, hope, and love and one event that decreased my faith, hope, and love. I will always use my personal name for God.

SECOND

I will listen attentively to my experience to discern the two plotlines in my story. I will do this by consciously attending to my fantasies and/or daydreams.

THIRD

As I begin part 2 in Forty Weeks, I will encounter several more foundational exercises. Like the exercises leading up to a whole-life confession, these additional exercises will help identify important narrative themes in my story that I can bring to my formal times of prayer. The exercises' meaning and energy come from my asking God for help and grace—from my relationship with God.

I will awaken to the present moment.
I will awaken to my spiritual nature.
I will not make any decisions based on fear.

This week, I will say this affirmation aloud once daily:
My sacred story takes a lifetime to write.

CB

Take this full week after your whole-life confession for this Ignatian daydream/fantasy exercise. It is inspired by St. Ignatius's "awakening" while he was recovering from his battle wound. Now is the perfect time to do this exercise, because after Reconciliation, you have much more clarity and peacefulness to see, by grace, the contours of your story.

Ignatius, while recovering from battle, discovered that his daydreams and fantasies were pulling his heart in two different directions. One direction was toward vain, self-serving, self-indulgent exploits rooted in his wounded human nature. The other direction was toward holy aspirations representing his authentic human nature and the deepest aspirations of his heart. These latter daydreams had been inaudible and out of view most of his life. The black noise of temptation and a false self-portrait both deafened and blinded his heart. Aided by grace, he awoke to the existence of his fantasies and daydreams and (also by grace) discovered that only one of the two storylines expressed his authentic human nature—the deepest dream of his heart.

You will discover that many daydreams and fantasies fight for room in the conscious and unconscious spaces of your heart. No matter their differences, or the fact that they might seem unrelated, they always fall into the two storylines representing the two trajectories of your heart. One set of daydreams or fantasies trend toward infinite Love, holy appetites, integration, humility, reconciliation, hope, peace, wakefulness, sobriety, and gratitude. The other set of daydreams/fantasies trend toward finite things, appetites low and earthly, disintegration, narcissism, resentment, cynicism, anxiety, unconsciousness, drunkenness, and lack of gratitude.

Begin this week by paying attention to your daydreams and fantasies. Let them see the light of day. You will find their traces everywhere:

✠ in the things you purchase, and the things you want to purchase

✠ in your favorite songs, movies, and stories

✠ in the podcast and TV programs that claim your passionate loyalty

✠ in the lives of artists, athletes, actors, saints, politicians—the heroes you emulate and admire and those you disdain

✠ in your programs of study and your job applications

✠ in the friends you have, and the friends you wish you had

✠ in the things that happened, and the things you wish had happened

✠ in the places you want to visit or make your home, and the places you want to leave and never return

✠ in the worlds you visit in cyberspace, and the ones you visit in your inner sacred space

✠ in what motivates you to exercise and discipline yourself, and what influences you to fall out of shape

✠ in the individuals and groups you love, and those whose love you reject

✠ in the people you offer forgiveness, and those you refuse to forgive

✠ in the people you envy, wishing you had their looks, talents, connections, wealth, happiness, or relationships

✠ in what causes you to practice your faith, and what causes you to forget and forgo its practice

✠ in the persons and events that stir your sexual lusts, and the persons and events that stir your childlike innocence

✠ in what opens your wallet to give to the needy, and what closes it to their need

✠ in the stories, images, and experiences that break your heart, and those that cause your heart to be joyful

✠ in the things that make you cry, and the things that make you laugh

✠ in the person or group you want to spend the rest of your life with, and the person or group you want to spend the rest of your life avoiding

✠ in what moves your heart to thanklessness, and what makes it swell with gratitude

The Prayer Exercise

Do this exercise in the context of your daily fifteen-minute prayer sessions, allowing it to permeate your actual daydreams. Your brief journal entry at the end of the day can itemize just one thing that brought you hope and peace that day and just one thing that eroded your hope and peace. In light of this fantasy exercise, focus on themes related to the two main daydreams/fantasies that you unconsciously or consciously entertain. An example: *"I daydreamed about x today and it brought me joy because...."*
Your own daydreams and fantasies may not be so sharply felt but will most likely align with the two themes described below.

NARCISSISTIC DAYDREAMS/FANTASIES

Anxiety, fear, lusts, compulsive appetites, resentment and anger, control of others, getting even/getting back, addictions, lost innocence, aggression, and vices populate these story lines. In short, they are linked to your broken heart and wounded human nature. These daydreams/fantasies generate electrical energy, excitement, and urges to things low and earthly. They inflate your ego and excite you while you are fantasizing or engaging them, but they leave you dry, empty, hungrier, and dissatisfied—even depressed—after the fact. Or out of your sadness, depression, anger, emptiness, and dryness, you may turn to them for satisfaction and release—like a narcotic—a painkiller for your heart.

GRATEFUL DAYDREAMS/FANTASIES

Peace, calm, self-control, forgiveness, surrendering angers and hatreds, appreciation of beauty and innocence, holy dreams and high ideals, inspirations to selfless love, desires for healing, and the joy of making a difference and living a meaningful life are their storylines. These storylines are linked to your God-given human nature and the deepest dreams of your heart. These daydreams/fantasies generate peace, tears, quiet hope, and aspirations to all things innocent, beautiful, and noble. They humble your heart and fill you with gratitude while you are fantasizing or engaging them, and they leave you fulfilled, content, and satisfied—even joyful—after the fact.

.

ɔ8

Lord, you will open my lips;
and my mouth will proclaim your praise.
For you do not desire sacrifice or I would give it;
a burnt offering you would not accept.
My sacrifice, O God, is a contrite spirit;
a contrite, humbled heart, O God, you will not scorn.
(Ps 51:17–19)

ꙅꙩ

Letters from Week Fourteen

Dear Fr. Bill,

St. Ignatius' daydreams have been the most interesting and helpful part of Forty Weeks so far, aside from my Whole Life Confession, obviously. Reading about his daydreams/fantasies has let me know I am not unique and there is definitely hope for me.

Right now I live in an extremely negative environment. I find myself in constant unavoidable contact with hundreds of men on a daily basis. Constant talk of sex, violence, drugs and other sins bombard me from all directions. I find myself listening to them and daydreaming/fantasizing about these things without being aware of it; like it comes naturally. What bothers me most is that it seems I am enjoying these daydreams until I realize what is happening and have to find a quiet place to pray. It is disheartening and scary that I can revert to my old ways so quickly without realizing what is happening.

I thank God regularly for the fact that I am experiencing grateful daydreams more and more. These dreams consist of me spending a lot of time in prayer. It's never clear in these daydreams where I am living. It is always obvious that I don't have much in the way of material possessions. I have plenty of time to commune with my Savior. I am doing good work although God has not shown me exactly what I am doing to glorify Him.

At the risk of characterizing this week's exercise too simplistically, I must say that my grateful, positive daydreams lifted me up much, much more than my negative, narcissistic daydreams dragged me down. The journal entries concerning the fantasies that brought me joy were much easier to recall than the ones that eroded my hope and peace. That's a fact, and all of the credit goes to the grace of God.

Respectfully,
Ritchie

Dear Ritchie

We learn the art of spiritual discernment by consciously recognizing our fantasies and daydreams and making distinctions between those that uplift us and those that drag us down. Most people have fantasies and never pay attention that these fantasies are running in the background like a movie. Awakening to the spiritual world requires us to wake up to what these fantasies are and how they are guiding our hearts! That is what it sounds like you are allowing the Holy Spirit to awaken in your life.

Yes, you are in a negative environment and will no doubt be influenced by what is around you. Don't be surprised that old fantasies and life-styles will pull at you constantly. This will likely happen till the day you die. The enemy of our human nature tries to discourage us by making us focus on the fact that these things still hold some power over us. But see how you were guided by the Holy Spirit to defend against the enemy. He called you to focus on gratitude and those dreams that uplift you.

Take great hope and encouragement that the holy dreams were much easier to recall than the narcissistic ones and that these were the ones that had the most power. That is because they are the ones that express the true desires of your heart and how Christ will continue to be your light and peace---"and all of the credit goes to the grace of God!"

You are in my prayers. Please keep me in yours.

Peace,

Fr. Bill

NOTES

Week 15

FIRST

I will ask for the grace of patience to start each day with renewed commitment, even if I miss a day's prayer. I will have my notebook at hand for each prayer period. I will remember to spend no more and no less than fifteen minutes in each formal prayer session. At the end of each day, I will continue to note in writing one event that increased my faith, hope, and love and one event that decreased my faith, hope, and love. I will always use my personal name for God.

SECOND

I am listening this week for the way that pride (narcissism) takes shape in my daily life. I will do this by engaging an attentiveness prayer that examines the two principal forms of narcissism (passive and aggressive). On Monday, Tuesday, and Wednesday of this week, I will reflect on one type of narcissism, and on Thursday, Friday, and Saturday, I will reflect on the other.

THIRD

I will continue to draw consolation from my letter to Jesus/whole-life confession. Also, I can bring insights on narcissism from my daily life into my prayer times. Sacred Story prayer is rooted in my asking God for help. Through grace, an intimate relationship between myself and God is being established.

I will awaken to the present moment.
I will awaken to my spiritual nature.
I will not make any decisions based on fear.

This week, I will say this affirmation aloud once daily:
Be not afraid.
Fear comes from the enemy of my human nature.

ଔ

Read this page and the next at the beginning of the week:

Recall how Ignatius of Loyola discovered a narcissistic pride at the root of all his manifest sins, addictions, spiritual dysfunction, and emotional imbalances. In Genesis, pride is the principal sin of Adam and Eve, or as we might define it today, narcissism.[11] The serpent tempted both Adam and Eve with eating the fruit of the forbidden tree by telling them that their "eyes will be opened" and they would "be like gods" (Gen 3:5). The rest of the story is the history of sin, sickness, and death.

The immense grief, sorrow, and guilt of paradise lost by human choice are memories burned deep in the heart of each and every woman and man who has lived, is living, or will ever walk this earth. But praise God, because it is through the wound, guilt, and grief of paradise lost that we come to understand the divisions in our hearts (Jer 17:9).

Although our sin separates us from God, it still points out the path that sets each woman and man on a journey back home to God and to our authentic self. St. Ignatius achieved his greatest enlightenment when he identified the pattern of sin in his story. Once he awoke to it, God used him powerfully in the work of redemption. God will do the same for each of us.

Awakening to our prideful narcissism is understood as a positive move toward deeper spiritual growth. It is not a depressing exercise to make us feel bad or fearful. If these negative emotions result from your prayer, set your eyes and heart on Christ Jesus, the Divine Physician. Recall that He looks on you with joy and love as you discover the things that diminish your hope and spiritual freedom. Allow Christ to work His healing graces in your story. Remember our affirmation for this week: fear comes from the enemy of human nature.

How does narcissism work? Narcissism, or pride (both words describe the same damaging spiritual darkness), makes me the center of the universe and the ultimate arbiter of all truth. Narcissism displaces God in order that I can be "like a god." From that first sin of narcissism flows humankind's banishment from paradise; the advent of pain, sickness, and death; the emergence of evolutionary evil in family structures, as evidenced by Cain's murder of Abel; and the fracturing of the human community as symbolized in the greed, competition, and overweening pride underlying the parable of the Tower of Babel.

Man and woman consciously displaced God as their center and source, and made themselves center and source. From this results the fracturing of creation's harmony. A terminal virus of sin now infects the core of all living things. The corruption caused by this virus has even altered life at the cellular, molecular, and biological level. Nothing in the created order has been left untouched or unharmed by the virus of this sin (Gen 3:17–19; Rom 8:18–27).

We are all born into it, and we all participate in it. Self-centeredness is an equal-opportunity employer. All serious Christian prayer disciplines target this core sin so that by the power of Christ's sacrifice, "creation itself would be set free from slavery to corruption and share in the glorious freedom of the children of God" (Rom 8:21).

It is spiritually valuable—exceedingly so—to understand what form of prideful narcissism your life circumstances have shaped in you. It might be helpful to realize that no side of pride's face is better than the other. Both are equally difficult to admit! Both forms of prideful narcissism displace God in our lives and serve to mask our wounded human nature—our heart's grief at paradise lost.

Prayer Exercise

With the Divine Physician's grace, ask to understand how you displace God as the center of your life. Ask to become aware of the grief, anger, and fear that grips you, and the void at the center of your heart and soul that only He can heal. The grace of a whole-life confession gives us renewed humility. It fosters a desire to open more to Christ's life and the spiritual growth, insights, freedom, hope, and peace it brings!

The following two exercises will help you identify your type of prideful narcissism. Spend the prayer periods of three days on each type (Monday, Tuesday, and Wednesday or Thursday, Friday, and Saturday). You decide which type to reflect on first and which one second.

Note that this week's prayer exercise is not to solve your prideful narcissism problem! That would be discouraging (and impossible)! It is enough for now to identify, with the Divine Physician's grace, a type of narcissism that you judge more present in your story. I want to emphasize that it was when Ignatius awoke to his prideful narcissism that God was able to really work with him. You will likely discover one or the other of these two principal manifestations of prideful narcissism at the root of all things difficult in your life.

Purposely, these two types are defined in very stark language so you can distinguish them clearly. You most likely will not feel them as strongly in your story as they are drawn here. So in your reflection and prayer, attend more to the type to which you are susceptible and not so much the intensity. Ask the Divine Physician to guide your prayerful awakening in peace, trust, and hope. These two faces of narcissism capture the principal forms of pride that life's circumstances generate in human nature wounded by Original Sin.

ও

The Passive Narcissist

Take the prayer periods of three days to pray with this description of the passive narcissist. It is vital to understand this type of Original Sin's pride manifesting in human dysfunction. Note briefly in your journal what you consider significant that causes anxiety or hope. Are the passive narcissist's qualities ones that typify your negative story?

This type of narcissism rehearses and repeats the anger, fear, anxiety, and grief of old wounds and hurts. The passive narcissist complains, is grasping, is cynical, and makes excuses for everything except his own bad behavior. The passive narcissist draws attention to himself in every thought, word, and deed and says he is the center of attention in these ways: "See how I have suffered." "See how I have been victimized." "See how unfairly I am treated." "See why I behave the way I do." "See why I am justified in...."

The passive narcissist works hard to blame others for her wounds and labors mightily in every thought, word, and deed to make sure others know of her suffering. The passive narcissist takes pride and finds power and comfort in her victim status, whether it is real or perceived. The passive narcissist works very hard to maintain her victim status and remain powerless, refusing to take responsibility for changing her situation, because changing the situation means confronting pain and offering forgiveness to those who helped her evolve this way. Changing also means losing her core identity of powerless victim. To lose this identity is to lose power and control. There are three main reasons for this.

First, losing victim status means literally losing power and control of the people and events in the passive narcissist's world. Second, he is disconnected from his authentic self, so losing the status of victim initiates an acute and fearful identity crisis, because life's meaning and definitions of success have been intimately linked with being a powerless victim. Third, as a result of the loss of power and control and the loss of his false identity, the passive narcissist will be confronted with the spiritual, psychological, and emotional wounds hiding behind the passive narcissism.

During your daily activities, pay attention to sudden anger, anxiety, fear, or grief that surfaces. Pray for graced insights to comprehend how sudden anger, temptation, anxiety, fear, or grief touch the deep spiritual, emotional, and physical wounds and Original Sins in your life. For those events that seem to jump out at you and capture your attention, consciously do this short exercise, speaking to Christ from your heart:

✠ Ask to be conscious of what you are reacting to rather than reacting impulsively, without thinking.

✠ Ask to feel the heart's fear, temptation, anxiety, anger, and grief present in the reaction.

✠ Ask for knowledge—for graced insight—to begin dismantling this immature, damaging, and self-glorifying process, which for a passive narcissist is particularly depressing and for an aggressive narcissist is particularly electrifying.

✠ Ask who or what initiated this particular pattern of reaction—of overpowering or of blaming others—and why?

✠ Ask for courage to face the negative story of being a passive victim, because facing it can cause panic when you are used to being its slave, but confronting it can bring you peace and freedom.

CB

The Aggressive Narcissist

Take the prayer periods of three days to pray with this description of the aggressive narcissist. It is vital to understand this type of Original Sin's pride manifesting in human dysfunction. Note briefly in your journal what you consider significant that causes anxiety or hope. Are the aggressive narcissist's qualities ones that typify your negative story?

This type of narcissism also rehearses and repeats the anger, fear, anxiety, and grief of old wounds and hurts. The wounded, prideful aggressor gets even, is grasping, and is determined to best others and to justify and excuse her behavior in the process. The aggressive narcissist draws attention to herself in every thought, word, and deed and says she is the center of attention in these ways: "See how special and gifted I am." "See that you never get in my way." "See, you will never overpower me." "See, I deserve what I have, because I earned it." "See, no one will ever hurt me again."

The aggressive narcissist works hard never to let anyone best him and labors mightily in every thought, word, and deed to make sure others get the message of his superiority. The aggressive narcissist takes pride in, and finds tremendous energy in, his triumphs over others, real or perceived. The aggressive narcissist works very hard to maintain his

winner status, for his negative story is now totally associated with being the winner. To lose winner status is to lose power and control. There are three main reasons for this.

First, losing winner status means losing the power and control of the people and events in the aggressive narcissist's world. Second, she is disconnected from her authentic self, so losing the status of winner initiates an acute and fearful identity crisis, because life's meaning and definitions of success have been intimately linked with the story of being the winner. Third, as a result of the loss of power and control and the loss of her false identity, the aggressive narcissist will be confronted with the spiritual, psychological, and emotional wounds hiding behind her aggressive narcissism.

During your daily activities, pay attention to sudden anger, anxiety, fear, or grief that surfaces. Pray for graced insights to comprehend how sudden anger, temptation, anxiety, fear, or grief touch the deep spiritual, emotional, and physical wounds and Original Sins in your life.

For those events that seem to jump out at you and capture your attention, consciously do this short exercise, speaking to Christ from your heart:

✠ Ask to be conscious of what you are reacting to rather than reacting impulsively, without thinking.

✠ Ask to feel the heart's fear, temptation, anxiety, anger, and grief present in the reaction.

✠ Ask for knowledge—for graced insight—to begin dismantling this immature, damaging, and self-glorifying process, which for a passive narcissist is particularly depressing and for an aggressive narcissist is particularly electrifying.

✠ Ask who or what initiated this particular pattern of reaction—of overpowering or of blaming others—and why?

✠ Ask for courage to face the negative story of being a passive victim, because facing it can cause panic when you are used to being its slave, but confronting it can bring you peace and freedom.

THE PASSIVE NARCISSIST	THE AGGRESSIVE NARCISSIST
SELF-IDENTIFIES AS A VICTIM	SELF-IDENTIFIES AS A WINNER
IS DETERMINED TO HAVE OTHERS NOTICE HOW SPECIAL THEY ARE BY POINTING TO THEIR UNFAIR SUFFERING	IS DETERMINED TO HAVE OTHERS NOTICE HOW SPECIAL THEY ARE BY DEFEATING ALL OPPONENTS
IS CYNICAL AND EXCUSES BAD BEHAVIOR BY INSISTING IT IS JUSTIFIED BECAUSE OF HOW MUCH THEY HAVE SUFFERED	IS CYNICAL AND EXCUSES BAD BEHAVIOR BY INSISTING IT IS JUSTIFIED BECAUSE THEY HAVE EARNED IT
WALLOWS IN SELF-PITY WHEN HURT, WHETHER THE HURT IS REAL OR IMAGINED	IS VINDICTIVE WHEN HURT, WHETHER THE HURT IS REAL OR IMAGINED
BLAMES ANYONE WHO CRITICIZES OR OPPOSES THEM	THREATENS ANYONE WHO CRITICIZES OR OPPOSES THEM
PROTECTS THEMSELF FROM BEING HURT AGAIN BY KEEPING WOUNDS AS FRESH AS POSSIBLE. IF ANYTHING IS TOO DIFFICULT OR PAINFUL, THEY WILL RETREAT INTO THOSE PAINFUL MEMORIES AND TURN INWARD, AWAY FROM OTHERS	PROTECTS THEMSELF FROM BEING HURT AGAIN BY ERADICATING VULNERABILITIES. IF ANYTHING IS TOO DIFFICULT OR PAINFUL, THEY WILL ACT IN A CONQUEROR ROLE AND DOMINATE OTHERS
WINS BY EMOTIONAL MANIPULATION	WINS BY DIRECT CONFRONTATION
IS SECRETLY ATTACHED TO THEIR OWN WOUNDEDNESS	IS SECRETLY ATTACHED TO THIER POWER OF DEFEATING OTHERS
IS TERRIFIED OF TAKING CONTROL AND PERSONAL RESPONSIBILITY AND HAS DIFFICULTY ADMITTING THIS TO ONESELF	IS TERRIFIED OF SURRENDERING CONTROL AND BEING VULNERABLE AND HAS DIFFICULTY ADMITTING THIS TO ONESELF

ଔ

Why, Lord, do you stand afar
and pay no heed in times of trouble?

Arrogant scoundrels pursue the poor;
they trap them by their cunning schemes.

The wicked even boast of their greed;
these robbers curse and scorn the Lord.

In their insolence the wicked boast:
"God does not care; there is no God."

Yet their affairs always succeed;
they ignore your judgment on high;
they sneer at all who oppose them.

They say in their hearts, "We will never fall;
never will we see misfortune."

Their mouths are full of oaths, violence, and lies;
discord and evil are under their tongues.

They wait in ambush near towns;
their eyes watch for the helpless
to murder the innocent in secret.

They lurk in ambush like lions in a thicket,
hide there to trap the poor,
snare them and close the net.

The helpless are crushed, laid low;
they fall into the power of the wicked,
who say in their hearts, "God has forgotten,
shows no concern, never bothers to look."

Rise up, Lord! God, lift up your hand!
Do not forget the poor!

Why should the wicked scorn God,
say in their hearts, "God does not care"?

But you do see;
you take note of misery and sorrow;
you take the matter in hand.

To you the helpless can entrust their cause;
you are the defender of orphans.

Break the arm of the wicked and depraved;
make them account for their crimes;
let none of them survive.

The Lord is king forever;
the nations have vanished from his land.

You listen, Lord, to the needs of the poor;
you strengthen their heart and incline your ear.

You win justice for the orphaned and oppressed;
no one on earth will cause terror again.
(Ps 10)

ℰↄ

Letters from Week Fifteen

Dear Fr. Bill,

I don't know whether or not it is to my credit but I was definitely not a passive narcissist. My ego would never allow me to be a victim or even try to play the victim for my own gain. There wasn't much I wouldn't do to feed my sinful pleasures, but I couldn't do that. If I experienced anger, fear, anxiety or wound and hurts, I would not acknowledge them and most certainly would not let others see them.

There is no question I was/am the aggressive narcissist. I self-identified as a winner. I projected myself as a winner. I projected a message of superiority. I spent a lot of time and energy trying to convince others of my triumphs. Simultaneously, I actually knew I was just an afraid, lonely, insecure and needy person. I was a fake, phony fraud.

Fr. Bill, Week Fifteen has been very good for me. Reading that "St. Ignatius achieved his greatest enlightenment when he identified the pattern of sin in his story" and realizing that the same is true for me, gives me extraordinary hope; unshakeable hope.

Facing my negative story is so important. It constantly reminds me that I am forgiven, and because of that, all things are now possible. Without embracing the fact that I am an unworthy sinner saved by God's grace, I would not have what I have today or the joy of looking to the future.

Respectfully,

Ritchie

Dear Ritchie:

I put the exercises on passive and aggressive narcissism after the Whole-Life Confession so that people would have enough hope and encouragement from the experience of God's forgiveness to more honestly face how the core sin of pride—narcissism—manifests in their lives. From your reflections above, I am encouraged once again that my timing for this exercise was right.

Pay attention to how your identification with aggressive narcissism, therefore, does not now discourage you, but gives you "unshakable hope." You know that pattern of sin was and is rooted in the broken heart of a young boy who was abandoned by his birth parents and who sought to defend himself from life's hardships by taking every shortcut to pleasure and power. You know it never worked and as you said above, your life is beginning anew.

You might want to take this insight about your own life and when you see and hear the many men around you talking about winning, drugs, sex and all the other negative things they desire. See in them children whose hearts need to be healed. Who knows, the joy you now have in looking to the future might one day mean bringing hope to men like these.

Peace,

Fr. Bill

NOTES

Week 16

FIRST

I continue to ask for patience to start each day with renewed commitment. I will not be discouraged by the times I have missed prayer but will instead ask God for help to be more faithful. I will bring my notebook to prayer and resolve to spend no more and no less than fifteen minutes in each prayer period. I will always use my personal name for God.

SECOND

This week, I am invited to learn the components of Sacred Story daily practice. My fidelity to the linked practice of these daily exercises will produce sustained spiritual growth and enlightenment. Ignatius was a strategist, and he understood that spiritual exercises must be regular, focused, and open to grace. It is up to me to ask God for help in using these resources for my healing and spiritual growth.

THIRD

I will continue to draw consolation from my letter to Jesus/whole-life confession.

> I will awaken to the present moment.
> I will awaken to my spiritual nature.
> I will not make any decisions based on fear.

I will practice sacramental Reconciliation monthly.
This week, I will say this affirmation aloud once daily:
The pathway to God's peace and healing runs through my heart's
brokenness, sin, fear, anger, and grief.

క్ర

Read this page at the beginning of the week:

The most important activity in any day is the time I take to direct my conscious attention—my mind and heart—to God in a prayer relationship. Not only is my relationship with God the most important dimension of life, it is also a relationship that takes time—a lifetime—to build! The depth of the relationship I desire will be evident in my fidelity to my prayer and sacramental life. As Scripture says, where your treasure is, so will your heart be (Mt 6:21).

Sacred Story Daily Practice

The Sacred Story prayer routine is a time-proven and highly effective discipline for waking up to God's life in you, and your life in God. Practiced daily, you learn to surrender to God. You will find interior freedom and peace so that your life's labor produces fruit that endures to eternity. Ignatius and the early Jesuits used similar prayers in conjunction with frequent sacramental Reconciliation as primary spiritual tools in their pastoral ministries in Europe and the New World.

The combined practice of regular prayer and sacramental Reconciliation has produced tremendous spiritual growth for countless thousands of souls and still does so today. Sacred Story prayer can bring this dual spiritual practice into your Christian life to help you encounter Christ daily. It would be hard to find a more effective prayer discipline for this purpose. This week's lesson teaches the prayer disciplines that serve as a support structure for Sacred Story prayer, which you will start next week. It will be a tremendous benefit for you to learn these habits of thought and introduce them into your daily life.

One of the chief victories of human nature's enemy in modern times is the violence of hyperactivity and a loss of interior silence. The prayer disciplines you learn about this week, the Sacred Story prayer you start next week, and a regular practice of Reconciliation will help you counter this unique modern form of violence and open your heart to the voice of God. These practices are simple, take little time, and if done faithfully, will move you forward on the path of holiness and integration with your sacred story. They are valuable spiritual practices for your life.

Bookmark This Section

You will need this week's reference materials throughout the rest of the forty weeks and beyond. Use this week's prayer periods to become familiar with them, and bookmark them so you can reference them often. Remember that you are not expected to implement these exercises this week. We will begin implementing them next week.

Cʒ

Prayer Exercise for Monday

Reflect on the instructions below for the "Prayer upon Waking," and use your fifteen-minute prayer period(s) today to understand this discipline. Note briefly in your journal what you consider significant. When you begin to incorporate this exercise into your day, you should be spending no more than fifteen to thirty seconds with it.

Prayer upon Waking (fifteen to thirty seconds)

Before arising from your bed, consciously awaken to Creation, Presence, Memory, Mercy, and Eternity (these concepts are explained more later this week). Note any significant movements in your heart and mind that come from your dreams. Note the state of your heart regarding any planned events of the day. Pay particular attention to feelings of peace or anxiety that stir in you. Anticipate any challenges that might confront you today, especially those linked to your wounded human nature that might stir fear, anger, or grief in you. With gratitude, offer the thoughts, words, and deeds of your day to God.

CB

Prayer Exercise for Tuesday

Reflect on the instructions below for the "During-the-Day Awakening" prayer, and take your fifteen-minute quiet period(s) today to understand this discipline. Note briefly in your journal what you consider significant. This exercise is linked to the exercises on sin, addiction, vices, Commandments, narcissism, and people in your life narrative.

During-the-Day Awakening
to Sins, Addictions, and Compulsions (fifteen to thirty seconds)

Prepare your heart to watch and listen to your day as it unfolds. Be attentive to the events and circumstances that evoke temptation and incite your attraction to things low and earthly. These are easily recognized, because they trigger your angers or addictions. They hook into your vices and the fault lines in your mind and heart. You are, in short, seeking to "wake up" to what makes living the gospel of Christ Jesus difficult. Discipline yourself to not react to these things outwardly.

Be curious about why you are tempted or angry. Remain open to the links between the events that spark your temptations, angers, addictions, narcissism, and attractions to things low and earthly. Be conscious of the theme and the fact of the temptation. Wake up, and watch the process with Christ so He can teach you how to grow in grace. When you are tempted or when you fail in the course of your day, Jesus is the Divine Physician who desires to help you. He judges you, but with compassion. He desires you to awaken to patterns of addiction, anger, narcissism, and chronic failures that rob you of freedom and peace, so they can be healed, you can be forgiven, and hope and peace can return to your life. Establish this ritual each time you are tempted and each time you fail by giving in to your core sins, wounds, addictions, angers, and narcissism:

✠ Declare the specific sin, addiction, narcissistic habit, or destructive compulsion as a false lover.

✠ Describe the specific sin, addiction, narcissistic habit, or destructive compulsion as coming from the enemy of your human nature.

✠ Descend with Christ into your memory, to see and feel your first experience of this specific sin, addiction, narcissistic habit, or destructive compulsion, asking Him to compassionately reveal the stress fractures, loneliness, and wounds in your heart that it promised to satisfy. (Once you have identified the first experience of various issues, you need only access the memory and then move to the next step).

✠ Denounce the specific sin, addiction, narcissistic habit, or destructive compulsion for its ruinous effect in your life.

✠ Decide for Christ to heal this wound, defuse the stress, anxiety, and fear feeding it, and transform its damaging effects on your life into sacred story.

Your goal in this short exercise is to invite God's grace to be present in your most difficult issues. Do the exercise two or three times a day on the most obvious sins, angers, and failures. And then move on. Your awakening and healing is on God's schedule, not yours. Over time, this will become a spiritual exercise that comes naturally. It takes people varying amounts of time to make it a habit. But it will become a positive spiritual habit that decreases your fears, reveals your truest self, and deepens your trust in Jesus as your protector and healer. It will also open you to Christ constantly at the most critical moments during your day, reminding you that He is Lord and Savior of your life. Remember, you are not doing this exercise to learn how to save yourself. You are doing it to turn to the Savior who forgives, loves, and heals the sins, addictions, angers, and compulsions from which you cannot save yourself!

೦ಽ

Prayer Exercise for Wednesday and Thursday

Reflect on the instructions on this page and the next for "Sacred Story Prayer at Midday and at Evening," and take your fifteen-minute prayer period(s) to understand the purpose of this discipline. The content for this main Sacred Story prayer will be given to you over the next ten weeks. It will take that long to learn the five meditations of Creation, Presence, Memory, Mercy, and Eternity and how to combine them into a single fifteen-minute prayer exercise. While we use the Creation, Presence, Memory, Mercy, and Eternity elements below to explain aspects of Sacred Story discipline, you will only fully understand these pieces once you have been introduced into their full practice over the next ten weeks. Consider this a preview, and do not be anxious if you "don't get it."

Sacred Story Prayer at Midday and at Evening (fifteen minutes)

Find a quiet place apart where you will not be disturbed. Bring with you the particular issues that surfaced in your day related to any specific annoyances or strong emotional events you experienced. Bring also your particular graces and inspirations.

During this time, you may kneel or sit, whichever is better suited to your prayer style and more conducive to contemplative reflection, prayer, and devotion. Keep your eyes closed or, if opened, in a fixed position, not allowing them to roam.

Take a full fifteen minutes for this exercise—no more and no less. You can consciously enter Sacred Story prayer for these fifteen-minute periods in one of two ways. Try both, and determine which best suits your character and personality. No matter which way you choose, at the beginning and at the end of the prayer time, in your imagination, see your whole life in God's hands, and say this antiphon inwardly, while breathing slowly and deeply:

"Creation...Presence... Memory...Mercy...Eternity."

First Way

Say "Creation," and continue meditating upon this word as long as you find meaning, connections, delight, and inspirations in considering it and some positive fruit in the graces you seek. The same method of reflection should be followed for each meditation in Sacred Story (Presence, Memory, Mercy, Eternity).

Second Way

With each breath you take, say interiorly, "Creation." And from one breath to another, ponder the graces and inspirations you seek. For this space of time, direct your attention mainly to the meaning of the word and graces you seek, the Person who is addressed, and why you need those graces. Follow this method with the other words (Presence, Memory, Mercy, Eternity) until you finish all the meditations in Sacred Story prayer.

For the body of the fifteen-minute prayer, after the opening antiphon and before the closing antiphon, you can be flexible. On some days, you may spend equal amounts of time on each meditation. On other days, you may spend most of your time on one meditation. Let your heart lead you, based on the events of the day and the images and emotions that emerge in your reflections.

As the lessons progress and you learn each meditation in Sacred Story prayer, only say the word[s] of the specific lesson for each week. Some weeks you will have only one word. Other weeks you will be combining two or more until you finally combine all five into your completed prayer.

After your closing litany, end the fifteen-minute Sacred Story Prayer at Midday and at Evening with one or the other of these two vocal prayers:

Our Father
This is the prayer favored by Ignatius for this discipline
Our Father, who art in heaven, hallowed be Thy name. Thy Kingdom come, Thy will be done, on earth, as it is in heaven. Give us this day our daily bread, and forgive us our trespasses, as we forgive those who trespass against us. Lead us not into temptation, but deliver us from evil. Amen.

Suscipe
This is the prayer of St. Ignatius that concludes his Spiritual Exercises

Take Lord, receive, my liberty, my memory, my understanding, my entire will. Whatsoever I have or hold, You have given to me. I surrender it all back to you to be governed by your will. Give me only Your love and grace. This is enough for me, and I ask for nothing more. Amen.

℃ß

Prayer Exercise for Friday

Reflect on the instructions below for "Daily Journaling" and "Prayer upon Retiring," and take your fifteen-minute quiet period(s) today to understand these disciplines. Note briefly in your notebook what you consider significant.

Daily Journaling (no more than two minutes)

Write in your journal daily, after you end your evening Sacred Story prayer session. It is not a diary but a logbook (of jottings, most accurately). What you write should be only single words or short phrases. The goal is to track the most significant events from your days. You are looking, first and foremost, for destructive patterns and trends in your life: patterns of fear, anger, and grief, and patterns of sin, compulsion, and addiction. In both of these patterns, you are also looking for links to persons, events, and issues. On the graced end of the scale, you are looking for gratitude, hope, and peace linked to your sacred story and the daydreams and fantasies coming from the Divine Inspirer.

The patterns and trends that are most relevant to Sacred Story in awakening to your life as a whole, and growing in interior freedom, are those that help you identify damaging, addictive, sinful habits at their roots. (This is the principal goal of the Particular Examen of St. Ignatius, which helps individuals name and target their core sins.) So be aware of patterns and trends that reveal triggering mechanisms that make you easy prey to habits, sins, angers, addictions, and vices. Pay attention in order to source the origins and "roots" of those habits from your early life. Remember that day's During-the-Day Awakening exercises, and ask for the grace to be aware of the importance of any significant events that open you to anger, fear, and grief or temptations, failures, and sins. Ask for God's grace to see your life integrated and holistic, as God does. God longs for your freedom, forgiveness, peace, and healing.

To help you in your journaling exercises, write the ideas discussed above by focusing your short entries within the following framework:

223

✠ Desolation from the Day: Write no more than two sentences on what decreased your faith, your hope, and your love for God and neighbor today.

✠ Consolation from the Day: Write no more than two sentences on what increased your faith, your hope, and your love for God and neighbor today.

People who engaged the journal exercise gained much more from the entire Sacred Story method than those who did not write in their journal. Those who persevered in the journal practice are the ones who learned to be brief and to do as instructed: write no more than a few words or a short phrase. You will not succeed in the journal practice if you take more than two minutes a day to accomplish it. Be brief but specific. (You can download a daily logbook for this purpose for free from the "Members" section of sacredstory.net.)

Prayer upon Retiring (fifteen seconds)

At day's end, listen to your heart for its state of spirit—peaceful or anxious—and what person or event inspires one or the other emotion. Speak a few words to God appropriate to your heart's peace or anxiety, and then invite God into your dreams.

ଔ

Prayer Exercise for Saturday

Reflect on the instructions below for the "Journal at Week's End" and "Journal at Month's End," and take your fifteen-minute quiet period(s) today to understand these disciplines. Note briefly in your notebook what you consider significant as you come to understand the purpose of this exercise.

Journal at Week's End

On Sunday (or Saturday, if that is your "weekend"), in place of the daily journal exercise, review the words and phrases from your journaling of that week. Ponder the words and phrases, and ask to see the story of your whole life (Creation, Presence, Memory, Mercy, and Eternity). Notice what particular insights or inspirations arise in you. Do not try to force insights. Most likely, you will awaken gradually to patterns and trends.

After you read over your journal entries from the week, write a brief entry of a few sentences that captures any insights you have gained about your life over the course of the week's prayer and reflection process. Be attentive for any connections between persons, events, temptations, sins, fear, anger, grief, and strong emotions.

Pay particular attention to insights that can help you unravel the manifest and root spiritual and psychological stresses (sinful habits, psychological stresses, addictions, and vices) that might be linked to significant events from your past history. Write these insights in a new section of your notes (perhaps entitled "Insights and Integration.") Date these reflections so you can watch your progressive growth and awakening.

Journal at Month's End

At the end of a month, in place of the journal at week's end, review your summary insights from these end-of-week exercises, and look for any patterns that are emerging in your life story, especially those linked to the matrix of spiritual and psychological stresses highlighted by these insights. In your "Insights and Integration" section, write several sentences (such as "I think...." "I believe...." "I discovered....") that reveal any changes you have experienced in your life as a result of grace, healing, forgiveness, or the insights you receive.

It is highly recommended that you initiate a monthly ritual of receiving the sacrament of Reconciliation. This discipline of grace and sacramental accountability will give you energy to engage the Sacred Story daily practice and will provide a clear focus for your journal exercises. Those who engage this discipline of monthly Reconciliation, accompanied with Sacred Story prayer, advance immeasurably more than those who forgo the graces of this great sacrament of insight and healing. Your journal practice is excellent preparation for sacramental Reconciliation.

When you receive monthly Reconciliation, consider following the same pattern as when you made your whole-life confession. Write your confession and speak directly to Christ and talk about the events of your life and where you need healing and peace. Do not tire of repeating the same issues, sins, and failures. Rely on and ask for the grace to see more and more clearly the roots and origins of the challenges in your life. St. Ignatius even suggested that his followers make a life confession every six months! He said it would help them make a new book of their lives. However, monthly Reconciliation is sufficient for measured spiritual, psychological, and emotional growth and enlightenment—unless you have grave matter that begs immediate attention.[12]

SACRED STORY DAILY PRACTICE AT A GLANCE

✠ **Prayer upon Waking**

Attune to the day ahead, and invite God's help.

✠ **During-the-Day Awakening**

Awaken to sins, addictions, habits, and compulsions.

Declare the false lover.

Describe it as coming from the enemy of your human nature.

Descend with Christ into your memory.

Denounce the false lover for its ruinous effect.

Decide to allow Christ to heal you.

✠ **Sacred Story Prayer at Midday**

Opening antiphon

Meditation on

Creation, Presence, Memory, Mercy, and Eternity

Closing antiphon

Closing vocal prayer

✠ **During-the-Day Awakening**

✠ **Sacred Story Prayer at Evening**

✠ **Daily Journaling**

Note significant event(s) of the day that increased and/or decreased your faith, hope, and love.

✠ **Prayer upon Retiring**

Attune to your heart; invite God into your dreams.

✠ **Journal at Week's End**

Review daily journals; listen for and note trends, patterns, links.

✠ **Journal at Month's End**

Review weekly journals; listen for and note trends, patterns, links; compose statements expressing growth and change.

✠ **Monthly Sacramental Reconciliation**

You will be renewed and powerfully graced.

✠ **Consult the Affirmations Frequently**

These are your thumbnail discernment aids.

ⓒ⅊

Lord, you have been our refuge
through all generations.
Before the mountains were born,
the earth and the world brought forth,
from eternity to eternity you are God
(Ps 90:1–2)

⅋ⅅ

Letters from Week Sixteen

Dear Fr. Bill,

Week Sixteen definitely reminded me of some things I'd stopped practicing or had forgotten since the first time I learned these spiritual disciplines. Fortunately, I've been adhering to some of these exercises for a few years now: prayer on waking; day's end prayer; and exercises during the day.

Contrary to your strict time limits, I find myself taking more than fifteen to thirty seconds for these. And I find myself needing to practice these more than the two to three times daily; lots of outside influences around here.

Prior to starting Forty Weeks anew, my two fifteen-minute Sacred Story prayers had sort of become regular, basic prayers concerning my daily fears, anxieties and needs while also expressing my gratitude for His love and grace.

I hadn't realized until this week how far I'd strayed from the Creation, Presence, Memory, Mercy and Eternity path; another reason to be grateful for the opportunity to experience this with you, Fr. Bill. I will be paying extra close attention in the coming weeks in order to get back on track.

You haven't addressed the possible need for more prayer aside from those assigned in Forty Weeks. I recite the Rosary twice daily. I read and meditate on the daily gospel from "Sacred Reading" the 2017 guide to daily prayer.

I spend time praying for God's will in the lives of so many men here in prison with me, and for those suffering everywhere — the homeless, hungry, addicted, those displaced by war. I feel I don't pray as much as I need or would like to.

Am I praying too much? Am I taking the focus off of Sacred Story prayer? Are all of my different prayers compatible? I cannot correctly express how important the peace I receive from praying and talking to my God of Mercy and Compassion brings me amid all the turmoil and anxiety of prison life. Any thoughts on all of this would be greatly appreciated.

Respectfully, Ritchie

Dear Ritchie:

Week Sixteen is a good one to bookmark. It details many of the spiritual disciplines that St. Ignatius thought beneficial to help one stay spiritually awake. It is just fine if you want to spend more than fifteen to thirty seconds on some of the shorter exercises. You do have the time to do so. Also, as you learn anew the Creation, Presence, Memory, Mercy and Eternity chapters in Sacred Story Prayer, you can spend a bit more time than the suggested fifteen minutes. But don't go over too much. The long-term goal is to find beneficial prayer disciplines that can be sustainable practices for your entire life.

All your other types of prayer sound just fine to me too, Ritchie, especially the Rosary, as it brings you so much peace. It is good that you are praying for the men in prison with you that they can find God's will in their lives. You might even want to pray for those God places on your heart by naming them to God in your prayers.

Someone might have done the very same thing for you years ago and their prayers are now bearing fruit! You are being drawn to pray for all the poor and suffering both in prison and in the world. It seems very clear to me that at least at this point in your life, this is one of the ways you are giving glory to God.

Peace to you Ritchie, and know you are in my prayers.

Fr. Bill Watson, S.J.

NOTES

Week 17

FIRST

I will ask for patience to start each day with renewed commitment. I will have my notebook at hand for each prayer period and resolve to spend no more and no less than fifteen minutes in each formal prayer session. I will always use my personal name for God.

SECOND

I will continue to draw consolation and insight from my letter to Jesus/whole-life confession.

THIRD

This week I am invited to learn the first meditation in Sacred Story prayer: Creation. My fidelity to the linked practice of these daily exercises will produce life-long sustained spiritual growth and enlightenment.

I will awaken to the present moment.
I will awaken to my spiritual nature.
I will not make any decisions based on fear.
I will practice sacramental Reconciliation monthly.

This week, I will say this affirmation aloud once daily:
God resolves all my problems with time and patience.

Sacred Story Prayer—Creation

Every day, consciously enter Sacred Story prayer during your set time(s). For these next weeks, we are building the five meditations of Sacred Story prayer. Set aside the other meditations, and focus on Creation for your fifteen-minute prayer sessions this week.

Remember the structure of the fifteen-minute Sacred Story prayer sessions you were introduced to last week. Be faithful to the structure. Ignatius was wise in developing the ritual, and rituals are very important. The ritual itself detailed below does not save you. Yet the ritual, faithfully practiced, makes it easier for you to open your mind and heart to the One who does save you! Rituals are good.

Remember that the complete Sacred Story daily practice has six parts:

1. Prayer upon Waking

2. During-the-Day-Awakening exercises over the course of the day

3. Sacred Story Prayer at Midday (this week, Creation prayer only)

4. Sacred Story Prayer at Evening (this week, Creation prayer only)

5. Daily Journaling immediately following Sacred Story prayer at evening

6. Prayer upon Retiring

During this week, we are only focusing on Creation for the fifteen-minute prayer period(s) so you can learn it by heart. There are four ways to learn a meditation: a single word, a single phrase, a single description ("Prelude"), and a single grace for which to pray ("Illuminative Grace").

All four elements compose a single exercise. It seems like a lot at first, but in time you will be able to understand the elements of Creation without having to refer to any text. One way to internalize the meaning of the meditation is to read through the prayer exercise text (the word, the phrase, the Prelude, and the Illuminative Grace) and then ponder those ideas while using one of the two ways to focus (letting yourself be led by the inspirations of the word or letting yourself be led by the conversation with the Lord about the graces you seek related to the word).

Remember, eventually we will be meditating on five different words but only spending significant time with those words that the Spirit is leading us to for that day. This is why it is important for us to learn both the substance for each of the words as well as the standard meditation process for the fifteen-minute periods.

Do not be anxious about learning everything at once—we are going slowly for a reason! This week, focus on internalizing the meaning of Creation and learning the rhythm of the fifteen-minute prayer period. The meditation text for Creation is below. (Remember, this is the summary of the word, which you will use as a guide during your meditation). Review the structure of the fifteen-minute prayer sessions. You will find these at the bookmark you left in week 16.

CREATION
I believe God created everything in love and for love;
I ask for heartfelt knowledge of God's love for me
and for gratitude for the general and particular graces of this day.

Prelude
God created the universe—all persons and all things—in love and for love. Every person and every thing in creation is linked in Love, through Christ, in whom and for whom everything was made. We are made to reverence God and each other and to delight in creation as both divine gift and support for our lives. The God of All knows me personally and loves me, even before I was knit in my mother's womb. So fearfully and wonderfully made am I! (Ps 139:13–14). My gratitude increases as my awakening to these truths is illuminated.

Illuminative Grace

Here I ask for what I desire: to know and feel God's tender and passionate love and to know myself as beloved—a treasure of God's heart in the grand symphony of creation. I pray for the grace of gratitude. In particular, I pray to know by whom I am created and why I am loved. I pray to know and believe that I am fearfully and wonderfully made.

ᘓ

When I see your heavens, the work of your fingers,
the moon and stars that you set in place—
What is man that you are mindful of him,
and a son of man that you care for him?
Yet you have made him little less than a god,
crowned him with glory and honor.
You have given him rule over the works of your hands,
put all things at his feet:
O LORD, our Lord, how awesome is your name
through all the earth!
(Ps 8:4–6)

ᘓ

Letters from Week Seventeen

Dear Fr. Bill,

CREATION: "The God of all knows me personally and loves me..."

Actually feeling God's love for me back in July 2013 made the difference. Knowing God loves me and feeling God's love for me are two totally different things. We all know God loves us. The old song says, "... because the bible tells us so". When I asked for His will to be done and then the most dangerous situation of my life had been erased, I didn't just thank God for answering my prayers to my satisfaction once again and then move on to other things in my life as I would have before. Instead, through nothing I did, I was consumed by God's love for me.

The sense that God loved me so much that it was His will for me not to endure this life-altering conflict filled me with such gratitude for His unconditional love that my life was changed. Today, my most fervent prayer is for everyone to open their hearts to God's love. Once it is truly felt there is no going back. "Behold, I stand at the door and knock..." Rev 3:20. Creation=love. Like you said, all persons and things are created in love and for love. And it starts with Christ's love for us.

Week Seventeen's prayer sessions were a joy to practice, giving me thirty minutes each day to recall and keep in mind what a huge part God's ceaseless love plays in my new life, something I hope and pray everyone will experience.

Respectfully,

Ritchie

Dear Ritchie:

The most important thing a person can learn in life is that they are loved by God. Not loved because you have done something important. Just loved because you are valuable and precious in God's eyes; are loved.

And always reflect in Creation, that all this was made for you to participate in the love of the Holy Trinity. The world and the cosmos were created so God could communicate his great love to us.

Relish it, Ritchie, and cherish it daily. This is why the Sacred Story Prayer begins with Creation. So we remember to be grateful for God's initiative allowing us to share in the Love of the Trinity.

Peace,

Fr. Bill

NOTES

Week 18

FIRST

As I engage Sacred Story prayer this week, I may find it helpful to recommit to my daily fifteen-minute sessions. I resolve to spend no more and no less than fifteen minutes in each formal prayer session. I will always use my personal name for God.

SECOND

For week 18, I am invited to open my heart to Presence, the second meditation in Sacred Story prayer. I will strive to trust St. Ignatius's wisdom and engage the prayer disciplines at least once daily as he suggested.

THIRD

Use your first prayer session to read through Presence, and then do the Sacred Story prayer exercise as suggested during your fifteen-minute prayer sessions for the rest of the week.

I will awaken to the present moment.
I will awaken to my spiritual nature.
I will not make any decisions based on fear.
I will practice sacramental Reconciliation monthly.
This week, I will say this affirmation aloud once daily:
I will always have difficulties in this life.

CB

Sacred Story Prayer—Presence

Every day, consciously enter Sacred Story prayer during your set time(s). For these next weeks, we are building the five meditations of Sacred Story prayer. Set aside the other meditations, and focus on Presence for your fifteen-minute prayer sessions this week.

Remember the structure of the fifteen-minute sessions you were introduced to last week. Be faithful to the structure. Ignatius was wise in developing the ritual, and rituals are very important. The ritual itself detailed below does not save you. Yet the ritual, faithfully practiced, makes it easier for you to open your mind and heart to the One who does save you! Rituals are good. Review the structure of the fifteen-minute prayer sessions. You will find these at the bookmark you left in week 16.

PRESENCE

I believe God is present in each moment and event of my life,
and I ask for grace to awaken, see and feel where and how,
especially in this present moment.

Prelude

The eternal God can only be experienced in the here and now, for everything in the universe is sustained by God's love in the present moment. When I worry about the past or fret about the future, my consciousness of God, of creation, and of my deepest desires is blocked. My challenge is to anchor both heart and mind firmly in the present—in each thought, word, and deed—as the story of my life evolves, in each moment, in God's presence.

Illuminative Grace

Here I ask for what I desire: to be present and awake to every feeling, thought, word, and deed—in the present moment. I beg for the grace to wake up to God's presence in every person, experience, and event—good or ill—that I encounter in my day.

☙

How lovely your dwelling,
O Lord of hosts!
My soul yearns and pines
for the courts of the Lord.
My heart and flesh cry out
for the living God.
As the sparrow finds a home
and the swallow a nest to settle her young,
My home is by your altars,
Lord of hosts, my king and my God!
Blessed are those who dwell in your house!
They never cease to praise you.
(Ps 84:2–5)

❧

Letters from Week Eighteen

Dear Fr. Bill,

PRESENCE: I would guess that realizing the need to awaken, see, and feel where and how God is present in each moment and event of our lives came about as a result of all the emphasis, time and agony Ignatius endured in his obsessive confession habit. I can see that worrying about the future or lamenting the past definitely would take up precious time which should be spent appreciating God's presence now. I must be in the present in order to acknowledge and appreciate His presence.

Respectfully, Ritchie

Dear Ritchie:

You have been awakening to your heart in all this process, Ritchie. A scripture on the uselessness of worrying about the past or future is one with which you are familiar and is always worth reading (Mt 6:25-34). It closely resembles the First Principle and Foundation from St. Ignatius:

First Principle and Foundation—St. Ignatius
A person is created to praise, reverence, and serve God our Lord,
and by this means to save his or her soul.
The other things on the face of the earth are created
for the person to help in attaining the end for which one is created.
Hence, one is to make use of them in as far as they help
in the attainment of that end,
and one must rid oneself of them in as far as they prove a hindrance.
Therefore, we must make ourselves indifferent to all created things,
as far as we are allowed free choice and are not under any prohibition.
Consequently, as far as we are concerned, we should not prefer
health to sickness, honor to dishonor, a long life to a short life.
The same holds for all other things.
Our one desire and choice should be what is more conducive to the end
for which one is created.

242

Foundations Prayer

Based on Ignatius' First Principle and Foundation
—William Watson, SJ

For and through whom everything was made, Is Christ Jesus.
I live because he loves me.
To praise and serve him alone with all my mind, heart, and strength
is my freedom--my only freedom.
I shall not prejudice any path in following him:
For I can praise him equally in my health and sickness.
I can distinguish myself in service to his Kingdom with great wealth,
modest means, or having nothing at all to call my own.
He is the anchor of my joy and peace whether I am disgraced or lauded.
In his all-embracing love I taste eternity,
whether my days are numbered great or small.
Christ Jesus alone is the treasure of my heart.
I shall ever listen for his call, and follow unreservedly.
For in everything I can love and praise him,
And find my eternal joy.
Amen.

Peace,

Fr. Bill

NOTES

Week 19

FIRST

As I engage the Sacred Story prayer this week, I will make a point of reviewing my prayer discipline and make any necessary changes to be more faithful to the daily disciplines I have committed to. I also resolve to spend no more and no less than fifteen minutes in each formal prayer period. I will always use my personal name for God.

SECOND

For week nineteen, I am combining meditations one and two in the Sacred Story prayer: Creation and Presence. I will enter my prayer at least once daily as St. Ignatius suggested.

THIRD

I will commit to reviewing the prayer structures from week 16.

I will awaken to the present moment.
I will awaken to my spiritual nature.
I will not make any decisions based on fear.
I will practice sacramental Reconciliation monthly.

This week, I will say this affirmation aloud once daily:
There are just two ways to cope with my difficulties.
One leads to life; one to death. I will choose life.

Review the structure of the fifteen-minute prayer sessions. You will find these at the bookmark you left in week 16. For this week, you are combining the first two meditations in Sacred Story prayer: Creation and Presence. Use your fifteen-minute prayer sessions this week to pray these two meditations together, following the wisdom you learned in week 16 for this practice.

CREATION

I believe God created everything in love and for love;
I ask for heartfelt knowledge of God's love for me
and for gratitude for the general and particular graces of this day.

Prelude

God created the universe—all persons and all things—in love and for love. Every thing and every person in creation is linked in Love, through Christ, in whom and for whom everything was made. We are made to reverence God and each other and to delight in creation as both divine gift and support for our lives. The God of All knows me personally and loves me, even before I was knit in my mother's womb. So fearfully and wonderfully made am I! (Ps 139:13–14). My gratitude increases as my awakening to these truths is illuminated.

Illuminative Grace

Here I ask for what I desire: to know and feel God's tender and passionate love, and to know myself as beloved—a treasure of God's heart in the grand symphony of creation. I pray for the grace of gratitude. In particular, I pray to know by whom I am created and why I am loved. I pray to know and believe that I am fearfully and wonderfully made.

PRESENCE

I believe God is present in each moment and event of my life, and I ask for grace to awaken, see and feel where and how, especially in this present moment.

Prelude

The eternal God can only be experienced in the here and now, for everything in the universe is sustained by God's love in the present moment. When I worry about the past or fret about the future, my consciousness of God, of creation, and of my deepest desires, is blocked. My challenge is to anchor both heart and mind firmly in the present—in each thought, word, and deed—as the story of my life evolves, in each moment, in God's presence.

Illuminative Grace

Here I ask for what I desire: to be present and awake to every feeling, thought, word, and deed—in the present moment. I beg for the grace to wake up to God's presence in every person, experience, and event—good or ill—that I encounter in my day.

ॐ

℃Ʒ

LORD, who may abide in your tent?
Who may dwell on your holy mountain?
Whoever walks without blame,
doing what is right,
speaking truth from the heart;
Who does not slander with his tongue,
does no harm to a friend,
never defames a neighbor;
Who disdains the wicked,
but honors those who fear the LORD;
Who keeps an oath despite the cost,
lends no money at interest,
accepts no bribe against the innocent.
Whoever acts like this
shall never be shaken.
(Ps 15)

℘

Letters from Week Nineteen

Dear Fr. Bill,

CREATION & PRESENCE: Creation and presence definitely belong together. God creating everyone and everything in love and for love, and then us. Acknowledging His presence in all of His creation is necessary because there is no love without Him. God is present in each moment and event of my life. This means His love is present in each moment and event of my life and all of his creation. I hope this makes sense.

Respectfully,

Ritchie

Dear Ritchie:

You need no help with this one. You understood the connections perfectly! This passage from Matthew's Gospel that I mentioned last week might however be something beneficial to pray with in light of these two meditations:

Therefore I tell you, do not be anxious about your life, what you shall eat or what you shall drink, nor about your body, what you shall put on. Is not life more than food, and the body more than clothing? Look at the birds of the air: they neither sow nor reap nor gather into barns, and yet your heavenly Father feeds them. Are you not of more value than they? And which of you by being anxious can add one cubit to his span of life? And why are you anxious about clothing? Consider the lilies of the field, how they grow; they neither toil nor spin; yet I tell you, even Solomon in all his glory was not arrayed like one of these. But if God so clothes the grass of the field, which today is alive and tomorrow is thrown into the oven, will he not much more clothe you, O men of little faith? 31 Therefore do not be anxious, saying, 'What shall we eat?' or 'What shall we drink?' or 'What shall we wear?' For the Gentiles seek all these things; and your heavenly Father knows that you need them all. But seek first his kingdom and his righteousness, and all these things shall be yours as well. Therefore do not be anxious about tomorrow, for tomorrow will be anxious for itself. Let the day's own trouble be sufficient for the day (Mt 6: 25-34).

You are in my prayers. Keep me in yours.

Peace,

Fr. Bill

NOTES

Week 20

FIRST
I resolve to ask God for help to be faithful to my prayer disciplines. I also resolve to spend no more and no less than fifteen minutes for these times of prayer. I will always use my personal name for God.

SECOND
For week 20, I am invited to enter the third meditation of Memory. As St. Ignatius suggested, I will engage my formal prayer at least once daily.

THIRD
Use your first prayer session to read through Memory, and then do the Sacred Story prayer exercise as suggested during your fifteen-minute prayer sessions for the rest of the week.

I will awaken to the present moment.
I will awaken to my spiritual nature.
I will not make any decisions based on fear.
I will practice sacramental Reconciliation monthly.
This week, I will say this affirmation aloud once daily:
"Impossible" is not a word in God's vocabulary.

❧

Sacred Story Prayer—Memory

Every day, consciously enter Sacred Story prayer during your set time(s). For these next weeks, we are building the five meditations of Sacred Story prayer. Set aside the other meditations, and focus on Memory for your fifteen-minute prayer sessions this week.

Be faithful to the structure. Ignatius was wise in developing the ritual, and rituals are very important. The ritual itself detailed below does not save you. Yet the ritual, faithfully practiced, makes it easier for you to open your mind and heart to the One who does save you! Rituals are good. Review the structure of the fifteen-minute prayer sessions. You will find these at the bookmark you left in week 16.

MEMORY
I believe every violation of love committed by me and against me
is in my memory, and I ask God to reveal them to me,
especially those that have manifested themselves today,
so I can be healed.

Prelude
I hold in my heart, by the power of God's grace, the memory of every
action—of every thought, word, and deed—done to me and done by
me, that has eroded my innocence. I affirm that these unloving
thoughts, words, and deeds have spiritual, physical, and emotional
consequences that wound me, others, and creation and for which Christ
had to suffer for my redemption. I believe all these unloving actions
have both generational and evolutionary consequences. At the root of
my own narcissism are some events that, more than others, have
significantly distorted my heart and mind. These events cripple my
desire and my ability to love selflessly and to freely forgive others.

Illuminative Grace

Here I ask for what I desire: to become conscious of my lost innocence; to have the grace to see and the power to touch the Original Sins and wounds, especially the most vital ones, which shape in me an anti-story instead of a sacred story. I ask for the grace of an illumined conscience to know intimately how these wounds and sins connect to everything I do that makes life burdensome; to know how and why these wounds so often compel me to violate God's life in myself, others, and creation. I ask God for the grace to wake up so I can see, feel, and name these thoughts, words, and deeds and bring them to the light of day, to be healed by the Divine Physician.

છ

Oh, that today you would hear his voice:
"Harden not your hearts as at Meribah,
as in the day of Massah in the desert,
Where your fathers tempted me;
they tested me though they had seen my works."
If today you hear his voice,
harden not your hearts.
(Ps 95:8–9)

છ

Letters from Week Twenty

Dear Fr. Bill,

MEMORY: As I've noted earlier in this Sacred Story process, I'd never believed very much in the idea that events and relationships from our early lives could matter or have anything to do with how we live our lives as adults. I think I used the term "psychobabble". Well, now I am a believer.

Going back to Weeks Six through Ten, in particular, "Looking for Links" was very helpful. The root/trunk/fruit chart is proof of a chain reaction which can be caused by just one instance of unloving thoughts, words, or deeds. Through the chain reaction, just one negative event can affect an infinite number of others.

We've discussed my childhood at length. We've connected the dots leading to my life today. I can see, while I listen, watch, and pray, how earlier unloving thoughts, words, and deeds influence the negative things I still do. I continue to pray for the ability to spot and connect these events.

Fr. Bill, once again I'd like to tell you how much I appreciate having you taking the time to work with me through Forty Weeks. Although I definitely learned a lot the first time I experienced Forty Weeks, this time I am truly blessed.

Respectfully,

Ritchie

Dear Ritchie:

It is a real grace that you have been able to overcome the cynicism of seeing early-life experiences that influence your adult life as merely "psychobabble." The discoveries you have made by God's grace understanding your early childhood experiences affecting your adult behaviors and attitudes have been profound and a real gift.

Keep expecting to "see" more and more connections as you continue on your journey with Christ Jesus. There is always more around the next bend. Jesus moves us closer and closer to Him and to our deepest desires.

It is a blessing to be able to walk with you on this path, Ritchie. It is especially gratifying to know you will be able to be of help to others with your own Sacred Story.

Peace,

Fr. Bill Watson, S.J.

NOTES

Week 21

FIRST

As I engage the Sacred Story prayer this week, I will continue to ask God's help to be faithful to my commitment. I will also resolve to spend no more and no less than fifteen minutes in each formal prayer session, as St. Ignatius suggested. I will always use my personal name for God.

SECOND

For week 21, I am invited to pray with the first three meditations in the Sacred Story prayer. As St. Ignatius suggested, I will commit to entering my prayer at least once daily.

THIRD

Use your first prayer session to read the reflection, and then do the Sacred Story prayer exercise as suggested during your fifteen-minute prayer sessions for the rest of the week.

I will awaken to the present moment.
I will awaken to my spiritual nature.
I will not make any decisions based on fear.
I will practice sacramental Reconciliation monthly.
This week, I will say this affirmation aloud once daily:
Sacred Story practice leads to my freedom and authenticity,
but does not always make me feel happy.

Review the structure of the fifteen-minute prayer sessions. You will find these at the bookmark you left in week 16. For this week, you are combining the first three meditations in Sacred Story prayer: Creation, Presence, and Memory.

Use your fifteen-minute prayer sessions this week to pray these three meditations together, following the wisdom you learned in week 16 for this practice. You can also refresh your memory on the Preludes and Illuminative Graces of these three meditations if you find it helpful.

CREATION
I believe God created everything in love and for love;
I ask for heartfelt knowledge of God's love for me
and for gratitude for the general and particular graces of this day.

PRESENCE
I believe God is present in each moment and event of my life,
and I ask for grace to awaken, see and feel where and how,
especially in this present moment.

MEMORY
I believe every violation of love committed by me and against me
is in my memory, and I ask God to reveal them to me,
especially those that have manifested themselves today,
so I can be healed.

ᘓ

Come, let us sing joyfully to the Lord;
cry out to the rock of our salvation.
Let us come before him with a song of praise,
joyfully sing out our psalms.
For the Lord is the great God,
the great king over all gods,
Whose hand holds the depths of the earth;
who owns the tops of the mountains.
The sea and dry land belong to God,
who made them, formed them by hand.
(Ps 95:1–5).

ᘒ

Letters from Week Twenty-One

Dear Fr. Bill:

I am definitely experiencing and benefitting from praying on the Creation, Presence, Memory, Mercy and Eternity meditations. At this time there is only so much I can write on this. As a result, I am afraid my reflections may appear to be lacking. I hope this is not the case. I suppose things will become clearer in the near future, or, you will help with this. Either way, I look forward to my future with Forty Weeks.

CREATON-PRESENCE-MEMORY: Acknowledging that God created everything in love and for love, and realizing His presence in all of His creation makes accepting all of the memories of my violations of love and of those against me easier to bear. All of the negative or bad in my past was for a reason. Because I now know that these violations are being used in His plans for healing me. Now I take God's love, present in all, and learn how all of these violations can move me toward my Sacred Story.

Respectfully,

Ritchie

Dear Ritchie:

You say in your opening to the letter that you only have so much you can say about the Creation, Presence, Memory, Mercy & Eternity prayers. That is fine. They will continue to take shape the more you pray them and they will become a part of the very substance of your spiritual life and your own story.

You share the conviction that the "violations of love" committed by you and against you are the very things that God will use for your hope and glory. This is a foundational element of our Christian faith that should make all of us grateful. The very things that we thought would destroy us and rob us of our humanity are the very wounds that Jesus Christ will use to bring blessings into our lives and the lives of others.

This is why we have the conviction that Christ in Glory has his wounds of crucifixion. The Son of God's wounds from a shameful, criminal's death are now the shining wounds that have redeemed us and the whole human race. A path to lead you out of self-pity and despair is to thank God for the "violations of love" that will become the source of your glory and hope!

You are in my prayers,

Fr. Bill

NOTES

Week 22

FIRST

I will preview my week and visualize the places and times for my prayer. They will be places apart—technology-free zones. I also resolve to spend no more and no less than fifteen minutes in each formal prayer session, as St. Ignatius suggested. I will always use my personal name for God.

SECOND

For week 22, I am invited to pray the fourth meditation in Sacred Story prayer: Mercy. Read through Mercy, and then do the Sacred Story prayer exercise as suggested during your fifteen-minute prayer sessions for the rest of the week.

THIRD

I will begin my week reviewing the prayer structure from week 16.

I will awaken to the present moment.
I will awaken to my spiritual nature.
I will not make any decisions based on fear.
I will practice sacramental Reconciliation monthly.
This week, I will say this affirmation aloud once daily:
My life's greatest tragedies can be transformed
into my life's major blessings.

Sacred Story Prayer—Mercy

Every day, consciously enter Sacred Story prayer during your set time(s). For these next weeks, we are building the five meditations of Sacred Story prayer. Set aside the other meditations, and focus on Mercy for your fifteen-minute prayer sessions this week.

Be faithful to the structure. Ignatius was wise in developing the ritual, and rituals are very important. The ritual itself detailed below does not save you. Yet the ritual, faithfully practiced, makes it easier for you to open your mind and heart to the One who does save you! Rituals are good. Review the structure of the fifteen-minute prayer sessions. You will find these at the bookmark you left in week 16.

MERCY

I believe that forgiveness is the only path to healing and illumination. I beg for the grace of forgiveness and the grace to forgive, especially for the general and particular failures of this day, and from my past.

Prelude

The path to Christian holiness and an illumined consciousness runs through the darkest memories and deeds of your life, strangely enough. These memories and deeds corrupt your innocence and blind your vision to the sacredness of all life. These memories and deeds can, by choice, act as a wall blocking the peace that leads to holiness and highest consciousness, or as a gate opening to them. The gate is unlocked by forgiveness and compassion, both received from God and then extended to all those entwined with the lost innocence that broke your heart. This includes those who hurt you, those whom you hurt, and the gifts of creation that you abused or misused as a result. This miracle of peace and enlightenment is attainable through Christ, who bore in love the wounds of every sin and dark deed since time immemorial.

Christ has the power to transform darkness, sin, and death into grace for the salvation of the world.

Illuminative Grace

Here I ask for what I desire: the grace to forgive any person who wounded my innocence or broke my heart. I pray to not only forgive them, but to have compassion and mercy on them. I ask for the grace of mercy and forgiveness for those whose hearts I have broken, those whose innocence I have wounded, and the gifts of creation that I have misused. I beg to know personally the One who absorbed in His heart and body every wound and every sin of this dark evolution across the millennia. I beg for the dual knowledge of sin and mercy as it affects my life story. I beg for patience, knowing that accepting and offering mercy and forgiveness leads me to holiness. This awakening to highest consciousness takes a lifetime.

☙

Fill us at daybreak with your mercy,
that all our days we may sing for joy.
Make us glad as many days as you humbled us,
for as many years as we have seen trouble.
Show your deeds to your servants,
your glory to their children.
(Ps 90:14–16)

❧

Letters from Week Twenty-Two

Dear Fr. Bill:

MERCY: Week Twenty Two's Affirmation – "My life's greatest tragedies can be transformed into my life's major blessings". Ain't that the truth! As I travel this road toward my Sacred Story I am coming to believe that every single instance in my life was necessary to get me where I am today – the good, the bad, the tragedies – everything. The realization and acceptance of the progression-from being hurt, to hurting others, and abusing or misusing the gifts of His creation is life-altering.

My name for God – My God of Mercy and Compassion, is no accident. Just as I am forgiven, I forgive others. Through His grace I am able to show some semblance of the compassion He has shown for me, to others. I mentioned in my Whole-Life Confession the victims I'd left in my wake. By abusing and misusing His creations, I disregarded His presence and abused His love.

Forgiveness has been granted for all of the causes – mine and others', and the domino effect of results that ensued.

Through God's mercy – his love, compassion, forgiveness and grace – this unworthy sinner is able to see and feel himself moving, sometimes very, very slowly, toward becoming the man he was created to be.

Respectfully,

Ritchie

Dear Ritchie:

Your reflections for this week on the Affirmation "My life's greatest tragedies can be transformed into my life's major blessings," mirror the revelations you discovered the previous week on "violations of love." Always allow yourself to reflect on the sins of your past <u>only</u> in light of the "God of Mercy and Compassion" that is now a part of your life. Our sins and transgressions can only be properly understood in light of the forgiving love of Christ Jesus.

We pray in the Lord's Prayer: "Forgive us our trespasses and forgive those who trespass against us." You have spoken many times already of forgiving family members. Continue to forgive those from your past when hurts resurface, as they will most likely all your life. Forgiveness is our antidote to the poison of anger and revenge that only leads to spiritual death. Forgive, always forgive. Continue to follow the example of the One who has and always will forgive you Ritchie. In that, you will become more and more like the God of Mercy and Compassion who is now your light and shield.

Peace,

Fr. Bill

NOTES

Week 23

FIRST

I will assess my fidelity to the fifteen-minute prayer periods and make the adjustments necessary to be more faithful. I resolve to spend no more and no less than fifteen minutes in each formal prayer session. I will always use my personal name for God.

SECOND

For week 23, I am invited to combine meditations one through four in the Sacred Story prayer. I will enter my prayer at least once daily, as St. Ignatius suggested.

THIRD

I will use my first prayer session to review the daily prayer structure and then use my fifteen-minute prayer periods for the rest of the week for the combined prayer.

I will awaken to the present moment.
I will awaken to my spiritual nature.
I will not make any decisions based on fear.
I will practice sacramental Reconciliation monthly.
This week, I will say this affirmation aloud once daily:
Times of peace and hope always give way
to times of difficulty and stress.

Review the structure of the fifteen-minute prayer sessions. You will find these at the bookmark you left in week 16. For this week, you are combining the first four meditations in Sacred Story Prayer: Creation, Presence, Memory, and Mercy. Use your fifteen-minute prayer sessions this week to pray these four meditations together, following the wisdom you learned in week 16 for this practice. You can also refresh your memory on the Preludes and Illuminative Graces of these three meditations if you find it helpful.

CREATION
I believe God created everything in love and for love;
I ask for heartfelt knowledge of God's love for me
and for gratitude for the general and particular graces of this day.

PRESENCE
I believe God is present in each moment and event of my life,
and I ask for grace to awaken, see and feel where and how,
especially in this present moment.

MEMORY
I believe every violation of love committed by me and against me
is in my memory, and I ask God to reveal them to me,
especially those that have manifested themselves today,
so I can be healed.

MERCY
I believe that forgiveness is the only path to healing and illumination.
I beg for the grace of forgiveness and the grace to forgive,
especially for the general and particular failures
of this day, and from my past.

൪

My heart is steadfast, God;
my heart is steadfast.
Let me sing and chant praise.
Awake, lyre and harp!
I will wake the dawn.

I will praise you among the peoples, Lord;
I will chant your praise among the nations.
For your mercy is greater than the heavens;
your faithfulness, to the skies.

Appear on high over the heavens, God;
your glory above all the earth.
Help with your right hand and answer us
that your loved ones may escape.
(Ps 108:2–7)

൭

Letters from Week Twenty-Three

Dear Fr. Bill:

CREATION-PRESENCE-MEMORY-MERCY: Another good affirmation this week: "Times of peace and hope always give way to times of difficulty and stress". Nobody ever said this journey was going to be easy. In Philippians 3:12-16 Paul speaks of his "straining forward" and "continuing my pursuit toward the goal". This is to be an ongoing battle, well worth the fight.

It would be so much easier if you would just go ahead and connect Creation, Presence, Memory and Mercy for me, but I know why that wouldn't work. The insights I've gathered from praying them individually and then, together are definitely more meaningful than if you just told me what to think.

It is through God's forgiveness and love, His mercy, that I am even able to understand and grasp His creation and presence. What I felt and wrote in week twenty-one would not have been possible without already having experienced God's mercy. Being forgiven and loved by Him is what has made everything possible.

Respectfully,

Ritchie

Dear Ritchie:

You like the Affirmation for this week too: "Times of peace and hope always give way to times of difficulty and stress." Many people forget to pray the Affirmations or return to them for sustenance and inspiration. This Affirmation's inspiration comes from a section of St. Ignatius' Rules for the Discernment of Spirits. In essence it affirms that when you are in a state of consolation, prepare for the state of desolation to follow. And when you are in a state of desolation, prepare for the consolation that will follow. The spiritual truth here is that we are always either in a state of spiritual desolation or spiritual consolation.

We are to prepare for the desolation while in consolation so that we don't become proud and think our consolation is the result of our own good works. It is only attributable to God's graces. We are to "arm" ourselves with prayer so we can withstand the lessons that we will learn from the desolation that is sure to come.

While in desolation, St. Ignatius wants us not to lose hope but realize that in time, peace and clarity will return. It is to again throw us on God's Mercy and ask for the grace to persevere in times of difficulty. So our consolation comes from God and our capacity to endure desolation comes from God. All is from the Lord! That is a lesson for us not to become proud.

The natural links between the five words in your prayer will become more obvious. Go back to the first part of Sacred Story and remember these five movements are the elements of St. Ignatius' awakening to grace after years of living in the darkness of his own sin and ego. The five movements also mirror the structure of the four weeks of the Spiritual Exercises. You will understand in time!

You are in my prayers,

Fr. Bill

NOTES

Week 24

FIRST

As I engage the last meditation in Sacred Story prayer this week, I will review my commitment to develop a rhythm that will carry me the rest of my life. To help me with that commitment, I resolve to spend no more and no less than fifteen minutes in each formal prayer session. I will always use my personal name for God.

SECOND

For week 24, I am invited to pray meditation five in the Sacred Story prayer: Eternity. Read through Eternity, and then do the Sacred Story prayer exercise as suggested during your fifteen-minute prayer sessions for the rest of the week.

THIRD

I will use my first prayer session to review the daily prayer structure from week 16.

> I will awaken to the present moment.
> I will awaken to my spiritual nature.
> I will not make any decisions based on fear.
> I will practice sacramental Reconciliation monthly.

This week, I will say this affirmation aloud once daily:

Times of difficulty and stress always give way to
times of peace and hope.

ᘓ

Sacred Story Prayer—Eternity

Every day, consciously enter Sacred Story prayer during your set time(s).
For these next weeks, we are building the five meditations of Sacred
Story prayer. Set aside the other meditations, and focus on Eternity for
your fifteen-minute prayer sessions this week.

Be faithful to the structure. Ignatius was wise in developing the ritual,
and rituals are very important. The ritual itself detailed below does not
save you. Yet the ritual, faithfully practiced, makes it easier for you to
open your mind and heart to the One who does save you! Rituals are
good. Review the structure of the fifteen-minute prayer sessions. You
will find these at the bookmark you left in week 16.

ETERNITY

I believe the grace of forgiveness opens my heart,
making my every thought, word and deed bear fruit
that endures to eternity.
I ask that everything in my life serve
Christ's Great Work of Reconciliation.

Prelude

The sacred story of all history, revealed on the last day, will show that
the lost innocence and the broken hearts of humankind inaugurated the
Great Work of Reconciliation. Because of Christ's mercy, each of us is
now being invited to take our part in this work. The grace of mercy and
forgiveness, received and offered, is the reconciling work that brings
true progress to the world; it is the only work that brings fulfillment and
bears fruit that endures to eternity. A holy life and the highest

consciousness attainable come in personally knowing the One who both reconciles my life and reconciles all creation. In this reconciling Love, I daily discern how to direct each thought, word, and deed to eternal glory—to the divine work of reconciliation.

Illuminative Grace

Here I ask for what I desire: to be graced daily with a profound consciousness of Christ Jesus's healing love, personally experienced, that will so enlighten my heart and mind that my every thought, word, and deed can serve His Great Work of Universal Reconciliation.

ɔ3

I will listen for what God, the Lord, has to say;
surely he will speak of peace
To his people and to his faithful.
May they not turn to foolishness!

Near indeed is his salvation for those who fear him;
glory will dwell in our land.
Love and truth will meet;
justice and peace will kiss.
Truth will spring from the earth;
justice will look down from heaven.

Yes, the Lord will grant his bounty;
our land will yield its produce.
Justice will march before him,
and make a way for his footsteps.
(Ps 85:9–14)

ଥ

Letters from Week Twenty-Four

Dear Fr. Bill,

I must admit that I am sort of stuck on the term "reconciliation". Until now I'd been under the impression that reconciliation was confession, penance, and communion. Aside from actual confession with a priest, I've been writing a short "letter to God" type confession as suggested in Week Sixteen. Now, in Week Twenty Four's Eternity meditation we have "Christ's Great work of 'Universal' Reconciliation" which I take to mean all of us turning from sin to Him.

I checked the Catechism, Part Two, Article Four, and it was a bit too complicated for me- reconciliation after baptism, reconciliation with the Church, etc. It was not helpful. In the Prelude to Eternity you talk of "reconciling work", "reconciling love" and "knowing the One who reconciles my life and all creation". I feel like I'm just not getting it. I would be grateful if you would expound on this a bit more for me.

"The grace of forgiveness opens my heart, making every thought, word, and deed bear fruit that endures to eternity." That is certainly my hope.

Respectfully,

Ritchie

Dear Ritchie:

I sense you are getting hung up on the word "reconciliation" and the various uses such as "reconciling work" and "reconciling love." Reconciliation is indeed a word that is used for the sacrament of Confession when we call it the sacrament of Reconciliation. Reconcile can also mean to resolve or settle.

So when something is reconciled, that which was unresolved or unsettled is now resolved and settled. So Christ's reconciling love resolves and settles all the conditions of sin and evil in the world, including the sin and evil in our own lives when we accept his "reconciling and forgiving love." It is really quite simple and I think you probably had this understanding all along. So the use of the word in this way was new for you. Now you know! Be at peace.

You are in my prayers, Ritchie, and I look forward to getting your next reflections. Keep me and my work in your prayers too. I count on them!

Peace,

Fr. Bill Watson, S.J.

NOTES

Week 25

FIRST

As I combine all five meditations in Sacred Story prayer this week for the first time, I will review my commitment and imagine a rhythm that will carry me for the rest of my life. To help me with that commitment, I again resolve to spend no more and no less than fifteen minutes in each formal prayer session. I will always use my personal name for God.

SECOND

For week 25, I am praying meditations one through five in the Sacred Story prayer. I will enter my prayer at least once daily, as St. Ignatius suggested.

THIRD

I will use my first prayer session to review the daily prayer disciplines from week 16. I will use the remainder of the week's fifteen-minute prayer periods for the combined prayer exercise.

I will awaken to the present moment.
I will awaken to my spiritual nature.
I will not make any decisions based on fear.
I will practice sacramental Reconciliation monthly.

This week, I will say this affirmation aloud once daily:
I will not tire of asking God for help, because God delights in my asking.

Review the structure of the fifteen-minute prayer sessions. You will find these at the bookmark you left in week 16. For this week, you are combining the five meditations in Sacred Story prayer: Creation, Presence, Memory, Mercy, and Eternity.

Use your fifteen-minute prayer sessions this week to pray these five meditations together, following the wisdom you learned in week 16 for this practice. You can also refresh your memory on the Preludes and Illuminative Graces of these five meditations if you find it helpful.

ᏆᎦᎠ

CREATION

I believe God created everything in love and for love;
I ask for heartfelt knowledge of God's love for me
and for gratitude for the general and particular graces of this day.

PRESENCE

I believe God is present in each moment and event of my life,
and I ask for grace to awaken, see and feel where and how,
especially in this present moment.

MEMORY

I believe every violation of love committed by me and against me
is in my memory, and I ask God to reveal them to me,
especially those that have manifested themselves today,
so I can be healed.

MERCY

I believe that forgiveness is the only path to healing and illumination.

I beg for the grace of forgiveness and the grace to forgive,
especially for the general and particular failures of this day,
and from my past.

ETERNITY

I believe the grace of forgiveness opens my heart,
making my every thought, word and deed bear fruit
that endures to eternity.
I ask that everything in my life serve
Christ's Great Work of Reconciliation.

 C&

May God be gracious to us and bless us;
may his face shine upon us.
So shall your way be known upon the earth,
your victory among all the nations.
May the peoples praise you, God;
may all the peoples praise you!
The earth has yielded its harvest;
God, our God, blesses us.
May God bless us still;
that the ends of the earth may revere him.
(Ps 67:2–4, 7–8)

&

Letters from Week Twenty-Five

Dear Fr. Bill:

CREATON-PRESENCE-MEMORY-MERCY-ETERNITY: The fact that God created everything in love and for love, that He is present in all of His creation and that we must stay in the present to appreciate this, the fact that everything I've done and all that was done to me was necessary to get me to where I am today, that I am loved and forgiven, make me the man capable of bearing fruit that endures to eternity. I am a new person—a new person in Christ.

I've been spending both daily prayer sessions on these five meditations. This week's affirmation is very helpful in this while I am trying to feel the connectivity in these meditations: "I will not tire of asking God for help because God delights in my asking." Amen.

Respectfully,

Ritchie

Dear Ritchie:

What can I add? It takes many people the better part of a lifetime to believe that God loves them and that he created the world and us because he wanted us to share in his love.

The more you pray with the meditations, the more "connectivity" you will feel and understand. And yes, never tire of asking God for help!

Peace,

Fr. Bill

NOTES

Week 26

FIRST

I visualize the week ahead and plan how I will engage my fifteen-minute prayer times. I resolve in my heart to allow God to help me be faithful to these set times of prayer. To increase my fidelity, I also resolve to spend no more and no less than fifteen minutes in any formal prayer period. I will always use my personal name for God.

SECOND

For week 26, I am invited to continue a life-long process of praying the five meditations of Sacred Story prayer. I will enter this prayer at least once daily, as St. Ignatius suggested.

THIRD

I will personalize meditations one, two, three, four and five: Creation, Presence, Memory, Mercy and Eternity.

I will awaken to the present moment.
I will awaken to my spiritual nature.
I will not make any decisions based on fear.
I will practice sacramental Reconciliation monthly.

This week, I will say this affirmation aloud once daily:
The urge to stop Sacred Story practice
always comes before my greatest breakthroughs.

℘

Ongoing Awakening to Sacred Story Prayer

A very significant exercise for us in the first weeks of learning Sacred Story prayer was finding the personal name for God that touches our hearts. Praying to God by saying this name often continues to be a powerful spiritual experience. Personalizing prayer and our relationship with God is an essential step in deepening our understanding of, and belief in, the God who is lovingly present to us each day of our lives.

Take what you are learning from praying with your personal name for God to understand why it is important to personalize the five meditations of Sacred Story. This week, you are invited to write your own single sentence for each of the meditations in Sacred Story. You are invited to continue working on this exercise until you know each of your sentences by heart. In this exercise, you are personalizing the Sacred Story of creation, the Fall, and our redemption in Christ to your own life story.

Engage all the other disciplines associated with Sacred Story prayer as part of your daily practice: Prayer upon Waking, During-the-Day Awakening exercise, daily journaling, and Prayer upon Retiring. Personalize Creation, Presence, Memory, Mercy, and Eternity during your fifteen-minute sessions this week. Use the blank spaces provided on the next page, or write the sentences in your personal journal.

CREATION

PRESENCE

MEMORY

MERCY

ETERNITY

∽

Come, children, listen to me;
I will teach you fear of the LORD.
Who is the man who delights in life,
who loves to see the good days?
Keep your tongue from evil,
your lips from speaking lies.
Turn from evil and do good;
seek peace and pursue it.

The eyes of the Lord are directed toward the righteous
and his ears toward their cry.
The Lord's face is against evildoers
to wipe out their memory from the earth.

The righteous cry out, the Lord hears
and he rescues them from all their afflictions.
The Lord is close to the brokenhearted,
And saves those whose spirit is crushed.
(Ps 34:12–19)

∽

Letters from Week Twenty-Six

Dear Fr. Bill,

Although I have spent quite some time now on the five meditations, it's slow going. I'm not getting something. The first four and their connection with each other came rather quickly and clearly for me. For some reason I've slowed down with the addition of Eternity. But rather than deter me I've become even more resolved, through prayer, meditation and practice, to get this. I know this is important. Hopefully, your feedback on my single sentence exercise is what will push me over the top.

Creation: God created everything in love and for love.

Presence: God is present in all of His creation and I must remain in the present in order to appreciate this.

Memory: Every violation of love committed by me and against me was necessary to prepare me for God's mercy.

Mercy: I am forgiven for the hurt I've caused, and the abuse and misuse of the gifts of His creation.

Eternity: I can only hope and pray that Christ's healing love will show through all of my thoughts, words and deeds.

Respectfully,

Ritchie

Dear Ritchie:

The reflection on Eternity can be seen this way: just realize you are doing a short review of your life in the five movements of the prayer, starting with gratitude and thanksgiving. You are listening to your history (short term and long term) and asking for grace to see where you missed the mark.

Then you are asking God for mercy and forgiveness. Finally and Eternally, you are moving back into your day with a focus on your ultimate goal which is life in the Kingdom with Christ. You are focusing on how you can live in the present moment with your eyes on the final prize. When I finish my Eternity meditation I say: "Lord, guide me along the everlasting way!" I hope this helps you.

Peace,

Fr. Bill

NOTES

Week 27

FIRST
I will visualize my prayer times this week and resolve to spend no more and no less than fifteen minutes in each formal prayer session. I will always use my personal name for God.

SECOND
For week 27, I am invited to continue developing a life-long process of praying the five meditations of Sacred Story prayer. As St. Ignatius suggested, I will enter my prayer at least once daily.

THIRD
I will continue my process of writing a personalized version of the five meditations.

I will awaken to the present moment.
I will awaken to my spiritual nature.
I will not make any decisions based on fear.
I will practice sacramental Reconciliation monthly.

This week, I will say this affirmation aloud once daily:
God gives me insights, not because I am better than others,
but because I am loved.

CB

Ongoing Awakening to Sacred Story Prayer

Sacred Story prayer is designed to carry us through our Christian journey to our heavenly home. It is also designed to open us to grace so that our story is shaped more and more by Christ's Sacred Story. Living our story in Christ is a labor of love, accomplished as we awaken to the truths of Creation, Presence, Memory, Mercy, and Eternity.

Let us resolve this week to continue our journey by praying with Creation, Presence, Memory, Mercy, and Eternity. By our openness and God's grace, our history and the history of the Church and world are changing. Make an act of faith this week that this is indeed true.

We also engage all the other disciplines associated with Sacred Story prayer as part of our daily practice. You can review these in week 16. Continue to use your personalized prayers of Creation, Presence, Memory, Mercy, and Eternity for the fifteen-minute sessions this week. Review the template from last week for this exercise.

CB

Many are the troubles of the just one,
but out of them all the Lord delivers him;
he watches over all his bones;
not one of them shall be broken.
Taste and see the goodness of the Lord.
(Ps 34:20–21)

SO

Letters from Week Twenty-Seven

Dear Fr. Bill,

In week Twenty-seven under the "Ongoing Awakening to Sacred Story Prayer" heading you wrote, "Sacred Story Prayer is designed to carry us through our Christian journey to our heavenly home". That is eternity. That is the fifth piece, the final piece of the five meditations. It's so simple, the journey from creation to eternity. There's nothing to "get" like I was concerned with last week and the week before. Was I not listening? The five meditations are our journey: my Sacred Story?

It all seems to be coming together for me now. One single sentence has opened my eyes. I sure hope I got it right.

As far as my one sentence exercise from last week, I apologize if you don't find it very creative. I couldn't find any better words than yours and the ones I'd used in the past. Nothing much had changed for me as far as the five meditations are concerned.

Respectfully,

Ritchie

Dear Ritchie:

So now you get Eternity….good! No need to apologize for using my words. In time, as your own story becomes clearer, you will find your own words. Let that time come naturally and don't rush it.

Peace,

Fr. Bill

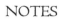

NOTES

Part Three
Entering the
School of Discernment

"Beloved, do not trust every spirit
but test the spirits to see whether they
belong to God, because many false prophets
have gone out into the world."

1 Jn 4:1

The Spiritual World

Spiritual discernment is challenging for a reason. Due to Original Sin, we have lost our capacity to readily distinguish truth from falsehood. To enter the path of discernment, we need to understand God and the universe God created. It is a universe that is both physical and spiritual. To help you enter the "school of discernment," Sacred Story prayer proposes a relational model (or paradigm) for God, human persons, and the created universe. Let us take a few moments to explore this relational paradigm.

First, we affirm a simple truth: God is Love. The essence of God as Love is God as Perfect Relationship. God is a Trinity of perfect, loving relationship. The Trinity—Father, Son, and Spirit—are three totally distinct, unique persons with no boundaries to their giving and receiving love. God is Love. It is a Love without beginning or end. God is Perfect Relationship. Love is always about relationship; the loss of love is always about the breaking of relationship. So everything not of God is anti-relationship, what Scripture calls the spirit of anti-Christ, "which is to come, but is already in the world" (1 Jn 4:3).

Second, God "created mankind in his image; in the image of God He created them; male and female he created them" (Gen 1:27). God willed human nature's form, freely creating persons as a perfect relationship of body and spirit.[13] The human nature God willed is the person as an embodied spirit. Human nature as embodied spirit is fashioned in God's own image. Consequently, persons are made to share in the Love that the Trinity enjoys—unique beings created to freely give and receive love with no boundaries.

For the human person, perfect love is the experience of being a completely unique individual and in that uniqueness, being completely transparent to one's beloved, who is also completely unique, perfectly transparent in the giving and receiving of love, perfectly giving, perfectly accepted, perfectly loved, perfectly loving, and eternally cherished! This giving and receiving of love, with no boundaries, was intended in God's plan to be realized between the persons and their Creator, and among the persons themselves. The relational paradigm of the Trinity is enriched immeasurably by God's free act of creation.

Third, the story of paradise in the book of Genesis reveals the state of perfect relationship between our first parents and God. This state of intimacy with God enabled a state of perfect justice and righteousness—a paradise! As long as our first parents remained in this state of spiritual intimacy with the Divine—as long as the state of perfect justice held—they were free from sickness and death.[14] This state of immortality was possible as long as they allowed God to be the very center of their lives—as long as they stayed in perfect, intimate relationship with God. In this state of perfect intimacy—their hearts undivided—they knew themselves. They had perfect interior harmony between their body and spirit.

Because they were innocent and radically transparent to their Creator, they cherished each other as sacred in God's eyes. As incarnate spirits they shared intimate knowledge, respect, trust, complementarity, uniqueness, separateness, and transcendent love. And they understood the creation. They had perfect relationship with creation, because they understood it as God's gift. God gifts the human persons with the power to name the plants and animals. We understand that this gift of "naming" includes the knowledge of creation's rhythms. They would understand how creation works to their benefit and their delight. The gift of Love freely given to our first parents by God was to expand in cosmic harmony.

The tragedy of Original Sin severs the perfect relationship between the incarnate spirits and the Creator:

> "When they heard the sound of the Lord God walking about in the garden at the breezy time of the day, the man and his wife hid themselves from the Lord God among the trees of the garden." (Gen 3:8)

The perfect relationship they had enjoyed now becomes filled with blame and grief. They will fight each other, and their offspring will fight them. Their perfect relationship with creation is now also cursed (Gen 3:17–19), and they lose immortality. They are vulnerable to sickness and disease. Free will, essential for love, also allows persons to sever their relationship with Love, with God. Relationship violated and severed is the true face of sin.

This is why abandonment and loneliness are the heart's deepest fears. As the most profound misery caused by sin, it is what Christ suffered on the cross, for all of humanity for all time, to a degree unimaginable: "My God, my God, why have you abandoned me?" Love itself suffered love's complete absence (Ps 22:1; Mt 27:45–46).

But God's work in creation cannot be undone by sin. The original unity is lost forever, but out of this tragedy, God creates an even more astonishing good. God would not create such beauty without a way to rectify even this tragedy with something more glorious. We are now invited to accept the mission of participating with Christ in His Grand Work of Reconciliation. We do this by opening to life as sacred story. We allow God to work His miracle of healing and forgiveness for the hope that we, as brothers and sisters of Christ and children of God, are destined to share:

> "I consider that the sufferings of this present time are as nothing compared with the glory to be revealed for us. For creation awaits with eager expectation the revelation of the children of God; for creation was made subject to futility, not of its own accord but because of the one who subjected it, in hope that creation itself would be set free from slavery to corruption and share in the glorious freedom of the children of God. We know that all creation is groaning in labor pains even until now; and not only that, but we ourselves, who have the first fruits of the Spirit, we also groan within ourselves as we wait for adoption, the redemption of our bodies. For in hope we were saved. Now hope that sees for itself is not hope. For who hopes for what one sees? But if we hope for what we do not see, we wait with endurance. In the same way, the Spirit too comes to the aid of our weakness; for we do not know how to pray as we ought, but the Spirit itself intercedes with inexpressible groanings. And the one who searches hearts knows what is the intention of the Spirit, because it intercedes for the holy ones according to God's will." (Rm 8:18–27)

Your discernment is made easier if you can see everything in light of the paradigm of perfect relationship—given, lost, and being restored in Christ:

✠ Perfect relationship of incarnate spirits in our unity of body and spirit

✠ Perfect relationship of created, incarnate spirits with our Creator God

✠ Perfect relationship of incarnate spirits with each other as unique individuals

304

✠ Perfect relationship between incarnate spirits as male and female, called to fruitful, respectful, loving, and joyful reverence

✠ Perfect relationship between created, incarnate spirits and the earth, which is given for our delight, refreshment, and sustenance

✠ Perfect relationship with the Church, the Body of Christ, as the community formed by Him for the work of Reconciliation, leading to a new heaven and a new earth

Every thought, word, and deed that seeks to affirm the meaning of perfect relationship and the human nature willed by God, everything that is working to heal damaged relationships, is a work of the Divine Inspirer—God the Creator.

Every thought, word, and deed that moves to alter the meaning of perfect relationship and the human nature willed by God, everything that is further undermining damaged relationships, is a work of the counter-inspirer—the enemy of human nature, who is from the beginning a murderer and a liar, the "father of lies" (Jn 8:43–45).

As you enter the school of spiritual discernment, keep your heart and mind focused on the relational paradigm. You are seeking the knowledge of your identity as a child of God, but informed by the truth of perfect relationship. Your authentic identity is a human nature, willed by God, as unity of body and spirit. You seek also the knowledge of your authentic God-given human nature as it has been violated and broken by Original Sin. And you seek this knowledge in light of what Christ is offering: by His life, death, and resurrection, you are offered the beginning of the full healing that will be completed in the world and the life to come.

In short, you are seeking the knowledge of perfect relationship and how in your own life and the world, that perfection has been broken but can also be restored, healed, and redeemed by the Divine Physician. You are also seeking knowledge of the thief and the robber—the enemy of human nature—who seeks to distort what authentic relationship is and to hide from you the truth of God and your authentic human nature. You are seeking to discern the two plotlines in your story: the one that leads to curse and death, and the one that leads to life and blessings. Ultimately, you are seeking to know truth from falsehood in all of your thoughts, words, and deeds.

ᗷ

So Jesus said again,
"Amen, amen, I say to you,
I am the gate for the sheep.
All who came [before me] are thieves and robbers,
but the sheep did not listen to them.
I am the gate.
Whoever enters through me will be saved,
and will come in and go out and find pasture.
A thief comes only to steal and slaughter and destroy;
I came so that they might have life
and have it more abundantly.
I am the good shepherd.
A good shepherd lays down his life for the sheep."
(Jn 10:7–11)

ᔒ

Letters from Part Three: Entering the School of Discernment

Dear Fr. Bill,

As I was reading the introduction to Part Three, I was once again reminded of how much sense Creation, Presence, Memory, Mercy, and Eternity now makes to me; "Given, lost and being restored in Christ;" "Seeking the knowledge of perfect relationship;" "How that perfection has been broken but can also be restored, healed and redeemed by the Divine Physician." I get it. I feel it.

John 4:1 and 10:7-11 are perfect for exactly where I am right now. Of course, you know that, that's why they're there. For a few years now my daily prayers have consisted of some form of the following:

"God of Mercy, I ask You to bless me with the ability to overcome all obstacles to my discipleship, including the ability to know the difference between
right and wrong,
good and bad,
smart and stupid.
I also ask to be able to intuitively know what to say or do in times of difficulty so that my actions will bring glory and honor to you."

Although my informal prayers may not be very eloquent, God knows what's in my heart and it appears I've been asking for spiritual discernment all along.

Respectfully, Ritchie

Dear Ritchie:

I very much like your prayer. It is simple and to the point, just what prayer should be! I think that others will find it a very good way to pray with the discernment section in Forty Weeks. Thank you for sharing it with me and the others who will journey with Forty Weeks: Letters from Prison.

Peace, Fr. Bill

NOTES

Week 28

FIRST

I will visualize the week ahead and imagine where and when I will find a technology-free zone for my time(s) of prayer. As before, I resolve to spend no more and no less than fifteen minutes in each formal prayer session. I will always use my personal name for God.

SECOND

I realize I am developing a deep, personal relationship with Christ. My lifelong process of praying Sacred Story prayer is a commitment to my relationship with Christ. As St. Ignatius found so fruitful, I will enter my prayer at least once daily.

THIRD

This week I enter the twelve-week school of spiritual discernment. It is essential for my progress to understand how the spiritual world works. My goal is to lay a foundation to understand Ignatius's guidelines for discerning the difference between the "voice" of God and the "voice" of the enemy of human nature. I will resolve not to become discouraged. The school of discernment requires spiritual exercise. Learning to distinguish the difference between the voice of God and the voice of the enemy of human nature takes practice. Most importantly, it requires listening, time, trial and error, prayer, patience, and God's grace.

I will awaken to the present moment.

I will awaken to my spiritual nature.
I will not make any decisions based on fear.
I will practice sacramental Reconciliation monthly.

This week, I will say this affirmation aloud once daily:
The insights and graces I need to move forward in life's journey
unfold at the right time.

℅

Cultivate the interior freedom to continue pondering the discernment reflections as they link to your own life. Understand them as an essential component to living your Sacred Story prayer.

Beginning in the School of Spiritual Discernment

As we begin discernment, continue with your daily prayer disciplines and the five meditations of Sacred Story. The materials for this third part of Forty Weeks are not new elements to integrate into the prayer discipline you are practicing. The discernment lessons are designed for you to learn more about how the spiritual world works. They are also an invitation for you to comprehend more fully the spiritual influences that are shaping your sacred story. Resist the temptation to incorporate these lessons on spiritual discernment into the structure of your fifteen-minute prayer periods. See them more as essential guidelines that will help you enter more fully into the daily disciplines of Sacred Story prayer

If you are praying the Sacred Story prayer faithfully, you will naturally encounter the dynamics taught in these guidelines on spiritual discernment. There is a reason for this. If you think and pray about Creation, Presence, Memory, Mercy, and Eternity in your Sacred Story prayer every day, the spiritual world awakens to you. The God of Grace who seeks to support you with divine inspirations, and the enemy of your human nature who seeks to disrupt your life with counter-inspirations, will both become apparent. If you seek daily to grow in faith, you will consciously encounter the spiritual world that supports your growth and the spiritual world that wants to disrupt your growth. While both forces have always been present in your life's story, you may have never before consciously noticed their activity.

These lessons on discernment will help you navigate these two spiritual currents so you can more readily move forward in your sacred story. If you do not now understand everything you are reading, you will one day, if you remain faithful to your prayer disciplines in the context of practicing your faith.

The first lesson examines God's intentional creation of human nature as a unity of spirit and body. We also examine why God willed the form of our human nature and created us as embodied spirits. Read the lesson several times this week and reflect on it. These truths need to be rediscovered and consciously reflected upon to help bring clarity to our lives. We are all influenced by the secularism of our age, to a greater or lesser degree, and need to wake up to what is real, because what is real may seem like spiritual fairy tales. But the principles of discernment we present here are the time-tested doctrines of our faith. If you do not believe or accept these fundamental Christian truths, Ignatius's discernment guidelines will make no sense whatsoever.

Church Tradition affirms that human nature, as a unity of spirit and body, was willed by God. We are human because our physical body is animated by an immortal, rational soul. No other creature is gifted with a rational soul to animate its physical body. Why did God will our human nature as a unity of physical body and rational soul? So God could be intimate with us. God communicates with our human nature by means of our spiritual soul. Complete intimacy with God is our destiny, our glory, and the purpose of our creation. Only a being with a spirit can know and love. A spirit's two chief faculties are the intellect (which knows) and the will or heart (which loves). Human beings are spiritual since humans both know and love.

Church Tradition also affirms that God created human beings as immortal beings. This is known as the condition of original holiness or original justice. The state of original justice means that the physical body and spiritual soul of our first parents were in complete harmony. The state afforded our first parents complete self-mastery. That state of sinlessness allowed all our thoughts, words, and deeds to be in complete harmony with the Divine.

We were without sin and thus without suffering, disease, or death. Immortality was the result of the total intimacy our first parents shared with God. Without complete spiritual intimacy with God, immortality would not be possible. Our first parents were at one in themselves, at one with each other and creation, and at one with God. Our spiritual nature, completely intimate with God, perfectly guided the lower nature of our material body. We call this period of history "paradise."

Our first parents were knowing beings (Homo sapiens). They knew themselves, God, and the purpose of creation's gift. They were the apex of God's creation and were given dominion to act as co-creators with God. To be co-creators means they were given power to cultivate and care for the earth and to name all living creatures (Gen 2:15–20). As woman and man, they had the power to give birth to other beings that would have an eternal destiny. Their role as co-creators could be accomplished with total integrity and justice because of their complete self-mastery. The triple corruption (1 Jn 2:16) of human nature "that subjugates us to the pleasures of the senses, covetousness for earthly goods, and self-assertion, contrary to the dictates of reason" had not yet poisoned God's plan for humanity and creation.

The Fall

The Tradition affirms that sin entered into creation originally from a spiritual entity, Lucifer, and the other spirits who irrevocably rejected God. Thus, sin first enters into God's creation in the spiritual realm, through a spiritual act of the will. It was an act of disobedience. Lucifer is the embodiment of sin, which is hatred of God and God's creation. Lucifer's hate, pride, and envy seek to destroy everything God creates. Lucifer operates through a gateway from his spiritual realm to the material realm so as to infect creation and activate its destruction. His gateway is the spiritual nature of our first parents. The perfect expression of hatred toward God is to destroy the beautiful, innocent immortals created to share in God's life.

Why Did God Allow Us to Disobey and Suffer?

God is love. Love always offers a choice to accept or reject divine love. If the woman and man cannot freely reject God's offer of life and love, God violates the freedom of the beings made in the divine image. Yet God would not have allowed this freedom if it would undo his plan for humankind. Our promise is that Jesus's Redemption will open a new heaven and a new earth with more blessing and glory than the first creation.

Lucifer's malevolent design starts by sabotaging the unity of human nature as a perfect relationship of body and spirit. His seduction begins by inviting persons to worship themselves instead of God. From this perversion of God's design, all other relationships will shatter. Lucifer's hope is that the virus of self-love—of narcissism—and the rejection of God's love that it manifests, will eventually evolve to destroy humanity and creation itself.

The time of paradise was real, and the plan to destroy paradise was also real. The plan to destroy creation required separating our first parents from their total intimacy with God. Here is the allegorical description in Genesis of the Original Sin that describes this heartrending primordial event:

> Now the snake was the most cunning of all the wild animals that the LORD God had made. He asked the woman, "Did God really say, 'You shall not eat from any of the trees in the garden?'" The woman answered the snake: "We may eat of the fruit of the trees in the garden; it is only about the fruit of the tree in the middle of the garden that God said, 'You shall not eat it or even touch it, or else you will die.' " But the snake said to the woman: "You certainly will not die! God knows well that when you eat of it your eyes will be opened and you will be like gods, who know good and evil." The woman saw that the tree was good for food and pleasing to the eyes, and the tree was desirable for gaining wisdom. So she took some of its fruit and ate it; and she also gave some to her husband, who was with her, and he ate it. (Gen 3:1–6)

This account is an allegory, a symbolic description of a real event that Tradition calls the Original Sin. We will never know the exact context for the Original Sin that ruptured God's plan for humanity and creation itself. And we cannot know the way the enemy of human nature insinuated itself into the consciousness of our first parents to get them to reject God and to make themselves gods, "masters" of the universe.

Yet the Genesis account provides valuable spiritual and theological material for reflection about the nature of temptation and the horrifying fall from grace that has evolved over time because of God's displacement from the center of human hearts. We see it in insatiable greed and grinding poverty; personal hatred and fratricidal war; the violation of the innocent in abuse and human trafficking; the legal murdering of children in the womb; the discarding of the weak, the vulnerable, and the aged; the lonely and despairing exploited by predators of all sorts; intellectual and scientific arrogance that subverts human nature and the created order; and self-serving political and financial collectives whose power is destabilizing and destroying families, nations, and creation itself.

Dissecting the story, we can imaginatively enter into this frightening and grief-filled catastrophe and see it with new eyes, through the relational paradigm: the plan of human nature's enemy to destroy the perfect ordering in love of all relationships, and to destroy God's creation.[15]

Stages of Original Sin Violation of Obedience and the Birth of a Divided Conscience: In the state of original justice, the woman and the man were completely intimate with God. Their spiritual nature was ordered solely to the Divine, and this gave them self-mastery over their lower physical nature. They also had the gift of immortality, because they listened only to God. The Latin root for obey means "to listen deeply." Lucifer inserts himself between our first parents and God. He did this by engaging them in seemingly innocent conversation. They violated obedience to God by elevating the voice of Lucifer to a status equal to

God. This foreshadowed unspeakable tragedy and loss. Turning from

---

What is Sin?

Every sin, in its essence, is a perversion and erosion of the perfect love and relationship that God gave to human persons as gift, life, and truth. And every sin in evil's evolution mimics the Original Sin. Each sin—whether it be a thought, word, or deed—spreads the virus of anti-Christ—anti-relationship as narcissism—to destroy human nature made in the divine image. Creation's perversion and destruction is the goal of evil's architect—the one St. Ignatius calls "the enemy of human nature."

God to listen and speak to Lucifer constitutes the first stage of Original Sin.

Stages of Original Sin

1. Violation of Obedience and the Birth of a Divided Conscience: In the state of original justice, the woman and the man were completely intimate with God. Their spiritual nature was ordered solely to the Divine, and this gave them self-mastery over their lower physical nature. They also had the gift of immortality, because they listened only to God. The Latin root for obey means "to listen deeply." Lucifer inserts himself between our first parents and God. He did this by engaging them in seemingly innocent conversation. They violated obedience to God by elevating the voice of Lucifer to a status equal to God. This foreshadowed unspeakable tragedy and loss. Turning from God to listen and speak to Lucifer constitutes the first stage of Original Sin.

2. Violation of Chastity and the Birth of Illegitimate Desires: In a state of original justice and with trusting innocence, the man and woman obeyed God, knowing the truth of their being, God, and creation. Engaged in conversation with the prince of lies, they were invited to see with new eyes what before had held no interest and incited no desire. But now, their hearts (consciences) were divided. They could not properly reason; nor could they maintain self-mastery over their physical nature. Cut off from God, their spiritual nature experienced the lust of self-assertion. They now contemplate (see with new eyes) an illegitimate desire opposed both to God and to their own human nature. All illegitimate desires are described in Tradition as appetites linked to the seven capital vices (pride, envy, anger, gluttony, greed, lust, sloth). This is the second stage of Original Sin.

3. Violation of Poverty and the Taking of What Does Not Belong to Me: Their total intimacy with God severed, the woman and the man had new desires and contemplated an electrifying, exciting, and

seemingly glamorous choice: to be like gods, knowing good and evil. God had told them that they would die if they ate this fruit. But Lucifer soothed them with lies to trick them into taking what they must have known in their hearts was wrong. The third stage in Original Sin is this: to experiment and find out for yourself who is telling the truth. And so our first parents took what they did not need and what did not belong to them. Devastation, heartache, and unspeakable tragedies followed.

The Three Stages of Original Sin in My Life

1.   By choice and/or habit: By choice and/or habit, the heart—conscience—is distant from God. I think I am following my own plans, but I am easily and subtly influenced to choose against God and my authentic self. I disobey my conscience. This lack of obedience ("deep listening") begins with my self-assertion. I make myself the final arbiter of truth. I break relationship with God and become independent of God, serving self over God.

2.   In this self-assertion, I open myself to all manner of illegitimate desires and entertain them. All these illegitimate desires are, in their essence, perversion and erosion of authentic relationships. Illegitimate desires are deemed "objectively wrong" by the Commandments, the gospel, and Tradition, but I judge them appropriate options, because I decide what I ought and ought not do. In so doing, I violate chastity. Violations of chastity are perversions and erosions of perfect relationship.

3.   I move from considering options to experimenting and trying what I like, because "It's my life." In this I violate poverty by taking what does not rightfully belong to me. Violations of poverty are perversions and erosions of relationship, because I take what I do not need or is not mine.

317

Jesus Redeems the Fall

Before the incarnate God-man Jesus begins His public ministry, He confronts this triple sin of our first parents. He confronts the temptation of Lucifer to turn the stones into bread. In this He confronts the violation of poverty by refusing to take what is not offered Him by the Father: "One does not live by bread alone, but by every word that comes forth from the mouth of God" (Mt 4:4).

Next, He confronts the violation of chastity and illegitimate desires by refusing to gain attention by plunging from the temple parapet: "Again it is written, 'You shall not put the Lord, your God, to the test'" (Mt 4:7).

Finally, He confronts the violation of obedience and the divided consciences it wrought by refusing to serve Lucifer and rule on this earth: "At this, Jesus said to him, 'Get away, Satan! It is written: "The Lord, your God, shall you worship and him alone shall you serve"'" (Mt 4:10).

The Sacred Story prayer journey challenges you to awaken to the voice of God in your own unique history, calling you to the poverty, chastity, and obedience that can bring peace and repair sin's damage. To do this effectively, it is essential to learn the language of discernment. The Discernment Guidelines presented in the coming weeks are modeled on St. Ignatius's classic Rules for spiritual discernment. For thirty years, Ignatius had made decisions based on self-assertion, with little thought of God. Both the desire and the choice to advance spiritually were totally new for him.

Ignatius's awakening forced him into uncharted terrain where he did not know how to navigate. He was not spiritually literate. He did not know himself—his authentic self—because he had lived controlled by sensual lusts and the desires of riches, honors of the world, and pride. All are values readily celebrated by our culture today.

God instructed Ignatius in discernment during his conversion journey. In his awakening process, he writes, "What is the new life we are living?" In this phrase he was discovering what Nicodemus was told by Jesus: "Amen, amen, I say to you, no one can see the kingdom of God without being born from above" (Jn 3:3).

Ignatius, in being born from above, was reconnected by grace to his spiritual nature and to God. He was awakening to realities he could not have known previously. He was learning that there were two "voices" and learning how to distinguish between them. By understanding the discernment guidelines that God revealed to Ignatius, we can awaken more easily to our authentic human nature.

To prepare ourselves, we will learn a new language of discernment and discover in our own life history the two voices "inspiring" us—one voice working to help us unite our spiritual and physical nature, and one voice working to keep us separated from God and divided within ourselves. You will learn how to distinguish in your thoughts, words, and deeds the voice of God from the voice of the enemy of human nature.

But they soon forgot all he had done;
they had no patience for his plan.
In the desert they gave in to their cravings,
tempted God in the wasteland.
They exchanged their glory
for the image of a grass-eating bull.
They forgot the God who had saved them,
who had done great deeds in Egypt,
They sacrificed to demons their own sons and daughters,
Shedding innocent blood,
the blood of their own sons and daughters,
Whom they sacrificed to the idols of Canaan,
desecrating the land with bloodshed.
They defiled themselves by their actions,
became adulterers by their conduct.
Save us, Lord, our God;
gather us from among the nations
That we may give thanks to your holy name
and glory in praising you.
(Ps 13–14, 20–21, 38–39, 47)

ॐ

Letters from Week Twenty-Eight

Dear Fr. Bill,

I see how original sin came to be. I understand the divided conscience and how I sometimes think I can be the sole arbiter of truth. Is discernment inherent? Is it more than good/bad, right/wrong?

I hope to be able to not only distinguish between the voice of the enemy and the voice of God, but to have the strength and fortitude to follow the right voice, to make my decisions based on the right voice.

It seems not much has changed since Adam and Eve. The process is still the same. Listen to the voice of the enemy, turn from God, contemplate illegitimate desires, and then think we can determine the truth. And we're off...

"Ignatius, in being born from above, was re-connected by grace to his spiritual nature and God." I'm getting there. I am definitely looking forward to growing in discernment.

Respectfully,

Ritchie

Dear Ritchie:

When we lost our innocence in the Original Sin, we also lost our capacity to know our hearts...we got lost. That is why Jeremiah says in 17: 9-10: "More tortuous than anything is the human heart, beyond remedy; who can understand it? I, the LORD, explore the mind and test the heart, giving to all according to their ways, according to the fruit of their deeds."

Discernment is a gift to give us back the knowledge of our hearts. Discernment helps us understand why what may "feel good" is actually bad, and why what "feels bad" might actually be good for us.

We must be reborn from above and work to allow God to become the center of our lives, like we were created to be. See the third chapter of John's Gospel.

It is very hard labor but Jesus promised to do all the heavy lifting. "Come to me, all you who labor and are burdened, and I will give you rest. Take my yoke upon you and learn from me, for I am meek and humble of heart; and you will find rest for yourselves. For my yoke is easy, and my burden light." Mt 11: 28-30.

You are in my prayers and keep me in yours.

Peace,

Fr. Bill

NOTES

Week 29

FIRST

I will visualize the week ahead to imagine where and when I can find a place apart—a technology-free zone—for my fifteen-minute periods of formal prayer. I will always use my personal name for God.

SECOND

This week, I continue the life-long process of praying meditations one through five in the Sacred Story prayer. I resolve to enter my prayer at least once daily, as St. Ignatius suggested.

THIRD

I continue my lessons in spiritual discernment. This week, I will come to understand how the world changed by the rupture of sin, and I will study God's plan to help us find our way home.

I will awaken to the present moment.
I will awaken to my spiritual nature.
I will not make any decisions based on fear.
I will practice sacramental Reconciliation monthly.

This week, I will say this affirmation aloud once daily:
My personal engagement with Sacred Story accomplishes, through Christ, a work of eternal significance.

Continuing in the School of Discernment

Take time, at your convenience outside of your prayer periods, to read and reflect on this second lesson in discernment. The lesson will examine two elements: first, the consequences of our first parents' decision to violate the freedom bestowed upon them by displacing God from the center of their lives; second, God's rescue plan to redeem us.

God desired that we be free and that we use that freedom to remain linked to God, our source of life. The complete unity of our higher spiritual nature with God is what made us human. This complete spiritual unity with God also bestowed balance and control over our lower physical nature. We controlled our bodily appetites. This complete unity of our higher spiritual nature with God also made us, body and soul, immortal. It was paradise.

The woman and the man silenced God's voice as the center of their consciences and replaced it with their opinions. In silencing God's voice, they cut the lifeline of God's grace. As a result, human nature, as an integrated unity of spirit and body, was shattered. The higher spiritual nature no longer guided the lower physical nature. The immortality of human nature as body and soul is lost. With their appetites cut off from the Divine spiritual compass, paradise was lost.

Before our first parents used free choice to make themselves the center of their own universe—to make themselves gods—spiritual discernment was not necessary. They knew the true God, they knew who they were, and they knew instinctively how to act with integrity and holiness. Truth was instinctive, based on the complete harmony they shared with God: discernment was automatic.

We cannot determine at what point in the two-hundred-thousand-year history of modern humans this rupture took place, but we affirm that it did occur. As a result, God's plan to save humankind and creation began. Our Judeo-Christian faith is a revealed religion. This means that

---

Covering Their Nakedness

In Genesis 3:7, Adam and Eve "see" their nakedness and "cover" themselves. Their seeing and covering demonstrates that their separation from God awakens them to know and feel that they no longer have control over their physical nature. They can objectify each other—use each other—and in their loss of innocence, are shamed by this discovery. Now begins the history of psychological and physical exploitation linked to the very gift God created to give life: human sexuality. The enemy of human nature knew this tragedy would result and relishes the agony it causes. The perfect complementarity of human nature created in the divine image, male and female, is shattered by narcissism. But God has a plan to rescue us and make all things new. It begins with the miracle of the wine at the wedding at Cana, which signifies the superabundance of grace that God pours out upon the covenant of marriage through Christ's life (Jn 2:1–12).

God reveals it to us; we do not create it. In the rupture caused by Original Sin, we lost the ability to instinctively know the truth about God, our human nature, and creation. God must reveal the idea of truth, good and evil, to His beloved creatures, which are now subject to corruption, disease, and death. It is no wonder that the first Commandment states: "I am the Lord your God; you shall not have strange gods before me."

The Ten Commandments reveal the moral truths—about God, about woman and man's proper relationship to God, and about their relationship to each other and to creation. God is revealing the knowledge of truth lost in paradise. God chose the Jewish people for this mission. The whole history of Israel is preparing for the coming of the Messiah who will save us from the devastation caused by Original Sin. Sin closes hearts to the truth, and so even the chosen people rejected God's messengers, the prophets. Christ fared no better and was executed. The Pharisees, with darkened consciences, even accused Jesus of collaborating with Satan (Mt 12:24).

What is Truth?

"'For this I was born and for this I came into the world, to testify to the truth. Everyone who belongs to the truth listens to my voice.' Pilate said to him, 'What is truth?'" (Jn 18:37–38)

At the beginning of the third millennium, many believe truth is relative. Even before the third millennium commenced, many pointed out that the greatest threat to the faith is not atheism but relativism. Jesus tells Pilate that he was born and came into the world to testify to the truth—the truth about God, the truth about human nature, and the truth about salvation. Truth does exist, and discernment's goal is to help us distinguish truth from falsehood in our sacred story.

Your Sacred Story prayer journey links you to the entire history of salvation. In your prayer and in your discernment, you participate in the holy labor of returning body and soul to God. You join Christ's Great Work of Reconciliation by your engagement. It is a labor to be sure, as St. Ignatius learned. Recall that he had lived for thirty years with his lower appetites in near complete control of his life. His awakening was guided by God and began while recuperating from battle. Ignatius was graced to notice a difference between two sets of fantasies or daydreams.

In the first daydream/fantasy, he imagines himself successful in marrying King Ferdinand and Queen Isabella's daughter. He describes this later as a vain fantasy. In the second daydream/fantasy, he imagines himself making a pilgrimage to Jerusalem and living like the saints.[16] Both daydream/fantasies make him feel good while he entertains them. But on deeper reflection, the afterglow of the first daydream leaves him dry and dissatisfied while the afterglow of the second daydream/fantasy leaves him feeling content and peaceful. With this awakening, he begins a lifelong practice of spiritual discernment.

Human Nature and Authentic Identity

Films, songs, books, and newspapers often define human nature positively and solely as our lower appetites. How these lower appetites might be divided from our spiritual nature and from divine influence is usually ignored. Today, many definitions of human nature are influenced by the theories of Sigmund Freud. Freud believed that sexual drives/desires are the root of all human psychological activity, so being authentic means discerning one's identity mainly by expressing one's sensual appetites. Yet to discern one's authentic identity requires being spiritually grafted to Christ. Only then can one discern both the higher calling we have as daughters and sons of God, and our true human nature. This "being born from above" reveals the truth about God, our authentic identity, and our mission to love as Christ loved.

What did he learn in this lesson? That the feelings associated with even imagined actions can reveal the truth about our identity. Learning to pay close attention to our feelings (our affective/emotional spiritual life) can reveal the signature of God in our authentic identity and the signature of human nature's enemy in our false identity. Ignatius was utterly amazed at this discovery. Never before had he noticed this subtle difference in his spiritual experiences.

As his Christian conversion deepened, St. Ignatius learned that there are three ways the human person can be "inspired." Inspirations can come from God, from the enemy of human nature, and from oneself. Next week, we will look at these three sources in more depth.

The first goal of spiritual discernment is to learn truth vs. falsehood about your human nature, about your identity as a child of God, and about God and His creation. The second goal of spiritual discernment is to choose thoughts, words and deeds that express your authentic identity as a child of God. You are called to surrender self-assertion in favor of humility so that your life's labor—your sacred story—produces fruit that endures to eternity.

Awaken this week to the truth that you are both body and spirit. You have a higher spiritual nature and a lower bodily nature. At one point, they were an integrated unity but now, they are divided (Jer 17:9). God desires to heal you spiritually ("Lord, I am not worthy to have you enter under my roof; only say the word and my servant will be healed" [Mt 8:8].) so that you can be at peace and gain eternal life. The enemy of human nature seeks to keep you spiritually distant from God so that your lower nature (your base appetites) guide your thoughts, words, and deeds, robbing you of peace and eternal life.

Both God and the enemy of human nature are working to achieve these very different ends. This is nothing to be afraid of, because you have given your heart to Christ. Christ will guide you to safety and holiness just like He did St. Ignatius. All the great teachers of the Church reinforce these central spiritual truths.[17]

၆၃

"And the Word became flesh and made his dwelling among us, and we saw his glory, the glory as of the Father's only Son, full of grace and truth." (Jn 1:14)

"God is Spirit, and those who worship him must worship in Spirit and truth." (Jn 4:24)

"If you remain in my word, you will truly be my disciples, and you will know the truth, and the truth will set you free." (Jn 8:31–32)

Jesus said to him, "I am the way and the truth and the life. No one comes to the Father except through me."

(Jn 14:6)

၈၁

Letters from Week Twenty-Nine

Dear Fr. Bill,

God has always desired that we be free and that we use that freedom to remain linked with Him. Although I did not fully realize it at the time, my lifeline to God's grace was re-connected four years ago when I recommitted to my Savior. "Sacred Story Prayer journey link you to the entire history of salvation."

The five meditations "Creation, Presence, Memory, Mercy, and Eternity" are real. They are truth and truth is not relative. Contrary to all we see and hear around us these days – opinions, interpretations, selfish perspectives- truth is truth and there's no way around it. There are no "alternate facts" or truths.

The fact that St. Ignatius was a great admirer of St. Francis of Assisi is quite heartening to me. I am also an admirer. I was first introduced to St. Francis by a friend, the best friend I ever had, a Franciscan priest, Fr. Mychal Judge, OFM. I greatly admired how he lived and as a result, I've done some reading on Francis. It is my hope to live my life in a way that would, somehow, in a small way, resemble how Francis lived the Gospel, while at the same time incorporating St. Ignatius' prayer model in my walk.

This chapter has opened my eyes even more to the fact that it's not just my words and deeds, but also imagined (daydreamed) actions that can reveal the truth about our identity. The first time I was able to relate to Ignatius was through the narcissistic daydreams we had in common. I'd been deeply immersed in this narcissistic fantasy land all my life.

Although I'd acted on a lot of these daydreams, there were many that were just wishful thinking, negative sinful thoughts that energized my egotistical, selfish existence. It is my goal that through these discernment exercises, I can learn truth vs. falsehood and awaken to that truth. I am not worthy, yet I do seek peace and eternal life.

Respectfully, Ritchie

Dear Ritchie:

What happened to you four years ago was the realization that God had always had a lifeline out to you but you just suddenly realized it. He never lets us go, even when we let him go. That should give you great hope!

You can't go wrong having the model of St. Francis (I took his name for my Confirmation) and the prayer disciplines of St. Ignatius. The fact that you desire to follow the example of these two men means that God has placed that desire in your heart and will fulfill it. Thank Jesus for those desires, Ritchie, and keep them alive in your heart.

Also, realize that Fr. Mychal Judge, OFM is one of your angels in heaven interceding for you. He was a great man who died serving others. You were blessed to have known him.

It is very enlightening, isn't it, to discover that our hidden fantasy life reveals much about who we are or want to become? Remember, there is a life of fantasy based on selfishness and one based on selflessness. Both fantasy worlds can be out of sight and hidden from those who are spiritually asleep. Part of the benefit of praying Ignatius' Examen prayer daily is that we begin to wake up to these guiding daydreams and have the capacity to follow those that are holy and work against those that are not.

Let us pray for each other.

Peace, Fr. Bill

Dear Fr. Bill,

Just as I was preparing to send you my reflections on Weeks Twenty-Nine through Thirty-Two, your letter and response to my last "batch" arrived. Perfect timing.

As I am learning through these lessons on discernment, feeling good is not always proof that I am doing the right thing or moving in the right direction. Your thoughts on weeks twenty-five through twenty-eight have seriously bolstered my confidence and my desire to move forward.

As I've alluded to before, the Life Connections Program keeps me pretty busy. Obviously, not so busy that I don't make time to do what is important to me and for my relationship with God, including Forty Weeks and all it entails. That said, I know that I definitely need to do another Whole Life Confession (properly) and I will get it done.

I definitely must be in the right place to do that. There will be a lull in the program fairly soon and I hope to do it then. Also, and I would definitely like your feedback on this, I think I probably need to describe and go into detail about life around here, how it affects the growth of my relationship with God and how it's affected my journey through Forty Weeks. Day to day life in here is surely different, even if not necessarily more difficult all the time. I'd be interested in hearing what you think.

My presentation should be coming up in a month or so and I've decided on the topic. It will be discernment. It's called "Word of the Day" and someone gives one four days a week. The W.O.T.D. is not usually of a religious nature, but can be, as long as the twenty-five-minute talk is not entirely religious. For instance-today's WOTD was "Experience" and the power phrase was "learn from it".

Nothing overtly religious but the speaker fits some spiritual connections in there. It is my hope to spend the majority of my talk on the secular dictionary definition and how it applies to our daily lives and then some time on our Catholic definition and its implications. Absolutely no chance of my sounding like a scholar of discernment ☺.

So, I need to come up with a power phrase like the one mentioned above, usually two to four words which supplement the W.O.T.D. If you have _any_ thoughts, hints, material or general help that may be useful _please_ do not hesitate to send it along. If you'd like, you wouldn't have to wait until you're ready to respond to Weeks Twenty-Nine through Thirty-Two. Any help would be appreciated and time is of the essence.

Respectfully,

Ritchie

"Don't bend to the Fear" has been helpful. Thanks.

Hello Ritchie:

It was very good to hear from you. I want you to know that Deacon Patrick has connected me with a second inmate who wants to do the Forty Weeks program. His name is Anthony and he is in a correctional facility back East. Please keep him in your prayers and I will have him pray for you, too!

It is good to hear that you are learning that just feeling good is not necessarily a sign that all things are right with the world. Discernment is subtle. Maybe that can be your power statement. What makes you feel good might not be good for you and what makes you feel bad might not be bad for you!

I will trust that you will come up with something for your talk. Ask the Holy Spirit to guide you and you will be guided. It is much more important that what you talk about comes from your own experience. In the end, you will have a much greater sense of accomplishment, Ritchie.

On redoing your Whole-Life Confession, just follow the template in the book and write out your letter to Jesus. If you follow that, you will know *all the things to say to Jesus from your heart! I will keep you in prayer for this experience.*

I am very glad the Life Connections program is keeping you busy and giving you a sense of hope for the future. I will keep you and all the folks in the program in my prayers.

Peace,

Fr. Bill

NOTES

Week 30

FIRST

I resolve to spend no more and no less than fifteen minutes in each formal prayer session. As before, I will visualize the week ahead and imagine where I can find a technology-free zone for my prayer. I will always use my personal name for God.

SECOND

I continue the process of praying meditations one through five in the Sacred Story prayer and, as St. Ignatius suggested, I will enter my prayer at least once daily. This prayer, like the rosary, will never grow old. It will take on more and more meaning, helping me deepen my faith and my wisdom and awaken me to God's truth and love.

THIRD

I will continue to open my heart to the lessons on discernment as I try to understand the three different sources of inspiration that can influence my thoughts, words, and deeds.

I will awaken to the present moment.
I will awaken to my spiritual nature.
I will not make any decisions based on fear.
I will practice sacramental Reconciliation monthly.
I will ask Jesus for help when I am troubled.

I will thank Jesus daily for life's gifts.

This week, I will say this affirmation aloud once daily:
Inspirations can have a divine or a demonic source. I pray for the grace
to remember how to discern one from the other.

ɔȝ

Continuing in the School of Discernment:
Guidelines for Foundational Healing and Spiritual Growth

Take time, at your convenience outside of your prayer periods, to read and reflect on this third lesson in discernment. We will examine the three distinct sources of inspiration that can guide our thoughts, words, and deeds.

Inspirations affecting your human nature (spirit-body) can originate from three different sources, according to St. Ignatius.[18]

1. Can originate with yourself
2. Can originate from a Divine Source: the Divine Inspirer
3. Can originate from a demonic source: the enemy of human nature, the counter-inspirer

There are three sources of spiritual inspiration, but only two spiritual states. St. Ignatius names the two states consolation and desolation. Next week, we will explore these two spiritual states in more depth.

Spiritual consolation is when one experiences, to a greater or lesser degree, an increase in faith, hope, and love.

Spiritual desolation is when one experiences, to a greater or lesser degree, a loss of faith, hope, and love.

Sources of Inspiration

✠ ✦ Human nature as spirit/body
✠ ✦ The Divine Inspirer
✠ ✦ The counter-inspirer

Types of Inspiration

✠ ✦ Consolation—increase of faith, hope, and love
✠ ✦ Desolation—loss of faith, hope, and love

Sources of Inspiration

To affirm that our human nature can be the source of inspirations makes perfect sense. We have our own thoughts and convictions and act on them. Such thoughts originate from within our being in several ways.

First, we can let our body make decisions. We can be led by our sensual appetites and give into them with little or no conscious thought about the consequences. Sometimes that giving in is due to sickness or addictions, but it is still the appetites doing our "thinking" and inspiring our actions.

Second, we can be inspired by what we might call embedded strengths/gifts in human nature from our Creator or by embedded diseases/weaknesses in human nature marred by Original Sin. Consolation from an embedded strength/ gift could be a bodily feeling that "life is good" after an excellent workout. It might also be a spiritual feeling of being happy to be alive, that "life is beautiful" when looking at a baby or a beautiful sunset.

Desolation from an embedded disease/weakness might be a bodily feeling that "life is miserable" when you have the flu, a chronic illness, or some type of bodily injury. It might also be a spiritual feeling that "life is difficult, burdensome, and not fair" if you are hurting in a relationship or suffering due to early life events.

If you are inspired spiritually by either the Divine Inspirer or the counter-inspirer, the inspiration will be communicated to you through your higher spiritual nature which was willed by God to guide your lower physical nature. We will look at this reality in coming weeks.[19]

You may continue your reflections on these spiritual realities by reading a homily by St. Bernard of Clairvaux and a short section from Vatican II's Gaudium et Spes: The Pastoral Constitution on the Church in the Modern World.[20]

Evil's Work is More Hidden than Sensational

Don't go looking for Exorcist-movie drama in your spiritual discernment. The counter-inspirer accomplished his greatest damage in the Original Sin when human nature was crippled. He knew you would be subject to disease and death and that the anger, cynicism, sickness, war, poverty, and injustice in human society would chip away at belief. A loss of faith, hope, and love would result, and belief in a "God of love" would diminish. Kindness avoided, forgiveness withheld, and self-centered behavior work to diminish faith, hope, and love. All have conspired to create the evolution of darkness present in our history. Exorcist-style evil does exist but serves the counter-inspirer's work mostly by making us blind to evil's greatest work: crushing the human spirit and making us believe that evil is more powerful than God and love. Yet the enemy of human nature—the counter-inspirer—has already lost his battle in Christ's victory. Be not afraid!

◌੪

My eyes long to see your salvation
and the promise of your righteousness.
Act with mercy toward your servant;
teach me your statutes.
I am your servant; give me discernment
that I may know your testimonies.
(Ps 119:123–125)

੪ට

Letters from Week Thirty

Dear Fr. Bill,

Affirmation: "Inspirations can have a divine or demonic source. I pray for the grace to remember how to discern one from the other."

I must admit that, even though it appears to be a simple statement, end note number seventeen which begins, "People today often form judgements about human nature based on the experience of human nature in its fallen state." really hit home.

The ability to be constantly conscious of the fact that "man has a wounded nature, inclined to the evil." would definitely be helpful while trying to navigate through my day, especially under my current circumstances. The very idea that through discernment, and the identification of the origins of our inspirations, we can somehow brook the divide of our hearts caused by Original Sin, is just another of the things I never knew I wanted or needed.

It is easy to discern consolations or desolations after the fact, especially at the end of my day when I am journaling, when I have a few minutes to go over my day. My whole and goal is to be able to stop in the course of my day and to instinctively label my current inspiration as Divine or demonic and move forward in a manner which would be in my best interest and bring glory to God.

Respectfully,

Ritchie

Dear Ritchie:

My comments on Week Twenty-Nine are instructive for your reflection here as well. Remember, there are thousands of inspirations that tug at us but they only have two main directions they can take us—towards or away from God. That is what you want to discern in your thoughts, words, and deeds and your fantasy life. St. Ignatius had the practice of regularly listening to the previous hour to determine which spiritual influences he had experienced.

It sounds a little neurotic that he did this so frequently but my sense is that he was so "lights out" for much of his life that he set a course to stay awake to the influences of both the Divine and the demonic and always as best he could, stay on the right course. God will show each of us the right way to use this great method of St. Ignatius to move from being "lights out" to full consciousness.

Peace,

Fr. Bill

NOTES

Week 31

FIRST

I will visualize my week to imagine where I can find a technology-free zone to spend my fifteen-minutes prayer sessions. I will always use my personal name for God.

SECOND

I continue the lifelong process of praying meditations one through five in the Sacred Story prayer. I commit to enter my prayer at least once daily as St. Ignatius suggested. This prayer will carry me for life. It will deepen my faith and my wisdom and awaken me to God's truth and love.

THIRD

This week I will continue to seek knowledge of spiritual discernment by examining two benchmark rules: spiritual consolation and spiritual desolation.

I will awaken to the present moment.
I will awaken to my spiritual nature.
I will not make any decisions based on fear.
I will practice sacramental Reconciliation monthly.
I will ask Jesus for help when I am troubled.
I will thank Jesus daily for life's gifts.

This week, I will say this affirmation aloud once daily:
Christ, who has walked before me, shares my every burden.
Christ, who has walked before me,
will help me resolve every crisis.
Christ, who has walked before me, knows my every hope.

♋

Continuing in the School of Discernment:
Guidelines for Foundational Healing and Spiritual Growth

Take some time this week to read and reflect on this fourth lesson in discernment. We will examine the two types of inspiration that can guide our thoughts, words, and deeds. First, let's briefly review the past three weeks. God willed that human nature be a perfect unity of body and soul. The gift of this blessed unity of human nature in paradise made us immortal. The turning from God, which we call Original Sin, broke the perfect unity of human nature: body and soul. Lust for power and dominance and the unbridled physical desires of our bodily nature (concupiscence) battled with our spiritual nature. In this battle, our authentic identity was distorted.

Our conscience was clouded, and we lost sight of right and wrong. Disease, strife, suffering, and death resulted. Original Sin broke our perfect unity with God's loving will. Also broken was the unity between male and female and their harmony with creation. Paradise was an ecstasy of harmonious relationships. Original Sin broke all relationships. Most tragically, it broke our hearts.

The revelation of the Ten Commandments to the people of Israel was one of the most significant gifts from God to help us relearn "right relationship." In the New Covenant, Christ is the ultimate revelation of God. Christ's life and message are the most perfect expression of how each of us is called to live. This is why we call our Judeo-Christian faith a

346

revealed religion. We did not come to the truth by our own reasoning processes. It had to be revealed to us.

The teaching Church has been entrusted with interpreting, passing on, and holding secure for all people the authentic message of Christ and the revealed Truths of God. It is the same Church that Ignatius served and

---

God Is Healing Our Broken Human Nature

Original Sin crippled our human nature. None of us will achieve perfection this side of eternity. Yet knowing that human nature was perfect once and will be perfect again informs the Church's interpretation of holiness. God's grace fosters healing in our souls, enabling us to gain a measure of mastery over the lusts and desires of our bodily nature. It also enables us to grow in forgiveness, selflessness, and charity. All of us are called to cooperate with God's grace for this healing and holiness. We are all encouraged by Christ not to be afraid but to be patient, as the process of healing takes a lifetime.

---

loved. His discernment rules are spiritual guidelines that help us understand the revealed truth of "right relationship" in our own lives, according to the revealed truths entrusted to the teaching Church.

Ignatius's discernment wisdom, in his rules, is discovered when individuals begin to pay close attention to inspirations that we identify through affective awareness. We are inspired in thoughts, words, and deeds from three sources: our own human nature (body and soul); the Divine Inspirer; and human nature's enemy, the counter-inspirer. These inspirations have one of two effects on us: they create either spiritual consolation or spiritual desolation. This week we begin looking at these two types of inspiration.

Two Benchmark Guidelines for Spiritual Discernment

To help your awakening and initiation into spiritual discernment, two benchmark guidelines will be beneficial in many life situations. It is important to understand that divine inspiration, or consolation, does not always feel good. Equally important is to realize that an unholy inspiration, or spiritual desolation, does not always feel bad. We will explore this seeming paradox in a later lesson. For now, it is sufficient to absorb the two benchmark guidelines and to understand that each is intended to influence the direction of our life in every thought, word, and deed either toward or away from God.

Benchmark One

Authentic Divine Inspirations, called Consolations, will:

1. Increase the heart's love for God and others,

2. Increase the virtues of docility, humility, and self-generosity, and

3. Not oppose the truths and teachings of Scripture, the Tradition, and the teaching Church.[21]

Consolation can be the consequence of the Divine Physician's Spirit working in you. This form of consolation helps strengthen your heart and soul, encouraging you to turn to God. Consolation helps you to choose thoughts, words, and deeds that express your authentic human nature made in the divine image.

Consolation can also be the consequence of the body/spirit aspect of your divinely shaped human nature. God created your human nature as a gift in the divine image and likeness. In spite of Original Sin's impact, cooperating with God's grace activates embedded life forces of your divinely shaped human nature, helping to heal biochemical, physiological, and emotional imbalances; energizing you; and enabling thoughts, words, and deeds that express your authentic human nature.

Benchmark Two

Authentic Counter-inspirations, called Desolations, will:

1. Increase narcissism, displacing God and others,

2. Decrease docility and humility and increase pride and self-satisfaction, and

3. Arouse hungers and desires that, although they feel good, will typically contradict the truths and teachings proposed by the Scripture, Tradition, and the teaching Church. This is because the author of counter-inspirations is opposed to Christ and will lead you away from life and truth.

Counter-inspirations will produce desires that feel authentic because they are linked to fallen human nature's physical lusts and spiritual pride. They are the familiar default drives of a broken heart and a broken human nature.

Desolation can be the consequence of the enemy of human nature working in you. This form of desolation helps weaken your heart and soul, encouraging you to turn from God. Desolation helps you choose thoughts, words, and deeds that are opposed to your divinely shaped human nature.

Desolation can also be the consequence of your own fallen human nature. God created your human nature as a gift in the divine image and likeness. Yet because of Original Sin's impact, not cooperating with God's grace erodes the embedded life forces of your divinely shaped human nature, helping to destroy biochemical, physiological, and emotional balance; de-energizing you; and increasing thoughts, words, and deeds that are in opposition to your authentic human nature.

፣

It is time for the Lord to act;
they have disobeyed your law.
Truly I love your commandments
more than gold, more than the finest gold.
Thus, I follow all your precepts;
every wrong way I hate.
(Ps 119:126–128)

፨

Letters from Week Thirty-One

Dear Fr. Bill,

"God willed that human nature be a perfect unity of body and soul." "Human nature was perfect once and will be perfect again." Through God's grace our souls can be healed, "enabling us to gain a measure of mastery over the lusts and desires of our bodily nature". I apologize for quoting so much but once again, the words you've used this week are much better than any I can come up with.

My conscience was, and is, often clouded. It's not as if I don't know right from wrong, but the fact that I didn't care was the problem. It was the enemy telling me it didn't matter, so what.

The Benchmark Guidelines for Spiritual Discernment are very helpful. Already, without yet learning how to implement the lessons on discernment, I have been able to recognize the origins of many of my inspirations.

Respectfully, Ritchie

Dear Ritchie:

So good to hear you are starting to understand the world of discernment. I will keep your advancement in my prayers! Let the phrases that strike your heart and enlighten your mind be ones that you go back to often. They speak to you and will continue to do so in the months and years ahead. Again, the goal is to wake up to the various inspirations acting upon us and follow those of Divine origin and reject those from the enemy of human nature.

Let's pray for each other.

Peace, Fr. Bill

NOTES

Week 32

FIRST

I resolve to spend no more than fifteen minutes in each formal prayer session and to do so in some place apart – a technology free zone. I will always use my personal name for God.

SECOND

For the sake of God's greater glory, I continue a lifelong process of praying with meditations one through five in Sacred Story prayer. I enter my prayer at least once daily, as St. Ignatius suggested. This prayer will carry me for life. It will deepen my faith and my wisdom and awaken me to God's truth and love.

THIRD

By God's grace, I continue opening my heart to learn spiritual discernment. This week, I explore definitions of spiritual consolation and spiritual desolation as divine inspiration and counter-inspiration.

I will awaken to the present moment.
I will awaken to my spiritual nature.
I will not make any decisions based on fear.
I will practice sacramental Reconciliation monthly.
I will ask Jesus for help when I am troubled.
I will thank Jesus daily for life's gifts.
This week, I will say this affirmation aloud once daily:

Christ, who has walked before me, knows everything I suffer.
Christ, who walks before me, will always lead me home to safety.

℃

Continuing in the School of Discernment:
Guidelines for Foundational Healing and Spiritual Growth

Take some time this week to read and reflect on this fifth lesson in discernment. We will examine the divine inspiration of spiritual consolation and the counter-inspiration of spiritual desolation. Start paying attention to your affective moods to feel the states of consolation and desolation in your story. This process requires a graced awakening, so ask God for the "eyes to see" your story through the lens of these spiritual lessons. Be patient as you slowly learn this way of understanding your story.

The practice of Sacred Story prayer makes one aware of the spiritual forces at work in one's life and in the world. Ignatius became a master at discerning these spiritual movements. He left guidelines for understanding how they work. You have learned already that there are three distinct sources influencing your thoughts, words, and deeds:

1. Your own emotional, psychological, and intellectual makeup, shaped by concupiscence and your unique history.

2. The divine inspiration of consolation, working to draw your thoughts, words, and deeds in the direction of your authentic human nature.

3. The counter-inspirations of the enemy of your true human nature, seeking to pull you away from your authentic self.

God (Divine Inspirer) and the enemy of human nature (counter-inspirer) each seek ultimate influence over how your history unfolds: God for eternal love and life, the enemy of human nature for eternal despair and death; God for eternal relationships, the enemy of human nature for eternal loneliness.

Is Prayer Helping or Hurting?

Some might say, "Until I started this prayer, I never felt bad, but now I do. I wonder if it is hurting instead of helping." If you find yourself asking the same question, you probably were feeling bad before you started the prayer discipline. You just were not aware of the pain or of your true feelings. There are many ways for us to "self-medicate" our pain, whether that pain is spiritual, emotional, or physical. The process of spiritual awakening brings to the light preexisting spiritual conditions that previously, we were simply not conscious of. Now that you are becoming more aware and actually feeling what is happening, you can ask for God's help, and God can help you. Sometimes the presence of discomfort and pain is the first step to healing. Welcome it, and invite Christ Jesus to heal your life and heart!

Both God and the enemy of human nature are aware of your strengths, weaknesses, wounded memories, hopes, dreams, and fears. God desires to stir your conscience towards freedom and light and bring you healing and hope.

God will build on your strengths, inflaming your holy desires and healing what is hurt and broken. The enemy of human nature seeks to silence your conscience and hide it in shadows. He will work to magnify your problems, diminish your holy desires, and inspire hopelessness.

We identify and distinguish divine inspirations from counter-inspirations by their intellectual and affective traits, or signature characteristics. Ignatius defines two distinct types of inspiration. The first type, caused by divine inspiration of the Spirit, he calls consolation. The second type, caused by the counter-inspiration of the enemy of your human nature, he calls desolation.

Divine Inspiration: Consolation defines the feelings and thoughts of a healing heart returning to God and/or residing in God. God always inspires movement towards reconciliation and union. The signature characteristics of divine inspiration include being passionate for God and loving all things in God, and tears of remorse and sadness when you fail—yet feeling loved by God despite your failures.

Spiritual Pleasure and Success

Illicit pleasures of our higher spiritual nature often reside in our attitudes like one's personal definition of success. I can be comforted by my own self-righteousness and contemptuous of others.

"The Pharisee took up his position and spoke this prayer to himself, 'O God, I thank you that I am not like the rest of humanity—greedy, dishonest, adulterous—or even like this tax collector. I fast twice a week, and I pay tithes on my whole income'" (Lk 18:11–12).

The Pharisee, while fulfilling the rule of law, was trapped in a false identity. Spiritual attitudes (world views and our definitions of success) need discernment to determine whether or not they are of God. Just because they are legal, does not mean they are of God!

You may experience tears of love for Christ who suffered the consequences of all sin, including your own. It is every increase in love, hope, and faith that magnetizes your heart towards holy things, and all experiences of peace and quiet in the presence of your Creator. The divine inspiration of consolation is manifest in humility that views eternal life, lasting love, and faith in God as the hope of the single-hearted and the ultimate goal of those willing to risk seeing reality as it truly is.

Counter-inspiration: Desolation defines feelings and thoughts that are the direct opposite of consolation's divine inspiration. The signature characteristics of counter-inspiration are darkness and confusion of a broken and wounded heart, soul, and spirit; magnetic and compulsive attractions to sensual and base appetites; restlessness, anger, cynicism, and temptations that make all things geared toward faith, hope, and love appear dull, absurd, and even destructive to your heart. You will feel a lazy, lukewarm, and sad spirit as if separated from God. The counter-inspiration of desolation is everything that magnetizes a broken heart toward cynicism, lusts, isolation, anger, despair, and aloneness. The counter-inspiration of desolation is manifest in an unyielding pride that views eternal life, lasting love, and faith in God as illusions of the simple-minded and the result of those unwilling to risk seeing reality as truly it is.

Consolations can make you feel bad when they move you toward your authentic human nature. The bad feelings caused by movement toward authenticity are something that applies equally to both your lower physical nature and higher spiritual nature. If you are accustomed to physical pleasures or lifestyles and relationships that fall outside the boundaries of the Commandments and/or Church teaching, the inspiration to cut loose from those pleasures can make you feel distress and anxiety. Remember that Ignatius panicked and felt distress when he realized that he would have to live without the pleasures of his first thirty years for the rest of his life.

The distress you feel when moving toward authenticity in your physical nature is also true when you are moving toward authenticity in your spiritual nature. If you are accustomed to spiritual pleasures that fall outside the boundaries of the Commandments or Church teaching, such as a false definition of success that has shaped your life, you may similarly feel distress, panic, or anxiety when contemplating a change. This is because you are uncertain of what lies beyond the false definition of success. It may feel like a frightening void.

Thus the movement toward authenticity can create fear and distress for both your physical and spiritual natures. The fear aroused by the invitation to live authentically needs to be strongly confronted, because you are being invited towards life, not death. You must learn to resist the fear when moving toward authenticity as defined by the Commandments and Church teaching.

Counter-inspirations called desolations can make you feel good even if they move you away from your authentic human nature. The good feelings caused by movement away from authenticity apply equally to both your lower physical nature and higher spiritual nature. If you are accustomed to physical pleasures that fall outside the boundaries of the Commandments and/or Church teaching, the inspiration to stay committed to those pleasures can make you feel relief—feel good.

The relief you feel when moving away from authenticity in your physical nature is also true when you are moving away from authenticity in your spiritual nature. If you are accustomed to spiritual pleasures that fall outside the boundaries of the Commandments and/or Church teaching, like a false definition of success that has shaped your life, you may similarly feel relief—feel good—in remaining committed to that false identity.

The inspiration to "stay just where you are" will most likely be supported by many logical justifications for why it is best not to change course. By staying put, you have consciously or unconsciously been manipulated by your fears. The fears aroused by the invitation to live authentically need to be strongly confronted, because you are being invited toward death, not life. You must learn to resist the fear when moving toward authenticity as defined by the Commandments and Church teaching.

This is an important discernment lesson. It is critical to understand that inspirations caused by the Divine Inspirer, as well as those caused by the counter-inspirer, can feel good or feel bad, depending on your lifestyle and the corresponding state of your heart and soul.

So always pay attention to discernment principles regarding authentic human nature as defined by the Commandments and Church teaching. It is advisable to keep an eye on the direction the inspirations lead (away from authenticity or towards authenticity) more than whether inspirations make you feel good or bad.

☙

From wanton sin especially, restrain your servant;
let it not rule over me.
Then shall I be blameless and innocent of serious sin.
The precepts of the Lord give joy to the heart.
(Ps 19:14)

❧

Letters from Week Thirty-Two

Dear Fr. Bill,

"Is prayer helping or hurting?"

Sacred Story Prayer meditations one through five, usually twice daily is becoming a natural part of my day and my prayer regimen. Praying on my beginning, through my life so far, receiving God's mercy and forgiveness along the way, and preparing for Eternity with Him, for fifteen minutes twice a day cannot fill me with anything but love and gratitude for my Savior. Like you said in your reply to Week Twenty-Six, keeping my eyes on the final prize is what helps me be able to live in the present moment.

I am constantly asking God for the "eyes to see" my story through the lens of spiritual lessons. I understand that the two types of inspiration- Divine (consolation) and Counter (desolation) are both aware of my strengths, weaknesses, wounded memories, hopes, dreams and fears. God wants me strong. The enemy wants me weak, with a silent conscience.

I realize that consolation is about a healing heart, moving closer to God, feeling the love of and for Christ, my Savior.

The counter-inspirer wants darkness, confusion of a broken heart and soul, attraction to base wants; everything I no longer want or need. What scares me the most is the enemy's attempts to have me doubt my faith, convince me that walking with my Lord here on earth will not lead to anything; that I should just live life to the fullest while I can.

The counter-inspirer wants me to go back to those old narcissistic daydreams that used to consume my days. They were so intense that there would have been no way to invite the Divine-inspirer in to relieve me of those fantasies if I hadn't read about Ignatius' own daydreams/fantasies. Until then I thought I was unique.

Sure, consolations are good, desolation is bad. But, I realize that during this journey, as I grow with discernment toward my authentic human nature, either inspiration can feel good <u>or</u> feel bad at any time, depending on the status of my heart, soul and lifestyle. I will definitely continue to pray on this and surely remain vigilant.

Respectfully,

Ritchie

Dear Ritchie:

As for spiritual advice for Week Thirty-Two, the most important thing that jumped out at me was the fears you describe that living for God will not "lead to anything." The fact that fear surrounds that idea and the fact that the thought of not being "led to anything" must make you feel desolate---loss of faith hope and love—is how you know the message is FALSE! Keep your eyes on Christ as St. Ignatius did.

When his conversion process had just begun, remember, Ignatius feared living for 70 years without the illicit comforts of his life of sinful narcissism. He "discerned" this fear as the voice of the enemy. Remember from the top of the letter: "Don't bend to the fear!"

Pray for me and I will pray for you.

Peace,

Fr. Bill

NOTES

Week 33

FIRST

As before, I will visualize the week ahead and imagine where I can find technology-free zones for my fifteen-minute period(s) of formal prayer each day. I will consider changing the number of prayer sessions each day (from one to two or from two to one). I will make a conscious choice to adjust my prayer schedule, if I judge it a wise decision that will deepen my daily commitment to Christ. I will always use my personal name for God.

SECOND

I pray for the grace to make a lifelong commitment to daily pray movements one through five in the Sacred Story prayer. I will enter my prayer at least once daily as St. Ignatius suggested. I recognize that this prayer will carry me for life, deepening my faith and wisdom, and awakening me to God's truth and love in thought, word, and deed.

THIRD

I continue to ask God's grace to understand spiritual discernment in my life. This week I will explore definitions of spiritual consolation and spiritual desolation as embedded attitudes or lifestyles that can shape my sacred story.

> I will awaken to the present moment.
> I will awaken to my spiritual nature.

I will not make any decisions based on fear.
I will practice sacramental Reconciliation monthly.
I will ask Jesus for help when I am troubled.
I will thank Jesus daily for life's gifts.

This week, I will say this affirmation aloud once daily:
I will strive to curb temptations to react to people and events.
I will ask myself what causes my anger and irritation at people and events.
I will seek to identify the source of my anger and irritation.

ଔ

Continuing in the School of Discernment:

Guidelines for Foundational Healing and Spiritual Growth

Take some time this week to read and reflect on this sixth lesson in discernment. We examined the divine inspiration of spiritual consolation and the counter-inspiration of spiritual desolation last week. This week, we focus on identifying the ways in which these spiritual states manifest as lifestyles. Continue to pay attention to your affective moods to feel the states of consolation and desolation in your story. Look too for embedded lifestyle attitudes that bear the signature characteristics of consolation and desolation.

Consolation and desolation manifest as lifestyles. We can consciously or unconsciously live a life that is either aligned with life or death. The book of Deuteronomy powerfully captures this reality. God placed before the people Israel two distinct choices:

> See, I have today set before you life and good, death and evil. If you obey the commandments of the LORD, your God, which I am giving you today, loving the LORD, your

God, and walking in his ways, and keeping his commandments, statutes and ordinances, you will live and grow numerous, and the LORD, your God, will bless you in the land you are entering to possess. If, however, your heart turns away and you do not obey, but are led astray and bow down to other gods and serve them, I tell you today that you will certainly perish; you will not have a long life on the land which you are crossing the Jordan to enter and possess. I call heaven and earth today to witness against you: I have set before you life and death, the blessing and the curse. Choose life, then, that you and your descendants may live, by loving the LORD, your God, obeying his voice, and holding fast to him. For that will mean life for you, a long life for you to live on the land which the LORD swore to your ancestors, to Abraham, Isaac, and Jacob, to give to them. (Dt 30:15–20)

If we have become insensitive to God's presence, we can be moving away from the Author of Life in our sacred story. We may not be aware of this because of a silenced conscience. If you live in a culture or a subculture that is also insensitive to the Author of Life, you can be doubly challenged to find the path back to life. If you are sensitive to the Author of life, then your sacred story is moving in the direction of producing fruit that endures to eternity. This will be true even if you live in a culture that is insensitive to life's Author. A culture oriented away from God can make choosing the good more difficult, but Christ guarantees the fruit produced. He promises:

Blessed are you when they insult you and persecute you and utter every kind of evil against you [falsely] because of me. Rejoice and be glad, for your reward will be great in heaven. Thus they persecuted the prophets who were before you (Mt 5: 11-12).

We can also choose to align ourselves with subcultures that are counter to the life proposed by the Commandments, Scripture, and the teaching Church. It is difficult to be objective about anti-gospel lifestyles when we are immersed in these subcultures simply because we become habituated to them.

These self-selected subcultures can diminish one's ability to gain objectivity or to discern effectively. These anti-gospel subcultures can be economic, political, artistic, ethnic, intellectual, sexual, athletic, addiction-based, and web-based, just to name a few. The main challenge is that we can cocoon in these cultures, allowing their definitions of happiness, success, the good, the beautiful, and the moral to isolate us from the data coming from deep in our heart or from any other source.

This process of cocooning marks the impenetrable individualism of the present age. For these reasons, consolation and desolation can be described more comprehensively as lifestyles, so one can measure the arc of one's life—one's life style—against the traditional categories Ignatius defined as the signature characteristics of human nature's Author or its enemy.

Thus your individual lifestyle can be discerned as either influenced by the Divine Inspirer or the counter-inspirer. You can identify the trajectory of your story first by reflecting on how you live. If your story and the balance of thoughts, words, and deeds are aligned with the Commandments, Scripture, and the teaching Church, then you are choosing life. If not, then it is time to pray for light.

Divine Inspiration as a Lifestyle

Are you evolving under the divine inspirations aligned to thoughts, words, and deeds harmonious with the Scripture, Commandments, and the teaching Church? If so, the Divine author of your human nature will provide "heart-verification" to alert you to thoughts, words, and deeds that can move you off the true path. The Divine Inspirer will awaken your reason and stir your conscience.

When this happens, you will feel sadness, anxiety, grief, and remorse, the result of thoughts, words, and deeds that lead away from God. God grants these feelings if you are moving toward the counter-inspirations of anti-love, anti-Christ. Such feelings can be difficult and intense. Yet they are a gift and a certain reminder that engaging the gospel values of your faith belief and practice will bring you the peace and hope you seek.

What Are Inordinate Attachments?

If we lack freedom before created things, St. Ignatius says we have an inordinate attachment. I can be inordinately attached to wealth, youth, health, people, material goods, or a definition of success for my life. An inordinate attachment can be almost anything I control (or want to control) that affects my sacred story. The goal is not to get rid of the things that are inordinate attachments. Ignatius tells us that we want to get rid of the attachment to the things. I may have $100 and be inordinately attached to it. Ignatius would advise that I neither keep nor give the money away, but pray for the spiritual freedom to either keep it or let it go. My discernment to keep or surrender is made according to whatever action advances me further along the path of my sacred story. The Foundations Prayer from week 23's E&W (available at sacredstory.net) articulates this principle of spiritual freedom from attachments.

Counter-inspiration as a Lifestyle

Are you evolving under the counter-inspirations opposed to love? Are your thoughts, words, and deeds opposed to the Commandments, Scripture, and the teaching Church? The enemy of your human nature is able to hold you in the grip of your disordered appetites by deceit and false appearances. What leads you away from God, from Love, appears pleasurable and is presented as good, life-giving, fashionable, enlightened, and sophisticated.

Leading away from the sheltering safety of God's love and your authentic human nature, these thoughts, words, and deeds, as excessive appetites, are aptly named false loves, and false loves speak powerfully to broken hearts. If you are in the grip of the counter-inspirations of these false loves, you will feel aversion to engaging the gospel values or be hostile to the Commandments and guidelines of the teaching Church. You will experience difficulty practicing and persevering in your faith.

This is an important discernment lesson. Think of divine inspiration (spiritual consolation) as a healthy lifestyle that may not feel healthy because it is not supported by the culture or subcultures in which you live. Think of counter-inspiration (spiritual desolation) as an unhealthy lifestyle that might not feel unhealthy because it is supported by the culture or subcultures in which you live. So as you learned last week, always keep an eye on the direction the inspirations lead, more than whether inspirations make you feel good or feel bad.

If you want to map some of the influences in your life, make a small chart of the various subcultures where you spend most of your time each week: corporate culture, work environments, internet, social groups and associations, exercise or athletic environments, groups aligned with arts and entertainment, political parties, and the cultures of film, television, and or radio where you spend time. Next to each subculture, write what you believe is its signature characteristic regarding its overall influence on your lifestyle. Does the subculture support divine inspiration or support counter-inspiration? In other words, is the subculture congruent with the values of Scripture, Tradition, and the teaching Church?

Some of these subcultures may be fixed parts of your life due to career, family, or region. Others may be affiliations by personal choice. Do some of the subcultures force you to conceal your religious beliefs? Do you have what St. Ignatius defines as an inordinate attachment to any of these subcultures and the values they espouse?

Does your affiliation with the subculture move you further along in your sacred story or obstruct your movement? Does your affiliation with the subculture increase the ease or difficulty of developing your authentic human nature as guided by the Commandments and Church teaching and traditions?

ᛒ

Set a guard, Lord, before my mouth,
keep watch over the door of my lips.
Do not let my heart incline to evil,
to perform deeds in wickedness.
On the delicacies of evildoers
let me not feast.
Let a righteous person strike me;
it is mercy if he reproves me.
Do not withhold oil from my head
while my prayer opposes their evil deeds.
(Ps 141:3–5)

ᛒ

Letters from Week Thirty-Three

Dear Fr. Bill,

It goes without saying, I continue to pray the five meditations, twice daily.

This week's daily Affirmation gets more use than all the others combined. I've been praying it and practicing it since I received Forty Weeks. If it wasn't for the time, energy, and peace of mind spent reacting to, or attempting to curb the temptation to react to people and events that cause me anger and irritation, I would be as calm and serene as a cloistered monk.

Consolation and desolation manifest as lifestyles. Our lives being either aligned with life or death is now much easier to see. All of the situations you teach about in Forty Weeks come down to two stark possibilities— life and death.

Life	*Death*
Consolation	*Desolation*
Sacred Story	*Anti-Story*
God Inspired Daydreams	*Narcissistic Daydreams*
Healthy	*Unhealthy*
Right	*Wrong*
Good	*Bad*
Drawing Closer to God	*Moving Away from God*

I would consider prison a sub-culture of the culture I was living in before I came to prison. It's kind of funny that I'd mentioned it in my last letter how it would probably be helpful to write more about life in here and how it affects my ability to walk, and grow in Christ. It is difficult at times.

To say there is insensitivity to the Author of Life would be an understatement. Everywhere I turn there is a roadblock to moving in the right direction. It doesn't take much to start doubting how much effort I am willing to put in in order to stay on the righteous path. It is easy to get lost in my old narcissistic thoughts and daydreams and be fooled by the "good" feelings they bring.

For a lack of a better term, I'll say that I must "keep my eyes on the prize". Although I do not choose to align with the counter sub-cultures, I am in it and I have nowhere to go except to Jesus — in my heart, and thoughts, words, and deeds. The prison sub-culture consists of all of the anti-Gospel sub-cultures you mentioned: economic, political, artistic, ethnic, intellectual, sexual, athletic, and addiction based. Luckily, I've been able to bond with a few like-minded (like-hearted) men and we support each other to get through this.

I still strive to live the Gospel as St. Francis did. That leaves little room for inordinate attachments. I know I am living a lifestyle which is Divinely inspired. My conscience has been awakened and I have been able, through God's grace, to see where my influences are leading me.

Respectfully,

Ritchie

Dear Ritchie:

The Affirmations capture many of the discernment lessons of St. Ignatius. Use them as you have been and they will be nice short-hand ways to keep your heart alert to the movements of the spirits that lead to life and that lead to death.

Prison is definitely a sub-culture in and of itself. I am sure that there is not much support for the direction you want your life to go. However, realize the most people on the "outside" are living in a culture that is quite hostile to the values of the Gospel, too.

Most of us have to go into our hearts to find the Lord. Your time will come when you can belong to a faith community on the outside once your prison time is up and a new journey begins. Until that time, the Lord has placed you in that "community" to strengthen your resolve and also to help others who might be open to the direction you are taking. Give thanks to the Lord for the blessings you will receive in prison. He has also given you some friends who are "like-hearted" to support you.

And remember, I write this on the Feast of St. Francis so he will also be guiding you daily.

Let's pray for each other.

Peace,

Fr. Bill

Dear Fr. Bill,

I hope this missive finds you well. I am extremely good right now. A whole lot of recent ups and downs, but all is well as I write this.

These past few weeks of discernment study have been awesome. Everything seems to be coming together. I've never been more hopeful about my state of mind, my relationship with my Savior, and my future, through eternity.

In addition to learning more of discernment, these most recent four weeks — thirty-three through thirty six have also reminded me of things I was taught to do in earlier weeks, but have let slip to the side. I'd been neglecting things which until I was reminded, seemed to be not so important. What a mistake! I will definitely be recommitting to listening, watching and praying; daily, weekly and monthly journaling; declare, describe, descend, denounce, and decide. And, of course, I will continue praying the five meditations daily — Creation, Presence, Memory, Mercy and Eternity.

If possible, it would be helpful if you would continue to send a few cards/tracts with each of your letters. The ones containing the five meditations, The Foundation's Prayer, and the Narcissists Examen. I've passed them around and have raised some interest in a few of the fellows here. Actually, feel free to send anything you may deem helpful to me or anyone I may pass it along to.

I received your response to Weeks Twenty-Nine through Thirty-Three today. Thank you for your insight, advice, and encouragement. We are in the home-stretch and I am quite excited to see what the future brings. There may be some hope for me yet ☺.

I think it's great that Deacon Pat has been able to connect you with another inmate who wants to do Forty Weeks. I will definitely keep Anthony in my prayers. Hopefully, I'll come across someone soon who is receptive to the program also. I'm sharing a bit with some the guys around here. We'll see what happens.

Thanks for everything, Fr, Bill.

Respectfully,

Ritchie

Dear Ritchie:

I write this note to you on the Feast of St. Francis of Assisi. He was the saint I took for my Confirmation name. I will ask for his guidance as I respond to your most recent letter.

It is good to hear that you are getting so much out of the weeks on spiritual discernment. You will find your capacity to understand those rules will only increase with each passing month and year as you stay engaged with the Examen prayer of Forty Weeks. And yes, do go back over those exercises that benefit your spiritual awakening.

Enclosed with this letter are five each of the cards you wanted. I will say a prayer that they end up in the hands of the men who need them the most and who are open to receive the Spirit's insights.

Thanks for praying for Anthony. Like I said, he is just at the beginning of the program. He is twenty years younger than you and has a much shorter prison sentence but still needs many prayers.

I used some of your letters for a Catholic Men's Retreat this past weekend. Your experience and reflections were helpful in unlocking some hearts and minds. So have hope that this project will help many people.

I am keeping you in my prayers, Ritchie and I know you are doing the same for me.

Peace,

Fr. Bill Watson, S.J.

NOTES

Week 34

FIRST

I will visualize my week ahead to identify places I can find technology-free zones for my fifteen-minutes prayer times each day. I am also learning that my resolution to spend no more and no less than fifteen minutes in those prayer periods increases my fidelity to the practice. I will always use my personal name for God.

SECOND

I will continue this thirty-fourth week by praying the five meditations of Sacred Story prayer. As St. Ignatius suggested, I enter my prayer at least once daily. Each time I pray, my heart opens more fully, and I am carried forward in my sacred story.

THIRD

I will ask God to help me understand the school of spiritual discernment. This week I will ponder St. Ignatius's wisdom on how I ought to act when influenced by the desolation of counter-inspiration.

I will awaken to the present moment.
I will awaken to my spiritual nature.
I will not make any decisions based on fear.
I will practice sacramental Reconciliation monthly.
I will ask Jesus for help when I am troubled.

I will thank Jesus daily for life's gifts.

This week, I will say this affirmation aloud once daily:
I will give thanks for what angers and upsets me;
identifying their source will set me free.

I will strive to listen, watch, and pray. Listen, watch, and pray.
I will listen, watch, and pray!

ᘓ

Continuing in the School of Discernment:
Guidelines for Foundational Healing and Spiritual Growth

Take some time this week to read and reflect on this seventh lesson in discernment. Last week we examined the divine inspiration of spiritual consolation and the counter-inspiration of spiritual desolation as embedded in our lifestyles. This week we will consider St. Ignatius's wisdom on how we can help defuse the impact of counter-inspiration's desolation when in its grip.

Four Principles for Defusing Counter-inspirations

Personal sin, addictions, and emotional/psychological wounds make a person vulnerable to spiritual desolation. When gripped by spiritual desolation, your faith, hope, and love is diminished. Ignatius offers indispensable guidance when you are under the influence of counter-inspirations and are spiritually desolate, discouraged, hopeless, and frustrated. If you closely adhere to these guidelines and act on them, you will avoid much pain and grief in your life. Do not despair if you do not understand the guidelines now. There will come a time when this wisdom will help you.

Ignatius offers four principles for how we ought to act when tempted by the counter-inspirations of desolation.

1. Never change course when in desolation!
When spiritually desolate and experiencing a loss of faith, hope, and love, never change course away from the positive resolutions and decisions you reached while under the influence of the divine inspiration of consolation.

Human nature's enemy feeds on spiritual/emotional wounds and on broken hearts. The counter-inspirations may seem logical, but they never lead to freedom, peace, or your heart's healing. None of the choices and decisions influenced by the counter-inspirations of desolation, no matter how utterly logical they might appear, will ever increase faith, hope, or love. One must be vigilant when tempted by an urgent or compelling need to act immediately. When you feel compelled by an anxious urgency to reach a decision or engage an action, this is a clear sign of counter-inspirations at work

2. During times of desolation, redouble efforts to open and orient your heart to God.
Use prayer, examination of conscience, and perhaps some simple penance or fasting to seek God's grace (Mk 9:29).

Counter-inspirations make it difficult to see and feel authentic human nature. Amplifying positive efforts on spiritual fronts might feel incredibly difficult. Yet St. Ignatius's experience demonstrated that we need, at these times, extra exercise of spirit and body to resist desolation. A determined spirit is necessary during such times. Also, be attentive to thoughts, words, or deeds that are based on inaccurate assessments of your authentic human nature. Allow the times of desolation to instruct you!

3. Actively trust God to provide the essential support and grace necessary to withstand these times of trial and purification.
The support you need will come from your natural abilities, assisted by divine grace. You may feel completely overwhelmed by temptations or

the darkness of spirit associated with disordered attractions and compulsive behaviors. Yet there is sufficient grace for salvation, even if the logic of the counter-inspiration indicates otherwise! Jesus, the Divine Physician, is very close to you during these times of purification. When you encounter the full force and darkness of counter-inspirations, be assured that God is present to you even though you may not feel God's presence.

Watch for Obsessive Thinking

You are always either in a state of consolation or desolation. These lessons are teaching you to notice these two spiritual states that have been with you all your life. If you find yourself becoming obsessive about tracking what state you are in at each moment of the day, then you have succumbed to counter-inspirations. Strive for an alert heart and mind. Pray to avoid an obsessive attitude. Being aware will serve your spiritual growth. Being obsessive will harm your spiritual growth.

Do not be deceived by the feelings, no matter how strong or mocking they might appear. This is especially true when your weaknesses, shame, and failings are painfully highlighted. Through trial and error, St. Ignatius learned that God is not absent. Trust Ignatius's wise counsel, and affirm your faith in God during times when you do not feel the Spirit. Instead, consciously thank God, who in complete faithfulness, will embrace you. Thank God aloud and affirm God's salvific role in your sacred story.

4. *Intentionally strive to cultivate patience, and persevere in the religious practices of your faith when influenced by the desolation of counter-inspiration.*

The divine inspiration of consolation always returns. In the interim, use the means of prayer, penance, and self-examination to resist and gain the most from these times of trial. To counter the anxiety you may experience, embrace desolations as an opportunity to deepen your maturing life with God. Be not afraid.

Considerable spiritual and human progress, as well as illumination, will result from your patience and perseverance during these trials. In time, you will discover that these times of stress, endured in faith, can produce the enlightenment, healing, peace, and hope you seek. Therefore, do not fear them.

Say aloud the one thing that makes you question God's love for you. Now hear the Lord say: "Nothing in the past or the future; no angel or demon; no height or depth; nothing in all of creation will ever separate you from my love in Christ Jesus" (Rom 8:38–39).

When to Make Decisions

Counter-inspirations are usually accompanied by anxiety, electrical excitement, and a compelling urge to act quickly and definitively. Never make decisions when you sense these emotional states.

Divine inspirations are usually accompanied by a deep and abiding peace and calm with no urge to act quickly or definitively. Only make decisions during times of divine inspiration's peace and calm.

Learning the difference between these two spiritual states of heart/mind will serve you very well. It is hard to resist the compulsive urge to act quickly when in the grip of counter-inspiration's anxieties. Resist! You will save yourself a great deal of pain the enemy of human nature desires to inflict upon you.

લ

Let your work be seen by your servants
and your glory by their children;
and may the gracious care of the Lord our God be ours;
prosper the work of our hands for us!
Prosper the work of our hands!
(Ps 90:16–17)

ખ

Letters from Week Thirty-Four

Dear Fr. Bill,

With discernment always at the forefront of my thought these days, it seems I am considering all things more intently. Again, this week, our daily affirmation is spot on: "I will give thanks for what angers and upsets me; identifying their sources will set me free. I will strive to listen, watch and pray; listen, watch and pray; I will listen, watch and pray". By listening, watching, and praying, by God's grace I <u>am</u> able to identify the source. So rewarding.

I never ceased to be amazed at how everything in Forty Weeks comes at the right time. The past week or so has been quite trying. Decisions needed to be made concerning if or how I am going to continue with the Life Connections Program. Changes are occurring, difficulties and roadblocks have arisen, and, as a result, my attitude had become less than acceptable – to me. I was neglecting my spiritual needs and responsibilities.

I've been anxious, angry and self-centered. I had made a decision that would not be in my best interest in the long run. I thought of "the urge to stop Sacred Story practice always comes before my greatest breakthrough". And then, just when I was about to make my decision final I read, ". Never change course when in desolation". And I was seriously in desolation!

I read Mark 9:29 and Romans 8:38-39 as you suggested. I spoke with one of our spiritual guides, received positive counsel, including the suggestion to read 2 Corinthians 4:1-18., particularly 7-10 and 16-18. All very good stuff. Needless to say, Fr. Bill, chapter thirty-four saved me from myself this week.

God <u>is</u> present no matter how dark things may seem, even if I can't feel Him. And the fact that there is no gray area- I am either in a state of consolation or desolation, makes things easier for me. Things get tricky.

The counter-inspirer is insidious, masking itself as good and logical. I look forward to the "...spiritual and human progress, as well as illumination..." that is sure to follow.

Respectfully,

Ritchie

Dear Ritchie:

It became clear to me in 1994 that I was 24/7 being bombarded by spiritual messages from both the enemy and from the Holy Spirit. Prior to this time in my life, I considered discernment something that happened only on a retreat. Now I know it is necessary all the time.

It is good that these lessons in Week Thirty-Four come at just the right time. YES! One of the most important lessons is to never make a decision in a time of spiritual desolation. Absolutely Never!!

The data you are getting is corrupt and the decision will be a bad one. It is difficult however to be patient because the false message is that if you "cut and run" you will be relieved from the difficulties you are experiencing. That is a false message. You will run only into greater long-term problems.

I am grateful that you learned this lesson prior to making a bad choice regarding your Life Connections program, Ritchie.

Peace to you,

Fr. Bill

NOTES

Week 35

FIRST

I resolve to spend no more and no less than fifteen minutes in each formal prayer period. At the beginning of the week, I will visualize where each will be, in some place apart: a technology-free zone. I will always use my personal name for God.

SECOND

For this thirty-fifth week, I resolve, by God's grace, to commit for life to praying meditations one through five in the Sacred Story prayer. As St. Ignatius suggested, I will enter my prayer at least once daily. Also, I may find it necessary to recommit to the simple, daily journal exercises explained in week 16.

THIRD

I ask God's grace to deepen my knowledge of spiritual discernment as this week I consider the three sources of desolation identified by St. Ignatius.

I will awaken to the present moment.
I will awaken to my spiritual nature.
I will not make any decisions based on fear.
I will practice sacramental Reconciliation monthly.
I will ask Jesus for help when I am troubled.

I will thank Jesus daily for life's gifts.

This week, I will say this affirmation aloud once daily:
Everyone has been mortally wounded spiritually, psychologically, and
physically by Original Sin and the loss of paradise.
Journeying with Christ to the roots
of my sins and addictions
will help break their grip.

ଔ

Continuing in the School of Discernment

Before proceeding, it is important to revisit the indispensable practice
of the daily, weekly, and monthly journal exercises.

A Review of the Journal Exercises

Early in the Sacred Story prayer journey, you wrote two things that
surfaced in your life each day: something that brought encouragement,
and something that upset you or generated fear, anger, or grief. By
briefly focusing every day on these two categories, you will be recording
the necessary data that will help you to understand Ignatius's spiritual
discernment rules in your own story and life history.

Every day, write one experience that increases faith, hope, and love.
Write a second experience that decreases your faith, hope, and love.
Make sure you write a complete sentence. For example, "The Sunday
homily about forgiveness helped me understand God's mercy and
brought me hope." or "The Sunday homily about forgiveness upset me
and made me wonder if God can ever forgive some of the things I have
done." The first experience increases faith, hope, and love; the second
diminishes faith, hope, and love.

These short statements are different than a diary or a regular journal. The statements help to track trends in your spiritual life. Done faithfully, you will begin to identify the signature of God's grace in your particular joys and encouragements, and the signature of the enemy of human nature's presence in your particular temptations and discouragements. For this week, every day, write two experiences you noticed from each source (instead of the usual one experience from each source). This exercise ought to be no more than one minute in length, as explained in the lesson from week 16.

At the end of each week, identify the most significant consolations and desolations. Write two short sentences at week's end that capture what you observe to be the most significant statement on each side of the spiritual divide: spiritual consolation and spiritual desolation.

At month's end, create a monthly summary from your eight weekly consolations and desolations. Sort through those statements (four consolations and four desolations), and identify the two that you consider have most increased and most decreased your faith, hope, and love. These monthly summary statements, for both consolation and desolation, might be a new statement that is a composite of the four you wrote. Or it may be one of the four you wrote that stands out as the most important in each category (consolation or desolation).

An analogy from the medical world might help. Imagine I am diabetic. Daily (or perhaps hourly) I have to monitor my blood sugar. I will become quite attentive to foods and drink that increase or decrease my blood sugar.

In like fashion, this simple writing exercise, done faithfully—daily, weekly, and monthly—will provide spiritual illumination on what increases and decreases your faith, hope, and love. Graced insights will reveal how God and the enemy of your human nature work in your life history. Grace will attract you toward peace and hope, while the enemy's influence will manifest in discouragement and despair.

Guidelines for Foundational Healing and Spiritual Growth

Take some time this week to read and reflect on this eighth lesson in discernment. Last week we examined four important ways to respond during a time of counter-inspiration's spiritual desolation. This week we consider three reasons Ignatius gives for why we experience spiritual desolation.

Three Reasons for Spiritual Desolation

Personal sin, addictions, and your emotional/psychological wounds make you vulnerable to spiritual desolation. When gripped by spiritual desolation, faith, hope, and love diminish. Ignatius offers indispensable guidance to assist you through the temptations of these counter-inspirations.

Recall that when you are spiritually desolate, you will experience discouragement, hopelessness, and frustration. By paying close attention to these guidelines and applying them daily, you will avoid much pain and grief in your life. Do not despair or get frustrated if you do not understand the guidelines now. There will come a time when this wisdom will be crystal clear.

God allows us to experience desolation to orient our hearts toward genuine love and our true human nature. We experience counter-inspiration's desolation for one of three reasons:

1. Wrong Choices
Desolation can be directly related to wrong choices in thoughts, words, and deeds made under the influence of the false logic of the counter-inspirations.

God removes the divine inspiration of consolation as a holy warning that you are straying from your authentic human nature. God acts this way to stir your conscience to remind you to return to authenticity. God allows the loss of consolation so you can feel the consequences of your thoughts, words, and deeds associated with counter-inspirational choices. Such false choices will, in due course, destroy relationships, creation, human life, faith, hope, and love.

Essentially, your false choices erode and destroy the very things that God provides, so you can find fulfillment, communion, and peace in this life and eternal joy in the next. Our own choices and the consequences of those choices lead us to experience the reality of counter-inspiration's desolation.

2. Healing
God can allow desolation, which is directly linked with your human growth and spiritual progress, in order to awaken your whole being—spirit, mind and body—to its spiritual, emotional, and psychological wounds.

Desolation reveals the ways in which your destructive desires and habits have taken root in your spirit, mind, and body. Desolation is evidence of how your wounds contribute to the division of your being. Spiritual progress and forward movement in your life story is only possible when you awaken and confront this damaging pattern.

We need to be courageous. Identifying and uprooting these appetites and habits can be likened to spiritual surgery. This awakening, and the spiritual renewal and healing it initiates, can at times be painful and intense, resulting in our feeling hopeless and/or abandoned. But recall that spiritual maturity cannot be evaluated by unpleasant feelings. Take courage and walk forward, trusting in God.

It is essential that you allow these deeply rooted destructive tendencies to surface, so that a new consciousness and freedom can be born. Giving God permission to move forward with your spiritual growth is the only way these habits, grounded in counter-inspirations, can be uprooted, defused, and healed.

Ignatius taught that God supports us most especially during these times when we can feel lost. At times, we might feel condemned by the darkness in our being: heart, mind, and body. These can be present events or ones we experience through memories. St. Ignatius advised, based on his own experiences of these intense moments, that God's grace is enough to support us.

You can have feelings of desolation associated with the awareness of your disordered appetites and a human nature wounded by sin. The feelings do not indicate how God views and feels about you. Since these feelings offer a false reading of your authentic human nature, do not be fooled into believing that God does not love and cherish you because you feel and experience these periods of darkness.

You are completely distinct from the darkness or the disordered, shameful appetites that you experience. God loves you and supports your most authentic self as you suffer the stripping away of the pain, sin, narcissism, and wounds that hide your authentic human nature.

Feelings of darkness are associated with your false self: the false loves; the broken heart and dreams; the narcissism and pride; the extravagant appetites and the destructive drives associated with your spiritual and psychological wounds. With your cooperation, God is gradually uprooting these from your heart.[22]

3. Growth
Counter-inspirations of desolation may appear during times of spiritual advancement.

After a period of purification marked by desolation, your heart finds peace in the divine inspiration of consolation. During these graced rests, you may be tempted to believe the illusion that you have arrived and/or reached the end of your spiritual journey. You experience this state of calm and peace as definitive and feel that you have achieved sanctity, completion, and holiness.

During these times, and almost imperceptibly, a spirit of pride and self-sufficiency takes hold in your heart. When this happens (when, not if!) the counter-inspirations of desolation return as a warning. This happened to St. Ignatius once. He felt that he was among the just and that his spiritual growth was complete, but then, having experienced desolation, he realized that he was actually only beginning on the road to salvation.

Everything achieved up to this point has occurred through God's grace and through your cooperation with that grace. Grace has reunited you with God, and as a result the virtues of humility, trust, and dependence are beginning to develop.

God allows desolations as a warning to remind you that although you have grown in authenticity and holiness, you are still susceptible to the narcissism and destructive pride that will halt all your progress toward further union with God. Be watchful for the first signs of narcissism and pride. They usually manifest when you start to fall away from your spiritual disciplines and other practices of your faith. You might say to yourself, "I am healed." or "I don't need those practices anymore." or "At least I don't heed them as much as I used to!" You are deceiving yourself and being deceived, to believe such things.

Therefore, cultivate humility during the consoling times of the divine inspiration. Use your periods of consolation as a preparation for the times of desolation. Be aware and awake, always anticipating the return of desolation.

Plan ahead for when desolation makes its return. During your time of consolation, remember how helpless you felt during your time of desolation. This serves as a reminder that God is the only one who stabilizes your heart with the divine inspiration of consolation.

When the counter-inspiration of desolation returns, pray to understand which of Ignatius's three reasons might be its origin. When under the influence of desolation, hold steady! Nurture humility and patience, doing everything possible to orient your thoughts, words, and deeds toward an awareness of God's presence in your life. Recall Creation, Presence, Memory, Mercy, and Eternity.

Remember that God holds you fast during the divine inspirations of consolation and holds you even closer during the cleansing times of desolation. Affirm your faith in God. Hold fast to the spiritual disciplines offered here as well as the other practices of your faith. Seek stability and fidelity in times of peace and calm as well as in times of turbulence and struggle.

CB

Behold, the eye of the Lord is upon those who fear him,
upon those who count on his mercy,
To deliver their soul from death,
and to keep them alive through famine.
Our soul waits for the Lord, who is our help and our shield.
May your kindness, O Lord, be upon us
who have put our hope in you.
(Ps 33:18–22)

ᔥ

Letters from Week Thirty-Five

Dear Fr. Bill,

Just like it says in the beginning of Week Thirty-Five, "I resolve by God's grace, to commit for life to praying meditations one through five in the Sacred Story Prayer". That's it. Done deal. I am committed to praying Creation, Presence, Memory, Mercy, and Eternity once daily, but I hope to continue twice-daily sessions. Also, I am recommitting to my daily, weekly and monthly journaling, which I definitely need to become more responsible at. Identifying and tracking the patterns of consolation and desolation should be helpful towards being able to employ discernment in real time during my day.

Three Reasons for Spiritual Desolation:

1. I can definitely see how I can experience desolation through my wrong choices in thoughts, words and deeds. One "innocent" or "harmless" moment of reminiscing about the "good old days" can easily snowball into negativity, permeating every aspect of my life. It doesn't take long or, much effort on my part. The fact that God would remove His divine inspiration as a "holy warning" definitely means he wants us to learn from our desolation so we can feel the consequences and, I suppose, make it easier to identify His divine inspiration of consolation when it is present.

2. I suppose I should appreciate God allowing desolation in order to awaken my whole being, but it kind of scares me that, maybe someday, I may not make it back. That I get stuck in my old habits, addictions and sins. The old narcissism of selfish, self-gratifying daydreams, the sinful life I was trapped in for almost fifty years. It is, at times, a very scary proposition. It is good and encouraging to know I am <u>not</u> the disordered, shameful appetites that I experience, that God loves and supports me and I work through this.

393

3. *Desolation may appear during times of spiritual advancement. I certainly hope so since I've been under the impression that I have been advancing spiritually, albeit sometimes very, very slowly, for some time now. I am reminded of another Sacred Story Affirmation: Times of peace and hope always give way to times of difficulty and stress. Times of difficulty and stress always give way to times of peace and hope. I must remain vigilant and always keep in mind that both inspirations are powerful. The Boy Scout motto comes to mind – "Be Prepared". I need to remain prayerful and hold steady.*

Respectfully,

Ritchie

Dear Ritchie:

When we make mental commitments, there are actually things that change in the neural networks of our brains that help us imbed new behavioral patterns. So the mind, heart and will all work together as God intended. If you keep telling yourself you are committed for life, that life will become a reality for you.

As long as you live, the pattern of consolation and desolation will move back and forth. Understanding the reasons for the desolation is critical, as you are learning in this week's exercises. In the first one, you want to know if you get too close to a hot flame and your body recoils. Desolation makes your spirit recoil and causes you to look at what is usually the most common reason it happens to us; failure to live our faith daily and do our spiritual work.

Secondly, the fear that you will "not make it back" is if course, from your old friend, the enemy of human nature. God has assured your victory and you simply thank him when you get fearful and say "Lord, by your power and grace you will bring me home. Thank you!"

Thirdly, God wants you to do the right thing because it is right, not because it always makes you feel consoled. So in order to get to the next step, consolation is removed (once you have learned the right things do to at a certain level) so you can jump to the next.

A young boy will be praised for the first time he ties his shoes on his own, but it would be a bit strange if he had to be praised every day for the rest of his life in order to do that task. Once we have learned something, it is on to the next lesson for our own spiritual growth and maturity!

Let's pray for each other Ritchie, that we can do a little better each day.

Peace,

Fr. Bill

NOTES

Week 36

FIRST

I resolve to spend no more than fifteen minutes in each formal prayer session and to visualize my week ahead for where these will be. I will choose a place apart. I will always use my personal name for God.

SECOND

I continue praying meditations one through five in the Sacred Story prayer in this thirty-sixth week. I enter my prayer at least once daily, as St. Ignatius suggested. If I have not been faithful to my journal exercises, I will recommit to this very important discipline.

THIRD

I ask God's grace to deepen my understanding of spiritual discernment as I consider two of the three strategies the enemy of human nature employs to stall my spiritual growth.

I will awaken to the present moment.
I will awaken to my spiritual nature.
I will not make any decisions based on fear.
I will practice sacramental Reconciliation monthly.
I will ask Jesus for help when I am troubled.
I will thank Jesus daily for life's gifts.
This week, I will say this affirmation aloud once daily:

I will not waste time worrying about my sins and failures.
I will use my time wisely and ask God to help
me understand the source of my sins and failings.
I will trust that Christ came to heal all my wounds.

ങ

Continuing in the School of Discernment:
Guidelines for Foundational Healing and Spiritual Growth

Take some time this week to read and reflect on this ninth lesson in discernment. Last week, we examined the three principal reasons we experience counter-inspiration's spiritual desolation. This week we look at two of the three attack strategies used by the enemy of human nature to obstruct our spiritual progress.

All three strategies use elements of our life story as weapons against us: our unconscious fears; our psychological and spiritual vulnerabilities; and our long-standing addictive, compulsive, and/or sinful habits. These sinful habits do not make us happy. But they are familiar behaviors, and the pain of the familiar is often preferred to the fear of the unknown.

Ignatius learned these three attack strategies from his own experience of being deceived during his conversion process. Learn from his hard-earned wisdom. You might be at a place in your life where you have not yet encountered any of these tactics. If that is the case, the explanations may not make sense now, but they will in time. Notice again that fear is the common basis for all lines of attack.

Three Strategies of the Enemy of Human Nature:
Frighten, Deceive, Viciously Attack

When you engage your faith practice daily, the enemy of human nature can employ three subtle and malicious lines of attack to discourage you. He will use the weaknesses associated with your vices, your extravagant appetites, your compulsive drives, your spiritual/psychological wounds, and your broken heart. This week we will consider the first two of the three strategies:

1. Frighten: Fear and panic attacks are strategically employed to block growth.
If you stay committed to the process of uprooting vices, sins, addictions, and destructive habits from your life and heart, you may be attacked with waves of fear and panic to turn you away from the healing process. If you waver in your commitment to the healing process, the fear and panic can intensify exponentially. In the extreme, you can be paralyzed by unrelenting terror and withering dread.[23]

Directly confront the menacing fear. If you hold steadfast to the commitments associated with your spiritual and psychological growth, the panic and fear will eventually abate. If you consistently confront the fears and hold fast to the healing process, you will notice that the strategy of "fear and dread" is just that: a strategy. As a ploy, the fear and the dread are never realized. Nonetheless, it is maliciously effective if and when you surrender to it.[24]

2. Deceive: Narcissism and false values masquerade as true love and authentic values.
Those committed to allowing vices, addictions, sins, and destructive habits to be uprooted from their life and heart will also confront other tricks. The enemy can portray narcissism as authentic love and vices as positive values. These are tactics of the father of lies to deceive you. The enemy of human nature knows that every heart searches for true love.

But every heart is also divided and broken by the effects of its multiple spiritual and psychological wounds. The counter-inspiration of desolation blinds your heart's perception of what is spiritually and humanly authentic, and what leads to eternal life. Your heart can be easily fooled and tempted by false promises of love. All false loves are illicit, because they are lusts masquerading as love. False loves are like mirages for parched and anxious hearts hoping to quench their thirst and find comfort. Instead of providing lasting peace, these illicit loves—illusions really—merely intensify longings, self-deception, self-preoccupation, and narcissism, ultimately leading to spiritual and psychological death.

Be Not Afraid!

The enemy of our human nature likes to conceal himself and manipulate us with our conscious and unconscious fears. It is a carefully planned strategy. The strategy of the enemy is to play on our greatest vulnerabilities, even menace us and taunt us with them.

A part of the carefully designed strategy is to keep us bending to our fears. The more we bend to them, the stronger the fears become the next time we consider opposing them. This is why it is imperative to call fear's bluff and confront the fear—whatever fear it may be. "Be not afraid" is one of the most common phrases in the Old and New Testaments. God uses hope. The enemy uses fear. Discern the difference in their "voices."

It is easy to observe the corrosive effects of sins and addictions in other individuals and other groups. But when you are in their grip, it is difficult to imagine these sins and addictions as anything other than a precious lifeline. God clearly sees the corrosive and poisonous effects of false loves on persons, families, societies, and nature. But those in their grip are seduced into believing in false love's comforts, because all false loves can appear as good, life-giving, and natural. The deception to believe false loves as good, life-giving, and natural is complicated by evil's evolution in political and financial collectives, in educational systems and philosophies, in family structures and social networks, and in culture and entertainment. Evil's evolution in all of these can support and reward those trapped in the deception.

The varieties of deception and seduction are as numerous as the ways a

---

Sin is Missing the Mark

The most common word in Greek for sin is hamartia, meaning to miss the mark. If we define sin primarily by what it does—destroy relationships—then sin means missing the mark in both our understanding and practice of "right relationship." Let's take a recurrent song lyric theme: "How can something that feels so right be so wrong?" If the love this lyric expresses stands outside gospel values, then "what feels so right" can be an experience of love that feels better than the lifelessness one had previously experienced. Or here's a variation on this lyric: "Feels so good to be loved so bad." This expression demonstrates the "false love" of lust that has become an addiction. Both types of love might feel better than what one had previously experienced. But both loves miss the mark on the true love God wants for us. They will not ultimately bring us to the fullness of our authentic human nature. This is why they are "wrong" in God's eyes and why Jesus does not bless them. Jesus wants much more for the Father's beloved children.

---

heart can be broken. God will not sanction these lusts because they issue from a violated heart and lead to your heart's further violation. Once acted upon, you will most assuredly violate the hearts of others. God is Love: the origin, the end, and the defender of the human heart. While God is infinitely merciful with our struggles, God cannot sanction anything that breaks your heart, destroys your authentic human nature, or leads to your spiritual death.

Bring all false loves to full consciousness. Examine them in light of the writings of saints, doctors of the Church, and the mystical Christian traditions of West and East. Identify and name your sins, addictions, and habits truthfully as false lovers. Speak about these false loves with a spiritual guide who holds sacred the Tradition and the Gospels

You will not be convinced of these false loves' unholy origin until you are honest about them. Examine your false loves in the light of day, not by the cover of night. Here in the light of grace, they will be revealed as neither true servants of the heart nor pathways to the Divine. By exposing them, you will not lose love and life, as you fear. You will find, eventually, the path to Love itself: the Christ who is worthy of your total devotion and self-surrender.

When you are in the grip of false loves, activate Ignatius's "Truth Paradigm" (as we first learned in week 16). With Christ at your side, consciously take these steps:

✠ Declare to Christ the specific sin, addiction, or destructive compulsion, and name it as a false lover.

✠ Describe to Christ the specific sin, addiction, or destructive compulsion as coming from the enemy of your human nature.

✠ Descend with Christ into your memory to see and feel your first experience of this specific sin, addiction, or compulsion. Ask Christ to compassionately reveal the stress fractures, loneliness, and wounds in your heart it promised to satisfy.

✠ Denounce, with Christ as your witness, the sin, addiction, or destructive compulsion, for the ruinous effect in your life, others' lives, and society.

✠ Decide for Christ to heal this wound, defuse the stress, anxiety, and fear feeding it, and transform its damaging effects on your life into sacred story.

C3

For I know well the plans I have in mind for you—
plans for your welfare and not for woe,
so as to give you a future of hope.
When you call me, and come and pray to me,
I will listen to you.
When you look for me, you will find me.
Yes, when you seek me with all your heart.
(Jer 29:11–13)

80

Letters from Week Thirty-Six

Dear Fr. Bill,

I definitely appreciate all that you included in Week Thirty-Six. Our sinful habits do not make us happy and the pain of the familiar is often preferable to the fear of the unknown. Also, so much of my falling into old thoughts, words and deeds, bringing on desolation, can be attributed to fear.

After reading the box entitled "Be not afraid", I sat in silent thought for a while and was able to remember incidents all the way back to elementary school when a simple fear of something as minor as not doing well on a test would lead to skipping school, doing something wrong during the time I would have been in school, having to lie about it, maybe skipping school again in order to not have to explain where I was last time, and on and on. I see how one little instance of fear can set the stage for an entire life of desolation – a vicious, sinful, narcissistic cycle.

If I am not constantly vigilant, if I am not in constant conscious contact with God, then I am even more vulnerable to the enemy's three lines of attack. I can definitely relate to the "fear and dread". I can't tell you how many times I've felt or actually said, "It's no use". I cannot surrender to this strategy.

Luckily, I've had thirty-five weeks to be able to realize my sins, habits and addictions: my false loves. I have a pretty good grasp on what is good and what is not good for me. Even when I am immersed in my destructiveness it usually does not take long to recognize it, even though some are more subtle than others.

Recognizing does not always mean I can or even want to get out of them right away. Once recognized I try to announce it aloud. I had gotten out of the habit of Declare, Describe, Descend, Denounce, and Decide. I will definitely re-incorporate these steps into my day.

Respectfully,

Ritchie

Dear Ritchie:

The most important insight you learned in Week Thirty-Six is that memory you had of grade school and out of fear of doing poorly, skipping school. That led to a lie and another lie and obviously more fear. So remember that the author of this fear is the enemy of human nature and his goal is to get to you act on the fear in order to increase your fears.

You would do well Ritchie, to let this early life experience be a spring board to look at other experiences in your life where the same pattern was present. This is one of the main tactics that the enemy will use to keep you off balance and distressed. He will keep using the same old tired tactic as long as it continues to be effective in messing you up. There is no need to pull out new tricks when the old ones work just fine! The enemy takes delight in your distress so work against him and his ways, Ritchie.

Do Not Be Afraid! And when you are, counter the fear by acting just the opposite of what it is telling you to do and keep your heart on Christ.

Peace,

Fr. Bill

NOTES

Week 37

FIRST

Visualizing the week ahead, I will decide where to spend my fifteen minutes in each formal prayer period. As before, I will select a place apart, a technology-free zone. I will always use my personal name for God.

SECOND

I will continue this thirty-seventh week by praying meditations one through five in the Sacred Story prayer. I will enter my prayer at least once daily, as St. Ignatius suggested. I will make a firm commitment to the simple, daily journal exercises, because they are an invaluable part of awakening to my sacred story.

THIRD

I will ask God's grace to help me master spiritual discernment. This week, I am invited to understand the third of the three strategies the enemy of human nature employs to stall my spiritual growth.

I will awaken to the present moment.
I will awaken to my spiritual nature.
I will not make any decisions based on fear.
I will practice sacramental Reconciliation monthly.
I will ask Jesus for help when I am troubled.

I will thank Jesus daily for life's gifts.
This week, I will say this affirmation aloud once daily:
I alone control Christ's ability to transform my life into a sacred story.
The process begins when I ask for the grace
to honestly name my sins and addictions.
The process continues when I invite Christ to illuminate my narcissism.
Only God's grace and mercy can write my sacred story.

ↅ

Continuing in the School of Discernment:
Guidelines for Foundational Healing and Spiritual Growth

Take some time on the weekend or during the week to read and reflect on this tenth lesson in spiritual discernment. Last week we examined two of the three attack strategies used by the enemy of human nature to obstruct spiritual progress. All three strategies use elements of our life story as weapons against us: our unconscious fears, our psychological/spiritual vulnerabilities, and our long-standing habits. These habits do not create long-lasting happiness, but they are familiar. The boredom and/or pain of the familiar is often preferred to the fear of the unknown.

This week we examine the third attack strategy used by the enemy of human nature to obstruct our spiritual progress. Just as in the first two lines of attack, fear is the weapon used here by the enemy of human nature.

3. Viciously Attack
When you commit to uprooting sin, addictions, and vices from your body and soul, you will be assaulted by attacks directed at the spiritual and psychological wounds that make you most vulnerable.

The enemy of human nature can viciously attack where your wounds have left you most vulnerable. Those wounds might be spiritual, emotional, psychological, or moral. Core spiritual and psychological injuries to your heart and mind affect your capacity for self-transcendence. They make it difficult to love selflessly and achieve higher consciousness. A wall, built with emotional and intellectual counter-inspirations, is erected around the injuries, darkening your conscience. It is characteristic of the enemy of human nature to reinforce these emotional and intellectual defenses.

The enemy's purpose is to keep your emotional and intellectual defenses firmly in place, to keep your conscience dark and your true human nature hidden. The enemy's assault is felt as a bolstering and intensification of powerful emotional and intellectual defenses, leading you deeper into self-centered, self-absorbed, self-defended, self-justifying, and narcissistic thoughts, words, and deeds. You become more proud. You are adamantly convinced and hardened in your judgments about the meaning of life, truth, and beauty. These hardened convictions often contradict the Scriptures, received Tradition, the teaching Church and the mystical Christian traditions of West and East.

The defense measures of hardened convictions share the various qualities of desolation's counter-inspiration.[25] The strategic attacks by the enemy of human nature keep you attached to self-oriented, defensive thoughts, words, deeds, and habits, reinforcing rigid reasoning systems and disordered attachments.

The enemy of human nature's chief goal is to permanently camouflage your heart's spiritual, emotional, and psychological wounds. He does this to hide them from an awakened conscience, so you never notice where or why you need healing. Jesus made reference to these forms of defensive structures. They keep people from believing in Him, even if He should rise from the dead (Lk 16:31), and they grieved Jesus because they harden hearts (Mk 3:5).

In our daily press, we can observe evidence of this tactic of the enemy of human nature. In one report, a teenager won a court case forcing a public high school to remove a banner in the school's gym that referred to "Our Heavenly Father." The student, a baptized Roman Catholic, stopped believing in God at ten years of age when her mother fell ill: "I had always been told that if you pray, God will always be there when you need Him," the student said. "And it didn't happen for me, and I doubted it had happened for anybody else. So yeah, I think that was just like the last step, and after that I just really didn't believe any of it."

Much of the media framed the story as a legal and constitutional fight to prevent state-sponsored religion. But another plotline can be detected in this story. The student is opposing religious expression because of deep childhood wounds. The student's mother fell ill and "God did not listen" to a prayer for healing. At the bottom of this story is a deeply wounded heart. On the surface we see a determined and fearless youth standing up to defend constitutional rights against the wrath of classmates and townspeople.

The student is a self-described atheist and revered as a hero by many (including much of the media). This student could be at the beginning of a lifelong crusade. And the enemy of human nature would urge this person on in that fight. The enemy will do anything to keep this person distracted from the interior wound so it cannot be healed. This fight will appear noble to the individual and to others. However, through the lens of discernment, it appears that the person is blind to the emotional and intellectual defense systems that have been constructed. Those defenses of pride, intellectual justification, and defiance conceal the fear and pain of a ten-year-old child's broken heart.

Many people fighting apparently noble causes, are terrified, wounded children running away from their pain. Further, the defense structures erected to protect the wound are hard to penetrate. Pride, rigid determination, anger, and attitudes of "crusader justice" conceal the

410

fearful and wounded heart within. One thinks of St. Paul's attacks on the Church before his conversion. At the opening of the Acts of the Apostles, Saul witnesses the murder of Stephen. Later, he starts a crusade to crush all followers of the Way:

> Now Saul, still breathing murderous threats against the disciples of the Lord, went to the high priest and asked him for letters to the synagogues in Damascus, that, if he should find any men or women who belonged to the Way, he might bring them back to Jerusalem in chains. (Acts 9:1–2)

The enemy of human nature manipulated Saul's anger to legitimize murder. His homicidal rage was cloaked in religious justifications to stomp out all who followed the Lord Jesus. Fear was likely at the root of Saul's rage. It is possible that fear was also a driving force in St. Ignatius's life. Against the advice of the other knights, Ignatius forced the hand of his commander to engage in a futile battle that nearly ended his life.[26]

Much of the violence perpetrated by persons, groups, and countries in our own day is generated by wounded hearts seeking revenge for their suffering. Violence, be it economic, academic, physical, psychological, or verbal, can be self-justified and is often hidden behind nationalism, false religion, laws, cultural norms, and/or mob mentality.

Observe how the enemy of human nature instigates intellectual arguments, fosters a sense of injustice, and promotes defiance against legitimate authority. Ask the Lord, "What motivates my crusade (or crusades)? Where do I hurt? Help me to heal, and forgive me in the same way that I seek to forgive others. Help me spend the energy of my life to produce fruit that endures to eternity."

Cʒ

For he is our God,
we are the people he shepherds,
the sheep in his hands.

Oh, that today you would hear his voice:
Do not harden your hearts as at Meribah,
as on the day of Massah in the desert.
There your ancestors tested me;
they tried me though they had seen my works.
Forty years I loathed that generation;
I said: "This people's heart goes astray;
they do not know my ways."
Therefore I swore in my anger:
"They shall never enter my rest."
(Ps 95:7–11)

ʒɔ

Letters from Week Thirty-Seven

Dear Fr. Bill,

It is true, the more determined I become to uprooting the things that cause me to push away from God, the more the enemy attacks. And he does know exactly where to hit me. All of my soft spots – my insecurity, pride, ego, vanity. He knows everything about me, especially my desire to be one with my Savior. He'll throw doubt and fear at me when he knows I'm most vulnerable. You used the right term, "strategic". The enemy attacks strategically, with pinpoint accuracy. But I must always remember – he is the enemy and he wants me to live a Godless life, mired in sin.

You would think that my sense of abandonment and lack of love and guidance as a child would have moved me in the direction of the one who would love me unconditionally and never leave me. Instead, I went in the opposite direction, doing everything possible to ensure I would remain alone, unloved and afraid. The enemy was there every step of the way, pushing me, encouraging me, and tempting me with all the sins, vice, and addictions I thought were necessary to make me "happy".

Acts 9:1-2 are good verses. I am reading a book on the travels, letters and epistles of the Apostle Paul and I have been attending a study of Paul's letter to the Romans; a weekly study that is very satisfying even though it has taken almost six months to get to chapter eight. On my own I have been reading Philippians and Timothy along with a ten-week study of the "Fruit of the Spirit", Galatians 5:22-23.

As if Paul's conversion wasn't enough to inspire me and give me hope beyond measure, it feels to me that every word he has written in the New Testament is directed straight at me, to my heart. The love that man had for Jesus and, as a result, for us, is almost beyond comprehension. Paul knew a little about sin and the need to remain vigilant. He told us it will be a battle.

Respectfully,

Ritchie

Dear Ritchie:

The enemy of your human nature is indeed both strategic and untiringly ambitious. He works 24/7 on you and all of us to distract us from our life in Christ. But never forget that Jesus Christ is also untiringly ambitious and he has defeated our enemy and fights for victory on our behalf 24/7. We shall not fear!

A reminder: St. Ignatius strongly advised us never to converse with the enemy, but always turn our hearts to Christ when temptations assail us. The enemy knows your weaknesses, this is true, and is strategic in his attacking you. However, something much more important is that Christ knows both your weaknesses and strengths and fights for you against the one you and I can't defeat on our own. This is our sure hope.

Continue to read and draw strength from St. Paul. He is a good mentor for you at this time in your life, Ritchie. It is my hope to complete this book of Forty Weeks and our correspondence on the Feast of the Conversion of St. Paul, January 25th 2018. Pray that I can get it done in time.

You are in my prayers. Keep me in yours.

Fr. Bill

Dear Fr. Bill,

Thanks so much for your response/insights for Weeks Thirty-Three through Thirty-Six. Also, thanks for the cards. I will disperse them with discretion.

Enclosed you will find my thoughts on the remaining weeks of Forty Weeks. Weeks Thirty-Seven through Forty have filled me with hope. Living my life as Sacred Story is very doable. With practice I will soon have no excuses for not knowing where I'm at, what going on with me spiritually.

"I don't know why I said that", "I don't know why I did that", or "I don't know where that came from" are phrases that I hopefully will not be using often in the future. I cannot adequately describe how much help you have been to me over the past year so since we first linked up. I am committed to practicing all of the disciplines I've learned in Forty Weeks for the rest of my life.

I am very glad that some of my letters have been helpful to others. I was hoping that since I've just about completed the preliminaries to living my life as Sacred Story, maybe you could facilitate contact between me and others who have experienced Forty Weeks?

Regarding your website, aside from what little Deacon Pat has told me about it, I don't really know what goes on there. Obviously, I do not have internet access, but I am interested in knowing more about it. Anything you can tell me or send me would be appreciated.

I look forward to hearing from you, as always. Thanks for everything. Your guidance is surely a gift.

Respectfully, Ritchie

Dear Ritchie:

It has been a grace for both you and me, your walking this path these past Forty Weeks. When we do things to help ourselves, we invariably are accomplishing things that will help other people. St. Ignatius said it best: "Seek first your own salvation before that of others."

The consolation you are experiencing is a confirmation of the path you have chosen to follow, both in Forty Weeks and the New Directions program at the petitionary. Hold on to the grace of this confirmation. You will need it in the future when, (when, not if) challenges present themselves to you.

Yet you will have the tools at your disposal of being able to ask those key questions on why you are doing certain things. You will also grow in understanding what part(s) of your past history the thoughts, words and deeds originate. Christ will walk with you every step of the way.

Should I be able to visit you after the book comes out, we can use my phone to view the website, Ritchie. Let me know if you would be allowed a visitor and if any photographs would be permitted.

You remain in my prayers.

Peace,

Fr. Bill

NOTES

Week 38

FIRST

I resolve to spend no more and no less than fifteen minutes in each formal prayer period. I will always use my personal name for God.

SECOND

As before, I continue this thirty-eighth week by praying meditations one through five in the Sacred Story prayer, entering my prayer at least once daily, as St. Ignatius suggested. I reaffirm the importance of the simple journal exercises and my monthly practice of sacramental Reconciliation.

THIRD

I will ask God's grace to keep my mind and heart open as I learn the ways of spiritual discernment in my sacred story. This week I am invited to reflect on the second series of discernment rules given by St. Ignatius. This second series of rules details temptations of a more subtle nature. Here the enemy of our human nature manipulates our undetected narcissism to obstruct or disrupt our spiritual growth.

I will awaken to the present moment.

I will awaken to my spiritual nature.

I will not make any decisions based on fear.

I will practice sacramental Reconciliation monthly.

I will ask Jesus for help when I am troubled.
I will thank Jesus daily for life's gifts.

This week, I will say this affirmation aloud once daily:
I will strive daily to pick up the cross, for it leads to my life.
The closer I get to holiness, the more I will
see and feel sin's disorder in my life.

૮ઝ

Continuing in the School of Discernment:
Guidelines for Integrated Healing and Spiritual Growth

Take some time this week to read and reflect on this eleventh lesson in discernment. Last week we finished a study of St. Ignatius's first set of rules on discernment. The first set of rules is called "Guidelines for Foundational Healing and Spiritual Growth." They are foundational rules because they are directed toward those who can be more easily distracted from their spiritual journey by sensual pleasures and delights from the enemy of human nature.

These rules help build the foundation of one's faith journey. The enemy of human nature seeks his victories at this level by fanning our cowardice and fear in the face of surrendering addictive and sinful thoughts, words, and deeds.

This week we examine St. Ignatius's second set of discernment rules. We call these "Guidelines for Integrated Healing and Spiritual Growth." They apply to those persons whom the enemy of human nature distracts from their spiritual journey with attacks to the reasoning processes. These rules are termed integrated because they facilitate healing of our human nature as a unity of body and spirit. The enemy of human nature seeks his victories at this level by creating illusions and hiding the truth of our thoughts, words, and deeds.

This week we consider five of the seven guidelines for discerning the difference between the Divine Inspirer and the counter-inspirer's tactics at this more subtle, nuanced level of spiritual development.

The Guidelines for Integrated Healing and Spiritual Growth are essential for discerning counter-inspirations of a more subtle nature. They are applicable when a person has matured to the point where vices, sinful habits, addictions, and extravagant appetites are no longer effective temptations to lure one from God.

When a certain level of spiritual, emotional, and psychological maturity has been reached, the enemy of human nature can best deceive with seemingly good, holy thoughts and feelings. He mimics the Divine Inspirer. He is no longer successful in undermining your authenticity and innocence with temptations to false pleasures and obvious discouragements. Direct appeals to narcissistic pride are no longer effective. Instead, the enemy resorts to twisting new and holy inspirations and habits against you, based on the undetected roots of your narcissism.

The enemy of human nature will then disguise counter-inspirations by having them appear as divine inspirations. Ignatius first discovered these new, indirect temptations in the midst of his battle with the crippling guilt of his scruples. The obsessive habit of reconfessing his past sins appeared as a good thing to do. The habit appealed to someone serious about spiritual growth. But the habit appealed especially to Ignatius's desire to be in control of his life and to save himself.

In his former way of living, Ignatius had tried to win fame at the battle of Pamplona by attempting to conquer the French almost single-handedly. Later, in his Christian life, his narcissism appeared under the "holy" guise of winning fame by conquering his sinfulness through his own agency: a different battle but the same concealed narcissism and pride at work.

Ignatius was miserable and experienced the constant reconfessing as damaging. Yet he would not relinquish the obsessive habit even when told to do so by his spiritual director. Ignatius seemed to be held bound by a "pious" and "holy" habit. In fact, he was bound by his narcissism and determination to save himself instead of allowing Christ to be his Savior. The enemy's counter-inspirations that characterized this episode were invisible to Ignatius, most likely because surrendering the habit meant a loss of control and a threat to his pride.

Ignatius was given grace to see the deception by observing the direction it was taking him: away from God. He realized that the inspiration was to "stop" the new life he was living. The enemy of our human nature can inspire desires and choices that are nonharmful or even objectively good. They appear as if they will help us evolve toward more perfect love and life.

Thus in Ignatius's situation, conscientious confession would appear to be a good choice to root out past sins and vices. But to someone susceptible to damaging scrupulosity, it could be the perfect tactic to turn that person from the path of faith and trust in God! And the enemy of human nature will search for any and all vulnerabilities to subvert our journey in faith.

Spiritual and religious persons are especially vulnerable to these more subtle temptations. The narcissism of these persons is concealed in a pious facade. A partial conversion has not sufficiently targeted the narcissistic pride that guides such a person's life. Those not sufficiently purified parade about like just and righteous people. The truth is, they are proud and arrogant. Jesus reserved some of His most serious criticisms for these religious hypocrites. (Lk 18:9–14).

Some things that are good, or appear as good, can gradually lead you away from the good you intend. They lead you away from God toward disintegration, separation, and death. This is exactly what happened to Ignatius. He was so disgusted with the trials and traumas of his obsessive reconfessing of past sins that he was suddenly inspired to be done with the new life he had embraced. As far as Ignatius was concerned, if he could not convert himself, and do it his way, he would not do it at all. This is narcissistic pride, plain and simple.

A habit that appeared noble was silently, slowly, and maliciously eroding his confidence in himself and his confidence in God, and it threatened the new way of life he had chosen. If the enemy of human nature could not lure Ignatius with the obvious vices and sins of his former life, then the enemy would manipulate Ignatius's new and holy inspirations, linking them to his yet undetected narcissistic pride. The enemy turned Ignatius's good habit against him.

It can be difficult to differentiate between divine inspirations and counter-inspirations, especially because a counter-inspiration can appear as a genuine good, or feel authentic. Ignatius offers these guidelines of discernment:

First, the Divine Inspirer works to give you true joy and happiness. This is accomplished by eliminating all sadness and upset caused by the enemy of your human nature. The counter-inspirer works against such joy and happiness. He does this most successfully by using false reasoning, subtleties, and layers of deceptions. The enemy's arguments will be logical yet leave you feeling anxious, discouraged, hopeless, and possibly cynical.

Second, the Divine Inspirer alone can work directly on your heart and soul. The Divine Inspirer can touch your soul at will. What does the Divine Inspirer promote by these spiritual visits?

✠ Increased love of God and love of innocence.

✠ Increased humility, selflessness, and surrendering control of your life to God.

✠ Increased docility of spirit: a spirit capable of listening deeply, accepting and affirming as true the Commandments, the teachings of Christ, and those divinely revealed and definitively proclaimed matters of belief held by the Church.[27]

Inspirations with these signature characteristics can be verified as coming directly from the Divine Inspirer.

Third, both the Divine Inspirer and the counter-inspirer can inspire, but with opposite goals. The Divine Inspirer seeks to promote genuine human freedom, authenticity, and spiritual/psychological growth in harmony with your authentic human nature. The counter-inspirer seeks to erode genuine human freedom and to disintegrate your spiritual and psychological health. The goal is to further damage your authentic human nature.

Fourth, the counter-inspirer can mimic some of the influences of the Divine Inspirer in thoughts, feelings, and desires. However, his purpose in doing so is to gradually lead you in the wrong direction, similar to Ignatius's experience with his damaging habit of reconfessing old sins.
Fifth, distinguishing the difference between Divine and counter-inspirations requires you to develop the habit of examining the overall trajectory of your thoughts and desires. If the beginning, middle, and end are all directed to what is genuine and right, the inspirations are from the Divine Inspirer. If the trajectory of the desires and thoughts:

✠ lead to something contrary to the Commandments or the precepts of Christ,

✠ distract and weaken your aspirations for selflessness, or

✠ in some way diminish the good plans and goals you had previously established, then it is very clear they are a product of the counter-inspirer. The goal of the enemy of human nature is to lead you away from genuine progress, authenticity, innocence, humility, obedience, and peace and to conceal his presence as he does so.

Ignatius was distracted by his re-confession habit, and his aspirations for following the path of conversion were undermined by it. When he realized this, he identified the influence of the counter-inspirer and surrendered the damaging habit. This choice began the process of dismantling his narcissistic pride at its root.[28]

Ignatius once remarked that human beings are no match for the subtle temptations of the enemy of human nature. But God is! God is indeed a match for the enemy's temptations. Never dialogue with the enemy of your human nature. Speak only to Christ, and let Christ deal with the enemy of your human nature. Trust your life, your heart, and your soul to Christ.

ભ

LORD, guide me in your justice because of my foes;
make straight your way before me.

For there is no sincerity in their mouth;
their heart is corrupt.
Their throat is an open grave;
on their tongue are subtle lies.
Declare them guilty, God;
make them fall by their own devices.
Drive them out for their many sins;
for they have rebelled against you.

Then all who trust in you will be glad
and forever shout for joy.
You will protect them and those will rejoice in you
who love your name.
For you, Lord, bless the just one;
you surround him with favor like a shield.
(Ps 5:9–13)

જી

Letters from Week Thirty-Eight

Dear Fr. Bill,

I see exactly what you and Ignatius mean in Week Thirty-Eight's The Guidelines for Integrated Healing and Spiritual Growth. There definitely comes a time in our growth, well, mine in particular, when sex, money, drugs and adulation will no longer work as a lure back into the old narcissistic, sinful life.

Sure, I still have my weak moments, and always will, when I briefly fall back into the old daydreams and fantasies. And my spiritual life will suffer for a short time. But it doesn't last long.

I'd like to think that I just snap out of it after a while. Actually, it's my constant conscious relationship with my Savior that opens my eyes and heart to what's really going on. It wasn't until reading this week's lesson, the eleventh lesson in discernment, that I realized the more subtle tactics of the counter-inspirer.

Fr. Bill, when we first started Forty Weeks together I told you of how I related to Ignatius' over-confessing by sharing my sense that I didn't have the faith necessary to move forward, to become the man God created me to be. I prayed so much and so often for the faith I thought I was lacking to no apparent avail, that I was becoming discouraged, like Ignatius.

That was definitely the enemy disguising his counter inspiration by sowing doubt in my heart and mind while convincing me that nothing could be more God-inspired than praying for faith. I honestly did not realize what was going on until I read Part Two, A journey to the Heart-Ignatius in Control in Week Three.

The enemy is relentless. I find myself stopping many times in the course of my day just to basically see where I'm at, what's going on, which direction am I heading, and consequently, who is inspiring me right now.

Respectfully,

Ritchie

Dear Ritchie:

The sensual sins and temptations eventually lose their grip on our hearts. They will always have some allure because of our weaknesses and old habits. An Irish Jesuit by the name of William Johnston in a book on the spiritual life[29] said that the last two vices to be burned out of the human heart are anger and lust. So, we must take hope from Proverbs 24:16: "Though the just fall seven times, they rise again, but the wicked stumble from only one mishap."

Let your great hope be the strategic prayer of the Examen you have learned. Stopping and listening to your story to see what direction your thoughts, words and deeds are moving you are your salvation. I like to think St. Ignatius did this discipline briefly every hour on the hour for two main reasons.

First, that he knew he needed to do it in order to keep his heart on true north. Second, he loved Christ so much he wanted to eliminate everything in his life that separated him from Jesus.

With Christ helping you, you will have the grace to remain faithful too because of your love of Jesus and his love for you.

Peace,

Fr. Bill

NOTES

Week 39

FIRST

I resolve to spend no more and no less than fifteen minutes in each formal prayer period. I will always use my personal name for God.

SECOND

I ask God's grace to help me commit to a lifelong habit of praying the five meditations of Sacred Story prayer. With God's grace, I will be able to enter my prayer at least once daily, as St. Ignatius suggested. God's grace will also help me to commit to my simple journal exercises and a monthly practice of sacramental Reconciliation.

THIRD

I am invited to continue reflecting on spiritual discernment by concluding the series of St. Ignatius's rules on integrated healing. This second series of rules takes into account temptations of a more subtle nature. Here the enemy of my human nature manipulates undetected narcissism to interfere with my spiritual growth.

I will awaken to the present moment.
I will awaken to my spiritual nature.
I will not make any decisions based on fear.
I will practice sacramental Reconciliation monthly.
I will ask Jesus for help when I am troubled.

I will thank Jesus daily for life's gifts.
This week, I will say this affirmation aloud once daily:
The more I experience sin's disorder,
the more tempted I will be to disbelieve my life as sacred story.
The way through the temptation
is to surrender my powerlessness to God.

ॐ

Continuing in the School of Discernment:
Guidelines for Integrated Healing and Spiritual Growth

Take some time on the weekend or during the week to read and reflect on this twelfth lesson in discernment. Last week our study of St. Ignatius's second set of rules on discernment examined five guidelines to utilize with temptations of a more subtle form. This week we examine the sixth and seventh guidelines. Remember these rules apply to those distracted from the spiritual journey by the enemy of human nature with attacks targeting their reasoning processes with illusions of truth, but not truth itself. We call these integrated rules, because they facilitate healing of our human nature as a unity of body and spirit.

Review the introductory narrative from week 38. These "Guidelines for Integrated Healing and Spiritual Growth" are essential for discerning counter-inspirations of a more subtle nature. They are applicable to those who have matured to the point where vices, sinful habits, addictions, and extravagant appetites are no longer effective in luring one away from God.

Sixth, develop the habit of tracing the trajectory of the thoughts and desires that have led you away from God and away from your authentic self. Do not become discouraged. This discipline takes practice. You will fall for the bait countless times. When you do, examine the initial inspiration, and follow it through the whole course of your

430

deliberations. Notice how you were initially inspired but then gradually, step by step, lost your peace of soul.

Notice how your former holy commitments and resolutions were undermined. From this objective vantage point, reflection will enable you to identify the particular strategy the counter-inspirer uses in your life story. This vigilance will help you develop spiritual radar for these deceptive tactics. You will also learn to identify your personal vulnerabilities that the enemy of your authentic human nature manipulates.

At this level of conversion, the enemy's tactics work on your concealed pride, vanity, and narcissism—the Original Sin of the human family. When you think or feel things like "I do not need God," or "I will control my own life," or "I will set my own rules," or "I will be my own savior," and you feel proud about it, rest assured, the enemy of human nature is at work!

Seventh, when you are progressing towards authenticity, innocence, and genuine human freedom, the effects of the Divine Inspirer are gentle and produce delight. A sense of electrical energy, anxious excitement, or a restless need to make hasty decisions is totally absent. Instead, a calm patience and tranquility abides. When making progress towards authenticity, you can detect the effects of the counter-inspirer by the rush of electrical energy, anxious excitement, or restlessness to make hasty decisions.

But you need to awaken to both the feelings (anxious or calm) and the trajectory (toward or away from authenticity) to accurately interpret what the feelings are signaling.

If you are moving toward God, the enemy of your human nature will inspire "black noise," creating anxious thoughts and urgent feelings. The enemy wants to discourage you from turning to God.

If you are moving away from God, God will inspire with alarm bells that you are entering dangerous territory. It can feel like the same anxiety and urgent feelings described above, but this time, it is your awakened conscience that God uses to alert you of an inauthentic trajectory.

Also, if you are moving away from God, the enemy of your human nature will inspire with thoughts that are appeasing, reassuring your complacency and attempting to conceal your movement away from God and from your authentic human nature.

When the inspiration produced in your heart and soul comes directly from the Divine Inspirer, you cannot be deceived or led astray. You will come to know the inspirations of the Divine Inspirer because of the effects on your heart and soul. These inspirations produce an intense sense of devotion and love of God and of innocence. They produce a sense of selflessness and willing surrender of your life to God's control. The inspirations help you understand and trust received Tradition, the Commandments, and the precepts of Christ as proclaimed by the Church.

However, you can be led astray in the afterglow of such inspiration and grace. You can be led astray by your own ideas or by the influence of the counter-inspirer. Be highly attentive during the time following divine inspirations. Be cautious and make no revisions, commitments, or plans during this time, unless you are clear as to the source of the inspiration.

The Divine Inspirer will lead you further along the path of love, innocence, humility, and self-surrender. The counter-inspirer will work toward disintegration and a weakening of your previous commitments and holy resolutions. The counter-inspirer will pull you further down the path of pride and encourage you to justify your angers. The enemy of human nature will inspire you to cling to whatever difficulties you have with gospel values as proposed by the Church.

Conclusion

Understand now how St. Ignatius's divine inspiration to reform his life was corrupted into a damaging habit of confessing old sins. The counter-inspirer accomplished this by manipulating Ignatius's narcissistic nature and long-standing vulnerabilities. If Ignatius had been deceived into walking away from his conversion journey, the Church would have been deprived of the gifts of his spirituality and the many saints who achieved holiness through it.

This was the counter-inspirer's hope for Ignatius. It will be the counter-inspirer's hope for you as well. The counter-inspirer understands the great good that you can accomplish for the Kingdom of Christ and will work to sabotage it at all costs. While we are incapable of matching the subtleties of the enemy of human nature, we can rest in the assurance that God is capable of battling our ancient enemy.

The Divine Inspirer will always offer the graces and insights to lead you home. God's victory is assured for you in Christ's birth, life, death, and resurrection. Have hope in Him. He will help you, just as He helped St. Ignatius. You will achieve the goal of love, the goal of forgiveness, and through your life's sacred story, the goal of service to the Great Work of Reconciliation that Christ has invited you to share with Him.

As you work with God's grace to let your life be transformed into sacred story, never be discouraged by your failings, sins, and weaknesses. The Divine Physician will never tire of forgiving you. Never tire of coming to Him for forgiveness. In this radical, loving trust, you encounter the unfathomable and unbounded mercy of God.

୭୪

Hallelujah!
Praise the Lord, my soul; I will praise the Lord all my life,
sing praise to my God while I live.

Put no trust in princes,
in children of Adam powerless to save.
Who breathing his last, returns to the earth;
that day all his planning comes to nothing.

Blessed the one whose help is the God of Jacob,
whose hope is in the Lord, his God,
The maker of heaven and earth, the seas and all that is in them,
Who keeps faith forever, secures justice for the oppressed,
who gives bread to the hungry.
The Lord sets prisoners free; the Lord gives sight to the blind.
The Lord raises up those who are bowed down;
the Lord loves the righteous.
The Lord protects the resident alien,
comes to the aid of the orphan and the widow,
but thwarts the way of the wicked.
The Lord shall reign forever,
your God, Zion, through all generations!
Hallelujah!
(Ps 146)

୫୭

Letters from Week Thirty-Nine

Dear Fr. Bill,

I am exceedingly grateful that I do not have much difficulty with the sixth guideline. I've always known that I need God. When I was in control of my life, setting my own rules, I was definitely aware that I wasn't living the way I should have been, that I was living a sinful life. I was aware of how I was living and thought it was wrong. I just didn't want to change. I thought I liked the way I was living, wouldn't change it for the world. That was the work of the enemy, the counter-inspirer.

I do experience difficulties concerning "anxious thoughts and urgent feelings" as stated in guideline number seven. I have a history of stress and anxiety issues which have, in the past and sometimes now, lead me to make rash decisions while in periods of desolation. The counter-inspirer convinces me that I must act Now, not giving me the time and desire to seek God's guidance.

I wouldn't go as far as hearing alarm bells, but the ability to realize in which direction I am travelling is becoming more natural. My many "During the Day Exercises: Awakening to Sins, Addictions and Compulsions" have become sort of short discernment sessions. In practicing declare, describe, descend, denounce and decide – discerning and accepting where this is coming from and where it is leading me is implied in the process. It wasn't clear to me back in Week Sixteen, but it is now.

You mentioned the "afterglow" of divine inspirations. I know what you mean. Sometimes I get to feeling almost invincible. It reminds me of the Affirmation: "Times of peace and hope always give was to times of difficulty and stress". Vigilance is important.

Respectfully, Ritchie

Dear Ritchie:

St. Ignatius was very wise. He said that if you can't pray for something because it is too hard for you to do, pray for the grace to desire to want to do it! So, this means that on tough things, all we need do is to admit to Jesus: "I can't do this and I don't even want to do it, so please help me." We can accomplish nothing on our own!

You have had anxiety for many years and it goes back to many issues when you were very young. This includes not feeling loved but abandoned. You know this about yourself. The enemy, as you have experienced, will use this old wound to get you to be anxious and make snap decisions. You know now to always wait for calmness to return. Decisions made during times of fear and anxiety are invariably bad decisions! Resist the urge to react by falling prey to the fear.

As you have discovered, times of consolation require vigilance. As we grow in our spiritual lives, the enemy seeks to make us trip by acting "as an angel of light." St. Ignatius, when in studies, was getting all manner of consolation at night time and this prevented him from getting the rest he needed to do his studies. He came to realize the consolations where "of the enemy" and stopped listening to them so he could sleep. Again, watch the direction inspirations lead you. If they lead away from your life in Christ, they should be challenged.

You are in my prayers.

Fr. Bill

NOTES

WEEK 40

FIRST

I resolve to spend no more and no less than fifteen minutes in each formal prayer period. I will always use my personal name for God.

SECOND

I ask God's grace to help me commit to a lifelong habit of praying the five meditations of Sacred Story prayer. With God's grace, I will be able to enter my prayer at least once daily, as Ignatius suggested. God's grace will also help me to commit to my simple journal exercises and a monthly practice of sacramental Reconciliation.

THIRD

This week I am invited to conclude my lessons on St. Ignatius's rules for spiritual discernment. This final section offers special discernment advice for those times that my deepening conversion to life as sacred story may prompt life changes of one sort or another.

૭૦

I will awaken to the present moment.
I will awaken to my spiritual nature.
I will not make any decisions based on fear.
I will practice sacramental Reconciliation monthly.

I will ask Jesus for help when I am troubled.
I will thank Jesus daily for life's gifts.
This week, I will say this affirmation aloud once daily:
It is never too late to open my heart to Christ
and live my life as sacred story.

C8

Additional Guidelines on Life Choices

Take some time this week to read and reflect on this thirteenth lesson in discernment. Last week we completed the study of St. Ignatius's second set of rules on discernment. These examined the sixth and seventh guidelines that indicate the presence of temptations of a more subtle form in our lives. This week we conclude the study of discernment by examining the guidelines St. Ignatius offers to those who, open to God's grace, contemplate making life choices.

These rules may not be applicable at this point in your spiritual journey. These guidelines will be helpful whenever you are required to make decisions based on faith in the future. The enemy of human nature is always at work to derail our conversion process, but we are not to be afraid. The Lord is our strength and shield. We must simply learn to be gentle as doves and wise as serpents (Mt 10:16).

As your conversion deepens, grace illumines your mind and heart. What had been in darkness is now revealed. You begin to awaken, to see the true nature of reality, the world, and your authentic human nature. Grace alone facilitates this journey out of spiritual unconsciousness and the darkened conscience of counter-inspiration. As you continue to awaken, you will discover why narcissism and pride are so much more difficult to identify and eliminate than are the sins of the flesh.

The pain of Original Sin, early life trauma, and lost innocence encourages your narcissism. The narcissistic ego is closed to the Spirit.

This ego rationalizes and legitimizes whatever it needs to fill its painful void. It is the ancient wound created by the self, displacing God as the heart's center. The defenses that hide your narcissism match the intensity of the hidden pain at the center of your heart. You defend the use of vices and addictions because they protect you from feeling the pain in your heart and keep you from turning to God for help and healing.

Your sacred story begins when you accept the Divine Physician's grace to honestly name your sin and let the heart's healing begin. You need God's grace to both break through and dismantle your defenses. This is the true path to mystical awakening. There are no shortcuts. There is no other way home. You have a unique path to holiness that no one else in all of history can follow. It is God's path for you. It is linked to the unique circumstances of your life. Let the Divine Physician heal you and lead you to wholeness and holiness.

The humility Ignatius discovered in surrendering control of his life—surrendering his pride and narcissism—allowed him to envision a new life, in and for Christ, that he had never known before. This awakened consciousness has its own graces and difficulties, as Ignatius well discovered. These graces abound, regardless of one's state of life and vocation. These graces bring illumination and clarity. They illumine the true portrait of your free and authentic self. They open you to the world, your Catholic faith, and the creator God. They reveal your past and present commitments, and your choices—both well- and ill-conceived. This is where Ignatius found himself after his spiritual and psychological trials at Manresa.

The grace of conversion transforms and heals divided hearts. The values you previously espoused that were contrary to the gospel give way to thoughts, words, and deeds that open you to opportunities never before imagined or thought possible. Purifying graces rush in with new opportunities for your life, filling the void of a heart on the mend. What else would you expect when your heart is touched directly by divine grace? When your heart is flush with the energy, the enthusiasm, and the vitality of God, Ignatius has clear advice.

Ignatius advises that a person in this stage of integrated conversion and healing, who has received these graces of illumination, must consider them very attentively. One needs to cautiously distinguish the initial consolation from the period that follows. In the afterglow of these illuminations and insights, when the consolations themselves have ceased, the soul is still passionate. It has been blessed with graces, and these graces have an afterglow. In the time of the afterglow, the heart and soul often form resolutions and plans that are not directly inspired or granted by God.

These ideas and resolutions can emanate from your own reasoning, creating ideas based on your own judgments. Or these resolutions can be the direct inspiration of the Divine Inspirer or the counter-inspirer. It is critical to distinguish the illuminations themselves and the period of time after the illuminations—the period of afterglow. Carefully, thoughtfully, and cautiously examine your afterglow reflections and plans, before approving them or acting on them.

This advice is especially important if you are transitioning from established habits and lifestyles. Those thoughts, words, and deeds, inauthentic expressions of your human nature, have deep roots and/or a long history. These long-established patterns of sin and dysfunction have created spiritual, mental, and psychological grooves. The grooves are your default narratives for defining "normal" and "success." These false-but-familiar narratives are narcissism's anti-story. They draw strength from your broken heart and wounded innocence.

We experience the spiritual and physical wreckage of the Original Fall in our wounded hearts. Our lost innocence is combined with the evolution of sin in our families, clans and social groups. The energy fueling our narcissistic anti-story shields us from pain and shame, both real and perceived. As you gradually receive the grace and illumination to relinquish the anti-story, you will experience a void.

Surrendering the false definitions of success, and the habits that support these false narratives, creates the void. You will feel a powerful compulsion to fill that void, a compulsion that is easily exploited by the counter-inspirer.

When you relinquish your anti-story, you will also have the desire to make up for lost time and to correct the mistakes of the past. These desires can also fill your heart with urgent and pressing agendas for change. These agendas may feel honorable and right.

This is true especially in light of your past misdeeds and errors. One must exercise caution, however, because these urgent and pressing agendas for change can lead away from the truths, positive resolutions, and commitments recently illumined by divine grace.

If you experience strong inspirations to change your life commitments, test them and the imagined future plans they represent. Do the inspirations of this follow-up period (after the initial consolation) strike the heart gently? Do they create delight and peace? Is there a notable absence of electrical energy or nervous urgency toward immediate action?

Or do the inspirations and ideas of this follow-up period strike the heart violently? Do they disturb the heart with electrical excitement and a compelling urgency to immediately enact the good ideas or plans being pondered? This latter effect is a clear sign that the inspirations and ideas will lead you away from life and love—fruit that endures to eternity—no matter how enlightened these ideas seem.

Be attentive! Be gentle as a dove and wise as a serpent. Honor the process of change. Wait for the signs of peace and humility, and test the decisions being pondered.

Conclusion

Spiritual discernment is an art that takes time to master. Its first phase involves knowing the objective rights and wrongs of thoughts, words, and deeds as taught by the Commandments, Christ, and the teaching Church. Spiritual discernment advances when you consciously attend to your affective/spiritual states and become aware of spiritual movements that are present in your life story. Next, you need to familiarize yourself with the language and signatures of the two different voices: that of the Divine Inspirer and that of the counter-inspirer.

Finally, you need to learn to trust your decision-making based on what you have learned from St. Ignatius's experience and wisdom. This means confronting fears that, in the past, incited cowardice on your part. It also means confronting narcissism's illusions that, in the past, incited self-satisfaction on your part. Confronting both of these will feel difficult, but you must trust Ignatius's wisdom and act rightly. You will make mistakes. But learn from your mistakes, always trusting God's infinite mercy. God has infinite patience for those honestly struggling to live a new life in Christ.

In all of this, God will be your support and guide. Turn your attention and heart to God. God will give you the insight, wisdom, and strength necessary to develop your spiritual self. Do not be fearful or discouraged as you gradually integrate the art of spiritual discernment into your life. The Divine Inspirer will offer all of the graces and insights needed to lead you home. Be not afraid!

Letters from Week Forty

Fr. Bill,

I am locked up in a Federal Penitentiary. I have been for quite a while now. There's not much good around here. Negativity is contagious. This week's Affirmation is simple yet important to me, "It is never too late to open my heart to Christ and live my life as Sacred Story". Not only am I just now doing this in my fifties – finally, but I also must re-commit daily, sometimes more often.

It is so easy to veer off course, to be led astray without being aware of it. The enemy uses others to do his dirty work. Being aware and willing to re-boot when necessary is key. All kinds of realization and justification seep into decisions that, if I would stop for just a moment and ponder the direction I am heading, could be righted without much effort at all.

I am still in the beginning stages of surrendering control of my life. At the same time I am "transitioning from established habits and lifestyles". I am not only talking about my life her in prison, but also what kind of life I will be leading in 2021 and beyond, after my release.

For the past four years I've been becoming more and more convinced of the life God wants me to live. I believe he has used my past life, the old me, to show me what is important and how to move forward. I don't know the details, only He knows, but my life of striving for money, material possessions; the "good life" is over.

Consequential service is my main goal: consequential service with humility. I will not be looking for earthly rewards. God has shown me over the past twenty years that I do not need much. Joy is gladness not based on circumstances. I have joy in my heart now. I am beginning to live my Sacred Story.

The awareness that I can live my Sacred Story under any circumstances is heartening. God's grace is wonderful. It's not always going to be easy, to say the least. It's a tough world. Diligence, awareness, constant conscious contact with my Lord and Savior, and the disciplines I have learned and continue to practice are the keys.

Respectfully, Ritchie

Dear Ritchie:

Someone said once, "where you fall, there dig for gold." That is, where you fail can be your best hope for spiritual awareness and growth. Perhaps St. Paul said it first in Romans 5:20 when he wrote: "Where sin abounds, grace abounds all the more."

Your life in federal prison has led you to Christ. It has become your monastery and your monk's cell. I know friends who live in monasteries, and they have problems and challenges too. There is no place on earth where it is easy to live a Christian life. But Christ is with us always not matter where we find ourselves.

I am quite confident that you are already living a life of consequential service. The process of this forty week journey and our correspondence will help, we hope, many thousands of individuals. When you are released at the end of your sentence, your consequential service will continue. We don't know how or where, but that you desire it is God's promise that it will come about. Hold on this sure hope. The disciplines you have learned and the person you have come to love, Christ Jesus, will lead you and me home to the kingdom.

The fact that our correspondence for Forty Weeks both began and concludes on the Feast of All Saints, Ritchie, is your sign from Christ that he has a plan!

You know you are in my prayers. Please keep me in yours.

Peace, Fr. Bill

ভ

The Lord is king, in splendor robed;
robed is the Lord and girt about with strength.
And he has made the world firm,
not to be moved.
Your throne stands firm from of old;
from everlasting you are, O Lord.
Your decrees are worthy of trust indeed;
holiness befits your house,
O Lord, for length of days.
(Ps 93:1–2,5)

ভ

NOTES

Week Eternity

Living Your Sacred Story Daily

You have engaged all the spiritual disciplines for Sacred Story. Now is the time to ask God for help to be faithful to the relationship with Him that the prayer invites. Continue praying all the meditations in your fifteen-minute periods. Keep practicing all the other daily disciplines you have learned. You have all the necessary instruction. What follows are all the spiritual disciplines and insights of Sacred Story, arranged for easy reference.

If and when you have difficulties, temptations, stresses, fears, or anxieties associated with the daily consciousness exercise or Sacred Story prayer (when, not if!), read "Sacred Story Affirmations" (available at the beginning and at the end of this book) and the "Guidelines for Healing and Spiritual Growth" ("Foundational" [weeks 30–37] and "Integrated" [weeks 38–39]). Remember the anxieties that Ignatius suffered as he began his journey. All spiritual and emotional crises soon pass. Christ Jesus will lead you home. Be not afraid!

✠ Prayer Upon Waking—Attune to the day ahead, and invite God's help.
This should take about fifteen to thirty seconds. After you wake up, lie

in bed and prevision the day ahead. What does it hold? Are you anxious or energized about the day ahead? What specific issues/persons/events are causing the anxiety and/or energy? Ask God to help you deal constructively with the anxieties or challenges, and give thanks for the events/persons that inspire energy. Ask God to keep you aware as the day progresses. Using the special name you identified, offer the day to God.

If you so desire, on Sunday morning, you can do a brief previsioning of the week in the same way you do for a single day. You might consider looking ahead to any special feast days or saint's anniversaries that week. Ask for their intercession for your sacred story at the beginning of the week and on their feast day.

✠ Exercises During the Day—Awakening to your life
Each one of these should take no more than fifteen seconds. Consciously note the most significant events that inspire aggravation (anger, upset, fear, or temptation) or joy (gratitude, hope, faith). Every day holds many of these events. Consciously attend to the events that seem most notable by the strength of the reaction they incite in you. At the time these notable events transpire, take about ten seconds to 1) turn to God in your heart and using your personal name for God, ask to understand why the event gripped you negatively or positively, and 2) ask for graced insight to understand if the event is linked to something from the past that needs exploration/healing. Then go on with your day.

The more you engage this consciousness exercise in the day, the more readily you will remember these events at the time of your fifteen-minute prayer reflections on Creation, Presence, Memory, Mercy, and Eternity. Every single event that happens in the day is in some way linked to one of these five meditations and your sacred story. But please note: do this exercise for notable events only (two or three times daily at most!). You will know which to attend to, because they will grab you by the gut or the heart.

✠ Sacred Story Prayer at Midday—
Creation, Presence, Memory, Mercy, Eternity

✠ Exercises During the Day—Awakening to your life

✠ Sacred Story Prayer at Evening—
Creation, Presence, Memory, Mercy, Eternity

✠ Sacred Story Daily Journal—Note two significant events of the day.
This should take no more than one minute. Before going to bed, jot down the two most notable events of the day—one negative (depleting hope) and one positive (increasing hope). All you need is to note two events. Write a short phrase to remember both what the event was and your reaction to it. Here are some examples:

Examples: Depleting Faith, Hope, and Love
office meeting—very dispirited about things working out in the future
letter from Joyce—very hurt that she excluded us from the event
my moral indiscretion on Saturday—How come I never seem to improve?

Examples: Increasing Faith, Hope, and Love
the incredible sunset Tuesday—Thank you God for your creation!
Saturday's confession—cried because of the priest's hopeful words
Bob's medical news—Thank you God for hearing our prayers!

✠ Prayer upon Retiring—
Attune to your heart; invite God into your dreams.

✠ Week's-end Journal—Listen for trends, patterns, and links.
This should take about ten minutes. Read your journal comments from the week. Notice any patterns or trends. Did any persons appear more than once? Can you discern patterns in the events depleting hope or increasing hope? Does a certain type of failure occur at "predictable

times"? Jot down any patterns you discover. Then write the two most significant "depleting hope" and "increasing hope" events from the week.

Examples: Patterns Discovered, with Suggested Insights/Actions

Fear of being criticized always precedes my gossiping about others. Perhaps I need to ask God's help on why I fear being criticized and examine what in particular I fear. I will also pray to hold my tongue, to see what I can learn from this discipline.

Every time I meet Carol or someone who reminds me of Carol, I get angry. I need to ask God to help me to forgive Carol.

I have constant anxiety around regular confession, because I am afraid that the priest will think I am not a good person. I need to learn not to let fear control my decisions.

Three times my boss appeared in my journal. Do I need to make a decision?

I seem more negative than positive about God's love for me. (I need to challenge this feeling and affirm God's love by focusing on gratitude.)

Example of Strongest "Depleting Hope" from Daily Journal

My moral indiscretion on Saturday—how come I never seem to improve?

Example of Strongest "Increasing Hope" from Daily Journal

Saturday's confession—cried because of the priest's hopeful words

Example of Note to Myself

My two examples above seem to be connected. I fear that I never seem to improve, yet I also felt great hope when I went to confession. I will trust the feelings of hope and not the feelings based on fear.

✠ Month's-end Journal—Listen for trends, patterns, and links.
This should take no more than fifteen minutes. Read over your weekly summaries, and do the same winnowing process with them as you did for the individual days.

✠ Renew with Monthly Reconciliation—You will be powerfully graced.
This should take one hour total, between preparation and confession. Spend thirty minutes reading over your journal summaries and writing a one-page letter to Jesus. Use the same pattern as your whole-life confession. Do not write more than one page! Discipline yourself to tell the Lord the most essential things for which you need His help and forgiveness, and no more. Take your letter to Reconciliation, and make your confession. Keep your letters, and use them for prayer. You will see your growth and begin to understand much better the outlines of your own sacred story and the Sacred Story of Jesus as well.

✠ Consult the Affirmations Frequently—
    They are your thumbnail discernment aids.

✠ Consult the Guidelines for Healing and Spiritual Growth—
You need them.
Guidelines for Foundational Healing and Spiritual Growth: weeks 30–37
Guidelines for Integrated Healing and Spiritual Growth: weeks 38–39

✠ Live Your Faith—
Engage its spiritual disciplines, serving God and neighbor.

Sacred Story Affirmations

My sacred story takes a lifetime to write.

Be not afraid! Fear comes from the enemy of my human nature.

The pathway to God's peace and healing runs
through my heart's brokenness, sin, fear, anger, and grief.

God resolves all my problems with time and patience.

๛

I will have difficulties in this life.

There are just two ways to cope with my difficulties.
One leads to life; one to death. I will choose life.

๛

"Impossible" is not a word in God's vocabulary.

Sacred Story practice leads to my freedom and authenticity,
but it does not always make me feel happy.

๛

My life's greatest tragedies can be transformed
into my life's major blessings.

Times of peace and hope always give way
to times of difficulty and stress.

Times of difficulty and stress always give way
to times of peace and hope.

๛

I will not tire of asking God for help,
since God delights in my asking.

The urge to stop Sacred Story practice
always comes before my greatest breakthroughs.

කෟ

God gives me insights,
not because I am better than others, but because I am loved.

The insights and graces I need to move forward
in life's journey unfold at the right time.

කෟ

My personal engagement with Sacred Story accomplishes,
through Christ, a work of eternal significance.

Inspirations can have a divine or a demonic source.
I pray for the grace to remember how to discern one from the other.

කෟ

Christ, who has walked before me, shares my every burden.

Christ, who has walked before me, will help me resolve every crisis.

Christ, who has walked before me, knows my every hope.

Christ, who has walked before me, knows everything I suffer.

Christ, who walks before me, will always lead me home to safety.

කෟ

I will strive to curb temptations to react to people and events.
I will ask myself what causes my anger and
irritation at people and events.

I will seek to identify the source of my anger and irritation.

I will give thanks for what angers and upsets me,
for identifying their source will help to set me free.

I will strive to listen, watch, and pray. Listen, watch, and pray.
I will listen, watch, and pray!

ꙮ

Everyone has been mortally wounded spiritually, psychologically,
and physically by Original Sin and the loss of paradise.

Journeying with Christ to the roots of my sins
and addictions will help break their grip.

I will not waste time worrying about my sins and failures. I will use my
time wisely and ask God to help me understand
the source of my sins and failings.

I will trust that Christ came to heal all my wounds.

ꙮ

I alone control Christ's ability to transform my life
into a sacred story. The process begins when I ask
for the grace to honestly name my sins and addictions.

The process continues when I invite Christ to illuminate my narcissism.

Only God's grace and mercy can write my sacred story.

ꙮ

I will strive daily to pick up the cross, for it leads to my life.
The closer I get to holiness, the more I will see
and feel sin's disorder in my life
The more I experience sin's disorder,
the more tempted I will be to disbelieve my life as sacred story.

The way through the temptation is
to surrender my powerlessness to God.

&

It is never too late to open my heart to Christ and
live my life as sacred story.

Christ, who is close to the brokenhearted, restores my lost innocence.

The path to my sacred story is
Creation, Presence, Memory, Mercy, and Eternity.

&

Two Benchmark Guidelines for Spiritual Discernment

To help your awakening and initiation into spiritual discernment, two benchmark guidelines will be beneficial in many life situations. It is important to understand that divine inspiration, or consolation, does not always feel good. Equally important is to realize that an unholy inspiration, or spiritual desolation, does not always feel bad. We will explore this seeming paradox in a later lesson. For now, it is sufficient to absorb the two benchmark guidelines and to understand that each is intended to influence the direction of our life in every thought, word, and deed either toward or away from God.

Benchmark One

Authentic Divine Inspirations, called Consolations, will:

1. Increase the heart's love for God and others,

2. Increase the virtues of docility, humility, and self-generosity, and

3. Not oppose the truths and teachings of Scripture, the Tradition, and the teaching Church.[30]

Consolation can be the consequence of the Divine Physician's Spirit working in you. This form of consolation helps strengthen your heart and soul, encouraging you to turn to God. Consolation helps you to choose thoughts, words, and deeds that express your authentic human nature made in the divine image.

Consolation can also be the consequence of the body/spirit aspect of your divinely shaped human nature. God created your human nature as a gift in the divine image and likeness. In spite of Original Sin's impact, cooperating with God's grace activates embedded life forces of your divinely shaped human nature, helping to heal biochemical, physiological, and emotional imbalances; energizing you; and enabling thoughts, words, and deeds that express your authentic human nature.

Benchmark Two

Authentic Counter-inspirations, called Desolations, will:

1. Increase narcissism, displacing God and others,

2. Decrease docility and humility and increase pride and self-satisfaction,

3. And arouse hungers and desires that, although they feel good, will typically contradict the truths and teachings proposed by the Scripture, Tradition, and the teaching Church. This is because the author of counter-inspirations is opposed to Christ and will lead you away from life and truth.

Counter-inspirations will produce desires that feel authentic because they are linked to fallen human nature's physical lusts and spiritual pride. They are the familiar default drives of a broken heart and a broken human nature.

Desolation can be the consequence of the enemy of human nature working in you. This form of desolation helps weaken your heart and soul, encouraging you to turn from God. Desolation helps you choose thoughts, words, and deeds that are opposed to your divinely shaped human nature.

Desolation can also be the consequence of your own fallen human nature. God created your human nature as a gift in the divine image and likeness. Yet because of Original Sin's impact, not cooperating with God's grace erodes the embedded life forces of your divinely shaped human nature, helping to destroy biochemical, physiological, and emotional balance; de-energizing you; and increasing thoughts, words, and deeds that are in opposition to your authentic human nature

When struggling with these issues, the "Guidelines for Integrated Healing and Spiritual Growth" will be of help (see weeks 38–39).

ATTENDING TO MY REACTION RESPONSES
OF ANGER, FEAR, AND GRIEF
General Awareness Exercises During the Day

When you experience your manifest sins and addictions

Using your own words, speak personally to Christ:

✠ Declare the specific sin, addiction, narcissistic habit, or destructive compulsion as a false lover.

✠ Describe the specific sin, addiction, narcissistic habit, or destructive compulsion as coming from the enemy of your human nature.

✠ Descend with Christ into your memory, to see and feel your first experience of this specific sin, addiction, narcissistic habit, or destructive compulsion, asking Him to compassionately reveal the stress fractures, loneliness, and wounds in your heart that it promised to satisfy.

✠ Denounce the specific sin, addiction, narcissistic habit, or destructive compulsion for its ruinous effect in your life.

✠ Decide for Christ to heal this wound, defuse the stress, anxiety, and fear feeding it, and transform its damaging effects on your life into sacred story.

When you are struggling with these issues, the "Guidelines for Foundational Healing and Spiritual Growth" (weeks 30–37) will be very helpful.

℃ℨ

ATTENDING TO MY REACTION RESPONSES
OF ANGER, FEAR, AND GRIEF
Particular Awareness Exercises During the Day

When you have identified your particular sin of narcissism
and react with anger, anxiety, fear, or grief

Determine if Original Sin's principal manifestation in your life story is in the form of aggressive or passive narcissism. Take notice of the sudden anger, anxiety, fear, or grief that creeps up during your day. Pay particular attention to how these emotions might be touching your narcissism, manifesting as sin and contributing to addictive tendencies. For those one or two standout events in a day that capture your attention, do this short exercise below.

Speak to Christ from your heart:

✠ Ask to be conscious of what you are reacting to rather than reacting impulsively, without thinking.

✠ Ask to feel the heart's fear, temptation, anxiety, anger, and grief present in the reaction.

✠ Ask for knowledge—for graced insight—to begin dismantling this immature, damaging, and self-glorifying process, which for a passive narcissist is particularly depressing and for an aggressive narcissist is particularly electrifying.

✠ Ask who or what initiated this particular pattern of reaction—of overpowering or of blaming others—and why?

✠ Ask for courage to face the negative story of being a passive victim, because facing it can cause panic when you are used to being its slave. But confronting it can bring you peace and freedom.

℘

460

ORIGINAL SIN'S NARCISSISM IN MY LIFE STORY

The *Passive Narcissist*	The *Aggressive Narcissist*
SELF-IDENTIFIES AS A VICTIM.	SELF-IDENTIFIES AS A WINNER.
IS DETERMINED TO HAVE OTHERS NOTICE HOW SPECIAL ONE IS BY POINTING TO HIS UNFAIR SUFFERING.	IS DETERMINED TO HAVE OTHERS NOTICE HOW SPECIAL ONE IS BY DEFEATING ALL OPPONENTS.
IS CYNICAL AND EXCUSES BAD BEHAVIOR BY INSISTING IT IS JUSTIFIED BECAUSE OF HOW MUCH THEY HAVE SUFFERED.	IS CYNICAL AND EXCUSES BAD BEHAVIOR BY INSISTING IT IS JUSTIFIED BECAUSE THEY HAVE EARNED IT.
WALLOWS IN SELF-PITY WHEN HURT, WHETHER THE HURT IS REAL OR IMAGINED.	IS VINDICTIVE WHEN HURT, WHETHER THE HURT IS REAL OR IMAGINED.
BLAMES ANYONE WHO CRITICIZES OR OPPOSES THEM.	THREATENS ANYONE WHO CRITICIZES OR OPPOSES THEM.
PROTECTS HERSELF FROM BEING HURT AGAIN BY KEEPING WOUNDS AS FRESH AS POSSIBLE. IF ANYTHING IS TOO DIFFICULT OR PAINFUL, THEY WILL RETREAT INTO THOSE PAINFUL MEMORIES AND TURN INWARD, AWAY FROM OTHERS.	PROTECTS HERSELF FROM BEING HURT AGAIN BY ERADICATING VULNERABILITIES. IF ANYTHING IS TOO DIFFICULT OR PAINFUL, THEY WILL ACT IN A CONQUEROR ROLE AND DOMINATE OTHERS.
WINS BY EMOTIONAL MANIPULATION.	WINS BY DIRECT CONFRONTATION.
IS SECRETLY ATTACHED TO THEIR OWN WOUNDEDNESS.	IS SECRETLY ATTACHED TO THEIR POWER OF DEFEATING OTHERS.
IS TERRIFIED OF TAKING CONTROL AND PERSONAL RESPONSIBILITY AND HAS DIFFICULTY ADMITTING THIS TO ONESELF.	IS TERRIFIED OF SURRENDERING CONTROL AND BEING VULNERABLE AND HAS DIFFICULTY ADMITTING THIS TO ONESELF.

SACRED STORY INTEGRATION AND AWARENESS TEMPLATE

The Sacred Story practices awaken you to patterns of sin and dysfunction, grace and healing. The Divine Physician helps you identify and unmask the diseases caused by Original Sin, so that you can continue integrated healing and grow in interior freedom. In this wholeness, you are able to serve the Great Work of Reconciliation.

No thought, word, or deed is ever neutral. Everything one thinks, says, or does contributes to the work of the Divine Inspirer or the counter-inspirer. This is not a reason to become obsessed about everything you think, say, and do. It is a reminder to be attentive to the spiritual reality of life, and to labor with God's grace, to choose Christ.

As you listen to your life each day, keep the Sacred Story template in mind. You are seeking a comprehensive view of the enemy of human nature's work to keep you asleep, and a comprehensive view of the Divine Physician's work to awaken you. Watch your life with compassionate, patient, and merciful attention. That is the way of the Divine Physician, who is working for your redemption and complete, integrated healing. As your memory awakens and you become conscious of your life's issues, you will become sensitive and discerning of movements in both directions as shown by the arrows in the template following:

Manifest Sins
The Fruit or Ornamentation
Manifest fear, anger, and grief, and moral weaknesses, vices, addictions, and sinful habits that are the most visible to you.
↓ ↑
Core Sins
The Trunk or Superstructure
Disobedience and narcissism, along with its fear, anger, and grief, that forms the trunk or superstructure of your daily life, feeding on originating sins and events.
↓ ↑
Original Sins
The Roots or Foundation
Ancient, originating events that rooted the patterns of disobedience and narcissism along with their fear, anger and grief.

THE FOUR STAGES OF IGNATIUS'S CONVERSION

STAGE ONE

AWAKENING

Ignatius's Awakening Experience Mirrors →	*His Examen Prayer*
A GRACED EXPERIENCE OF GOD'S LOVE OPENED IGNATIUS TO... ↓	GIVE THANKS FOR FAVORS RECEIVED ↓
A DISSATISFACTION WITH VAIN FANTASIES, WHICH LED TO SURRENDERING TO HOLY DAYDREAMS, CHARACTERIZED BY CONSOLATION, WHICH IN TURN... ↓	PRAY FOR GRACE TO SEE CLEARLY ↓
CAUSED HIM TO REVIEW HIS LIFE AND ACTIONS, LEADING TO... ↓	GIVE A DETAILED ACCOUNT OF CONSCIENCE: GENERAL AND PARTICULAR ↓
GRIEF WITH YEARNING FOR PENANCE AND REPENTANCE FOR HIS PAST SINS, CULMINATING IN... ↓	ASK PARDON FOR ONE'S FAULTS ↓
IGNATIUS'S PASSION TO AMEND HIS LIFE AND A DESIRE TO LOVE GOD WHOLEHEARTEDLY.	RESOLVE AND AMEND TO SERVE GOD

STAGE TWO

FIRST CRISIS—SPEAKING TRUTH TO POWER

Ignatius's Experiences →	*Discernment Principles Revealed*
AN ENEMY VOICE EVOKED IGNATIUS'S FEAR OF A LIFELONG STRUGGLE WITH HIS SINFUL HABITS. ↓	THERE IS CONSCIOUS FEAR AND ANXIETY OVER SURRENDERING SINFUL AND ADDICTIVE HABITS. ↓
IGNATIUS REJECTED THE "ENEMY OF HUMAN NATURE" AND CONFRONTED THIS ENEMY'S FALSE PROMISES. ↓	ONE CONFRONTS THE THREATENING "VOICE" OF SIN AND ADDICTION WITH THE TRUTH THAT THEY BRING DEATH, NOT LIFE. ↓
PEACE WAS RESTORED AFTER IGNATIUS TRUTHFULLY NAMED SIN AND ADDICTION AS DEATH DEALING.	FINALLY, PEACE RETURNS AND ANXIETY DISSOLVES.

STAGE THREE

SECOND CRISIS—SURRENDERING CONTROL
AND ADMITTING POWERLESSNESS TO SAVE ONESELF

Ignatius's Experiences →	Discernment Principles Revealed
IGNATIUS'S STRUGGLE WITH SCRUPLES HID HIS VAINGLORY. ↓	THE INITIAL CONFRONTATION WITH ONE'S ROOT SIN ↓
IGNATIUS CONSTANTLY RECONFESSED TO SEEK SALVATION BY WILLPOWER ALONE. ↓	THE EFFORT TO CONTROL ONE'S ROOT SIN ONLY BY PERSONAL EFFORT OR FORCE OF WILL ↓
IGNATIUS EXPERIENCED SUICIDAL IMPULSES, DISGUST, AND THE DESIRE TO WALK AWAY FROM HIS NEWFOUND FAITH. ↓	DESPAIR AND DESIRE TO GIVE UP FAITH WHEN HUMAN EFFORT ALONE FAILS ↓
IGNATIUS TRACED THE SPIRIT OF DISGUST TO A DEMONIC SOURCE. ↓	INSIGHT THAT DESIRE TO REJECT THE SPIRITUAL JOURNEY IS A TEMPTATION ↓
IGNATIUS ABANDONED HIS COMPULSIVE CONFESSING OF PAST SINS.	THE ADMITTING OF POWERLESSNESS TO SAVE ONESELF AND THE SURRENDERING OF PRIDEFUL ACTIONS

STAGE FOUR

LIFE-LONG PATIENCE WHILE GOD WRITES OUR SACRED STORY

Ignatius's Experience	Universal Principle	Mystical Path
IGNATIUS, JUSTIFYING HIMSELF, ANXIOUSLY RECOILED AND FOCUSED ON HIS SINFULNESS. ↓	PANIC OVER ONE'S SALVATION DUE TO WEAKNESS AND SINFULNESS →	PURGATION ↓
IGNATIUS, NO LONGER FEARFUL, REGRETTED NOT HAVING RESPONDED SOONER TO GOD'S GRACES. ↓	SADNESS AT SLOWNESS OF ONE'S RESPONSE TO GOD'S LOVE AND INVITATION TO INTIMACY →	ILLUMINATION ↓
IGNATIUS FELT INTENSE JOY AT THE THOUGHT OF DYING AND BEING WITH GOD. →	AN ARDENT, ALL-EMBRACING LOVE OF GOD AND DESIRE FOR COMPLETE UNION WITH THE TRINITY →	UNION

SACRED STORY PRAYER MEDITATIONS

Pray the whole fifteen-minute Sacred Story prayer once or twice daily, and consciously repeat to Christ Jesus the five-word litany whenever you are in the grip of fear, anxiety, or grief or dealing with sins, addictions, and destructive compulsions.

CREATION
I believe God created everything in love and for love; I ask for heart-felt knowledge of God's love for me, and for
gratitude for the general and particular graces of this day.

PRESENCE
I believe God is present in each moment and event of my life, and I ask for the grace to awaken, see and feel where and how,
especially in this present moment.

MEMORY
I believe every violation of love committed by me and against me is in my memory, and I ask God to reveal them to me, especially those that have manifested themselves today, so I can be healed.

MERCY
I believe that forgiveness is the only path to healing and illumination. I beg for the grace of forgiveness, and the grace to forgive, especially for the general and particular failures of this day, and from my past.

ETERNITY
I believe the grace of forgiveness opens my heart, making my every thought, word, and deed bear fruit that endures to eternity. I ask that everything in my life serve Christ's Great Work of Reconciliation.

മ

Our Father

Our Father, who art in heaven,
hallowed be Thy name.
Thy Kingdom come, thy will be done,
on earth, as it is in heaven.
Give us this day our daily bread,
And
forgive us our trespasses,
as we forgive those who trespass against us.
Lead us not into temptation,
but deliver us from evil.
Amen.
(This is the prayer favored by Ignatius for this discipline.)

Suscipe

Take Lord, receive,
my liberty, my memory, my understanding, my entire will.
Whatsoever I have or hold,
You have given to me.
I surrender it all back to you
to be governed by your will.
Give me only Your love and grace.
This is enough for me,
and I ask for nothing more.
Amen.
(This is the prayer of St. Ignatius that concludes his Spiritual Exercises)

Your ways, O Lord, make known to me;
teach me your paths. Guide me in your truth and teach me,
for you are God my savior, and for you I wait all the day.
Good and upright is the Lord; thus he shows sinners the way.
He guides the humble to justice, and teaches the humble his way.
All the paths of the Lord are kindness and constancy
toward those who keep his covenant and his decrees.
The friendship of the Lord is with those who fear him,
and his covenant, for their instruction.
(Ps 25:4–5,8–9,10,14)

NOTES

Abide in Me

A Daily Relationship with Christ as Savior,
Divine Physician, and Lord of All

I invite you to pray with the first few verses of chapter fifteen from the Gospel of St. John. Take as many minutes, hours, or days as you wish to pray with St. John. There is no hurry.

> I am the true vine, and my Father is the vinedresser. Every branch of mine that bears no fruit, he takes away, and every branch that does bear fruit he prunes, that it may bear more fruit. You are already made clean by the word which I have spoken to you. Abide in me, and I in you. As the branch cannot bear fruit by itself, unless it abides in the vine, neither can you, unless you abide in me.

> I am the vine, you are the branches. He who abides in me, and I in him, he it is that bears much fruit, for apart from me you can do nothing. If a man does not abide in me, he is cast forth as a branch and withers; and the branches are gathered, thrown into the fire and burned. If you abide in me, and my words abide in you, ask whatever you will, and it shall be done for you. By this my Father is glorified, that you bear much fruit, and so prove to be my disciples.

> As the Father has loved me, so have I loved you; abide in
> my love. If you keep my commandments, you will abide in
> my love, just as I have kept my Father's commandments
> and abide in his love. These things I have spoken to you,
> that my joy may be in you, and that your joy may be full.
> (Jn 15:1–11)

The Ignatian Examen that inspires Sacred Story prayer became an active part of my Jesuit life in 1994. Having entered the Society of Jesus in 1973, I had already lived for twenty years as a Jesuit—eight of those years as a priest. My practice of this prayer was inconstant for many years. By most measures, one could say that I had a Christian vocation. I mean this in much the same way that one looking at a Catholic married couple with children or a single person doing service work would agree that each of these persons has a Christian vocation.

A life of prayer and daily Mass, a yearly eight-day retreat, and a fair amount of theological living (faith-oriented reading plus lots of God/Church conversations) made me feel I had a real religious life. And I did. The question for me had become instead: was I fully living a Christian vocation? The answer to that is much more complex. For simplicity's sake, let me say that I have learned more clearly that a Christian vocation is not equivalent to simply belonging to a religious order. To use an analogy, a Christian marriage is different from being Catholic and married with children.

My Christian vocation requires that I daily open myself to Jesus and allow my actions, emotions, desires, loves, hurts, fears, and plans (especially my precious plans) to be shared with and shaped by Jesus's influence. Sharing means that I submit myself to Jesus and let Him have a say in what I am doing and whom I am daily becoming, what I hold on to and what I relinquish. Acting in a Christian way means that I no longer belong to myself. Rather, I belong to Christ.

Some good friends of mine who have been married for several years recently shared with me one of the biggest adjustments they have had to make as a result of being married. They can no longer make plans in blissful isolation but have to consult with each other about practically every aspect of their lives. This consultative sharing can be both a joy and an annoyance. Each one is called out of the prison of their own ego and invited to love, sacrifice, and make adjustments so that the other can grow and flourish. We really grow when we are called out of ourselves. But there is joy in sharing intimately in the life of the Beloved. We are created for the joy of sharing intimately in the life of the other. We are made in the image and likeness of God who is relationship.

A Christian vocation requires an intimate relationship with Christ. It requires making this relationship a priority on a daily basis. Sacred Story prayer, more than any other spiritual discipline I have encountered in my forty years in religious life, brings me face-to-face with Christ in a relationship that calls me out of myself. It is the most effective path that has enabled me to be true to the man and priest that God desires me to be. It is not always easy, and I do not want to minimize the challenge it has been in terms of my honesty and openness. It is a joy and an annoyance for exactly the same reasons as with any serious relational commitment. I have had moments of aggravation and difficulty in praying Sacred Story. I have also experienced times when I did not want to pray because I knew I would be confronted with things I would prefer to ignore.

Here is a typical example. Some time ago, I was struggling internally with someone who, I judged, had wronged me. I was hurt, frustrated, and upset from what I perceived to be an injustice against myself. I discovered I was not at all upset when this person experienced misfortunes, for I felt this person deserved it. In prayer, I was not speaking with Jesus about this person. Instead I found myself rehearsing conversations in my head about how I had been wronged. My focus was on myself.

One day I was awakened to my lack of Christian charity. Instinctively I understood that I needed to bring my feelings about this person to Jesus, and yet, I resisted. A part of my heart wanted to simply rehearse my justified hurts. It took several Sacred Story prayer periods for me to begin to speak from my heart to Christ about what I was feeling. The insight that I needed to reach out and forgive this person came in a split second. I was also able to accept some of the fault lines in my own personality, which may have contributed to the initial difficulties. It is amazing how that clarity comes with honesty. This was a graced experience!

However, upon leaving the time of Sacred Story prayer, a new inspiration took hold. Perhaps it is unwise to forgive? I could lose ground. The re-emerging frustration and darkened spirit—the counter-inspiration—accompanying this new inspiration was in marked contrast to the peacefulness I had experienced previously in the time of Sacred Story prayer. In testing the spiritual inspirations, it was clear which inspiration was from the Divine Inspirer and which inspiration was from the counter-inspirer. Honestly, I was strongly tempted to ignore the truth of my spiritual discernment and go with the refusal to forgive. But I was being invited by God to disarm. I was invited to be vulnerable. It was an invitation to greater spiritual freedom, the freedom that Ignatius calls detachment. Freedom sounds good, but it is not something we always really want.

This event was a wake-up call, because it clearly presented the difficult choice of forgiveness. It may sound odd, but it gave me the conviction that Jesus is interested in everything I am doing. Every thought, word, and deed I have is important to Christ. He wants to be part of everything I experience. Sacred Story, prayed faithfully, has made me aware of what being in relationship with Jesus means. I feel the effects of the surrender that is necessary for a real relationship with Jesus, and I feel it in a particularly powerful way twice a day. I have chosen to make spiritual surrender the center of my Jesuit life. And praying Sacred Story prayer has revealed how many areas of my daily life I keep off-limits from Christ.

A strong intellectual tradition is a characteristic of the Society of Jesus; it is a good in and of itself. But there is something that Ignatius wanted Jesuits to value above learning: virtue, the spiritual life, and the surrender of our will and our hearts to Christ. The human gifts we cultivate only reach their fruitfulness in light of a well-grounded spiritual life. In section 10 of the Jesuit Constitutions, entitled "How the Whole Body of the Society is to be Preserved and Increased in its Well-being," Ignatius says the following:

> Thus it appears that care should be taken in general that all the members of the Society devote themselves to the solid and perfect virtues and to spiritual pursuits, and attach greater importance to them than to learning and other natural and human gifts. For these interior gifts are necessary to make those exterior means efficacious for the end which is being sought. (part X [813] 2)

This advice is written for Jesuits, and for the care and growth of the Society of Jesus. Yet it offers good pragmatic Ignatian wisdom that is applicable to any vocation or situation in the Church. Human gifts and qualities reach their perfection and the height of their potency when the bearer of those gifts and/or qualities is grafted to the vine of Christ—when they surrender to Christ. This holds true for the talents of the athlete, the intellectual acumen of the college student, the artistic skills of the singer or architect, the healing gifts of the doctor or nurse, the ministry of religious and priests, the leadership skills of the politician and the professional business person, and the love of husband and wife for each other and for their children.

The personal decision I face daily—twice daily—is how much of my life will I allow to be grafted onto the vine of Christ? How much will I allow myself to abide in His Love? Jesus must have been looking at grapevines when He spoke this passage from John's Gospel. The vine or stalk is the source of all nutrients. Only shoots which grow directly from it, or have been grafted onto it, bear fruit. As I look back over my life, I can see that I have produced all sorts of fruit by my own effort. What has become a much more important question at this point is, how much of what I produce is the fruit of my relationship with Jesus? In other words, have I allowed myself to become a "daily disciple" of Jesus by being in relationship with Him? Am I grafted onto the vine of Christ?

The bottom line of my experience of Sacred Story is that I am being challenged to open all of my heart and my life to God's grace. While the commitment to the Jesuits and the priesthood always felt full-time and lifelong, the relationship with Jesus seemed to have an on-again, off-again feel to it. Quite frankly, I was more in control than Christ. Now I feel that I have truly begun to commit to Jesus. Twice daily I need to come to Him with my ups and downs, my joys and angers, my loves and victories, my failures and grief, and my constant need.

My constant need: what does that mean? It means that Sacred Story prayer makes me more aware of my weaknesses, my failures, and my need for redemption. I have been graced with the eyes to see the reason for Christ's redeeming sacrifice, more clearly than ever before. It is a sacrifice and grace I cannot live without. Perhaps it is the same discovery of the alcoholic or drug addict. One day, the addict finally wakes up and realizes that the life they thought they controlled is actually out of control.

The only way to salvation is to surrender to love's sobriety and embrace. The alcoholic genuinely in touch with the truth of his life knows he is always recovering and is never fully recovered. He must live constantly with the knowledge of his vulnerability and turn to God for help and aid. It is a life of submission, humility, and holy dependence.

Is the invitation to submission, humility, and holy dependence the best way for me to convince you to stay committed to Sacred Story prayer? Is this good marketing? Perhaps not, but I am convinced that while your issues may be different from mine, your experience will pull you into the same position of humility, submission, and dependency on God when confronted with the truth of your weakness and need.

What could possibly be attractive about living this way? Praying and living Sacred Story enables a person to be vulnerable, humbly submissive, and dependent on God. I can rely on Jesus, who has promised to give me what I need: "If you remain in me and my words remain in you, ask for whatever you want and it will be done for you" (Jn 15:7). These words utterly change a person and her worldview. Jesus offers this relationship so that her joy "may be full."

How so? Because I experience that even in the weakest and most vulnerable condition of my life, Love does not walk away from me. Love has irrevocably committed Himself to me. He sacrificed for me so that I could be whole, and He wants the knowledge of this great love to be known by me on the most intimate level. He has also promised that this life of discipleship gives great glory to the Father in heaven. Allowing myself to abide in His love will bear fruit that will give glory to the Father of Jesus Christ. What an awesome reality!

At the beginning of a retreat or in my daily Sacred Story prayer, I try to commit to this relationship. The renewal of my vocational commitment to Christ in the daily engagement with Sacred Story prayer is a means to deepen the knowledge of my radical dependence on God. It fosters the joy of a personal relationship with Christ Jesus that grounds me and opens me up to the deepest yearnings of my heart.

The more I open my heart to a serious relationship with Christ, the more I come to understand the joy for which I have been created. You also have been created for this joy. That is why I am confident you will

477

remain in the embrace of Sacred Story and the Lord Jesus, who loves you beyond all reckoning. The Love that grounds the universe holds you in His Heart.

ೞ

Glorious Lord Christ,
You who are the first and the last,
The living and the dead and the risen again;
You who gather into your exuberant unity
Every beauty, every affinity, every energy,
Every mode of existence;
It is you to whom my being cried out with a desire
As vast as the universe,
"In truth you are my Lord and my God."[31]

ഇ

NOTES

NOTES

NOTES

NOTES

NOTES

NOTES

NOTES

About the Author

Fr. William Watson, S.J., D.Min., has spent over thirty years developing Ignatian programs and retreats. He has collaborated extensively with Fr. Robert Spitzer in the last fifteen years on Ignatian retreats for corporate CEOs. In the spring of 2011, he launched a nonprofit institute to bring Ignatian spirituality to Catholics of all ages and walks of life. The Sacred Story Institute is promoting third-millennium evangelization for the Society of Jesus and the Church by using the time-tested Examination of Conscience of St. Ignatius.

Fr. Watson has served as director of retreat programs at Georgetown University, vice president for mission at Gonzaga University, and provincial assistant for international ministries for the Oregon Province of the Society of Jesus. He holds master's degrees in divinity and in pastoral studies 1986, from Weston Jesuit School of Theology: Cambridge, Mass.). He received his Doctor of Ministry degree in 2009 from The Catholic University of America in Washington, DC.

FORTY WEEKS ~ LETTERS FROM PRISON
MINISTRY FOR INMATES

To Inmates, Chaplains and Friends:

If you are an inmate and have a copy of *Forty Weeks Letters from Prison* and would like to have someone to correspond with you over the course of the program as I did with Ritchie, please write to us at the address below. We will work to find you a good spiritual guide and friend to help you with your questions.

To initiate the process, send us in two pages your life story and why you want to begin this walk with Jesus over the course of forty weeks. We will read what you say and work to find you a good spiritual guide and friend to correspond with you and help you along the way as I did with Ritchie.

If you are a prison chaplain or a friend who wants to participate in our letter writing program or help us with this project, please go to our website (https://sacredstory.net/forty-weeks/) and you will find a link to give us the information we need to get you involved.

FORTY WEEKS ~ Letters from Prison is collaborating with award winning songwriters and singers on an album titled, Worth of Souls. The record label, Stone Angel Music Inc. and Sacred Story Institute are still working to find a way to get this music to the incarcerated in prisons as *Letters from Prison* goes to press. In the meantime, we will provide a link for free downloads to interested prison chaplains and those who work with the incarcerated. Contact us at: https://sacredstory.net/forty-weeks/ and fill out the interest form under Prison Ministry.

Sacred Story Institute
Letters from Prison Project
1401 E Jefferson, STE 405
Seattle, WA 98122
https://sacredstory.net/forty-weeks/

Sacred Story Press
Seattle, USA
sacredstorypress.com

Sacred Story Press explores dynamic new dimensions of classic Ignatian spirituality, based on St. Ignatius's Conscience Examen in the Sacred Story prayer method, pioneered by Fr. Bill Watson, S.J. We are creating a new class of spiritual resources. Our publications are research-based, authentic to the Catholic Tradition, and designed to help individuals achieve integrated spiritual growth and holiness of life.

We Request Your Feedback

The Sacred Story Institute welcomes feedback on Forty Weeks. Contact us via email or letter (see below). Give us ideas, suggestions, and inspirations for how to make this a better resource for Catholics and Christians of all ages and walks of life. Please also contact us for bulk orders and group discounts.

admin-team@sacredstory.net
Sacred Story Institute & Sacred Story Press
1401 E. Jefferson, Suite 405
Seattle, Washington 98122

ENDNOTES

---

[1] While the overall recidivism rate for prisoners released from federal institutions is around 75 percent after three years, the recidivism rate for those going through Life Connections is closer to 10-15 percent. This is dramatic by any standards. It is effective because it uses researched and evidenced-based interventions. They learn to correct thinking errors that contribute to criminal behavior. They learn to empathize with victims so as not to victimize in the future. They learn to cope and manage their emotions and problem solve in a constructive manner. They learn to become accountable for their behavior.
To the editor: By Mel Bockelman / Overland Park, Kansas
http://www.leavenworthtimes.com/article/20150808/OPINION/150809519
Posted Aug 8, 2015 at 12:36 PM

[2] Paul Doncoeur, SJ, The Heart of Ignatius, (Baltimore: Helicon, 1959), 34

[4]. There is no need to read the Scripture passages during your fifteen-minute prayer periods. If your heart leads you to read these Scripture passages apart from the fifteen-minute prayer periods, you are encouraged to follow your heart!

[5]. A suggestion: Use this name to address God every time you naturally think of God throughout the day. For example, you may say in your heart before a meeting: "Lord Jesus, be with me now." Say it, and then just move on with your meeting. Do not make this a tedious exercise, but one that feels natural and relaxed. You do not have to think long and hard about God. The purpose of this spontaneous prayer is just a short, friendly reminder of God's presence. Use this name if you find yourself conversing with God during the day.

[6]. Ignatius is very specific that spiritual exercises should be kept to the exact time allotted for them. The only exception he makes is that an exercise may be extended by one minute if one is having difficulty, or is experiencing some upset or turmoil. Ignatius believed that this brief extension of an exercise in times of difficulty works positively to help us confront and not be cowed by spirits of darkness and the psychological and emotional anxieties they manipulate.

[7]. If you feel called, you can reflect on the entire Decalogue as enumerated in the Catechism of the Catholic Church (CCC, 561–672). You can either purchase an inexpensive paperback, or you can access the text online:
http://www.vatican.va/archive/ccc_css/archive/catechism/p3s2c1a1.htm

[8]. "Compulsion, impaired control, persistence, irritability, relapse, and craving—these are all the hallmarks of addiction—any addiction." Gabor Maté, In the Realm of Hungry Ghosts: Close Encounters with Addiction (Berkeley: North Atlantic Books, 2010), 136-9.

[9]. Catechism of the Catholic Church (CCC) 1469--John Paul II, RP 31, 5.

. Our studies have shown that those who committed to two times a day for prayer were more faithful in cultivating a sustainable daily practice. Also, research revealed that those who practiced a simple logbook or journal exercise were also more faithful to the prayer disciplines.

11. See endnote 13.

12. From the Catechism of the Catholic Church [CCC #1854-64] on THE GRAVITY OF SIN: MORTAL AND VENIAL SIN:

> Sins are rightly evaluated according to their gravity. The distinction between mortal and venial sin, already evident in Scripture, became part of the tradition of the Church. It is corroborated by human experience.

> Mortal sin destroys charity in the heart of man by a grave violation of God's law; it turns man away from God, who is his ultimate end and his beatitude, by preferring an inferior good to him. Venial sin allows charity to subsist, even though it offends and wounds it.

> Mortal sin, by attacking the vital principle within us - that is, charity - necessitates a new initiative of God's mercy and a conversion of heart which is normally accomplished within the setting of the sacrament of reconciliation: When the will sets itself upon something that is of its nature incompatible with the charity that orients man toward his ultimate end, then the sin is mortal by its very object, whether it contradicts the love of God, such as blasphemy or perjury, or the love of neighbor, such as homicide or adultery. But when the sinner's will is set upon something that of its nature involves a disorder, but is not opposed to the love of God and neighbor, such as thoughtless chatter or immoderate laughter and the like, such sins are venial.

> For a sin to be mortal, three conditions must together be met: "Mortal sin is sin whose object is grave matter and which is also committed with full knowledge and deliberate consent."

> Grave matter is specified by the Ten Commandments, corresponding to the answer of Jesus to the rich young man: "Do not kill, Do not commit adultery, Do not steal, Do not bear false witness, Do not defraud, Honor your father and your mother." The gravity of sins is more or less great: murder is graver than theft. One must also take into account who is wronged: violence against parents is in itself graver than violence against a stranger.

> Mortal sin requires full knowledge and complete consent. It presupposes knowledge of the sinful character of the act, of its opposition to God's law. It also implies a consent sufficiently deliberate to be a personal choice. Feigned ignorance and hardness of heart do not diminish, but rather increase, the voluntary character of a sin.

> Unintentional ignorance can diminish or even remove the imputability of a grave offense. But no one is deemed to be ignorant of the principles of the moral law, which are written in the conscience of every man. The promptings of feelings and

passions can also diminish the voluntary and free character of the offense, as can external pressures or pathological disorders. Sin committed through malice, by deliberate choice of evil, is the gravest.

Mortal sin is a radical possibility of human freedom, as is love itself. It results in the loss of charity and the privation of sanctifying grace, that is, of the state of grace. If it is not redeemed by repentance and God's forgiveness, it causes exclusion from Christ's kingdom and the eternal death of hell, for our freedom has the power to make choices for ever, with no turning back. However, although we can judge that an act is in itself a grave offense, we must entrust judgment of persons to the justice and mercy of God.

One commits venial sin when, in a less serious matter, he does not observe the standard prescribed by the moral law, or when he disobeys the moral law in a grave matter, but without full knowledge or without complete consent.

Venial sin weakens charity; it manifests a disordered affection for created goods; it impedes the soul's progress in the exercise of the virtues and the practice of the moral good; it merits temporal punishment. Deliberate and unrepented venial sin disposes us little by little to commit mortal sin. However venial sin does not break the covenant with God. With God's grace it is humanly reparable. "Venial sin does not deprive the sinner of sanctifying grace, friendship with God, charity, and consequently eternal happiness."

While he is in the flesh, man cannot help but have at least some light sins. But do not despise these sins which we call "light": if you take them for light when you weigh them, tremble when you count them. A number of light objects makes a great mass; a number of drops fills a river; a number of grains makes a heap. What then is our hope? Above all, confession.

"Therefore I tell you, every sin and blasphemy will be forgiven men, but the blasphemy against the Spirit will not be forgiven." There are no limits to the mercy of God, but anyone who deliberately refuses to accept his mercy by repenting, rejects the forgiveness of his sins and the salvation offered by the Holy Spirit. Such hardness of heart can lead to final impenitence and eternal loss.

[13]. GOD WILLED HUMAN NATURE [CCC #362-8]:

The human person, created in the image of God, is a being at once corporeal and spiritual. The biblical account expresses this reality in symbolic language when it affirms that "then the LORD God formed man of dust from the ground, and breathed into his nostrils the breath of life; and man became a living being." [Gen 2:7.] Man, whole and entire, is therefore willed by God (emphasis supplied). In Sacred Scripture the term "soul" often refers to human life or the entire human person. [Cf. Mt 16:25-26; Jn 15:13; Acts 2:41.] But "soul" also refers to the innermost aspect of man, that which is of greatest value in him, [Cf. Mt 10:28; 26:38; Jn 12:27; 2 Macc 6:30.] that by which he is most especially in God's image: "soul" signifies the spiritual principle in man.

The human body shares in the dignity of "the image of God": it is a human body precisely because it is animated by a spiritual soul, and it is the whole human person that is intended to become, in the body of Christ, a temple of the Spirit: [Cf. 1 Cor 6:19-20; 15:44-45.]

Man, though made of body and soul, is a unity. Through his very bodily condition he sums up in himself the elements of the material world. Through him they are thus brought to their highest perfection and can raise their voice in praise freely given to the Creator. For this reason man may not despise his bodily life. Rather he is obliged to regard his body as good and to hold it in honor since God has created it and will raise it up on the last day. [GS 14 § 1; cf. Dan 3:57-80.]

The unity of soul and body is so profound that one has to consider the soul to be the "form" of the body: [Cf. Council of Vienne (1312): DS 902.] i.e., it is because of its spiritual soul that the body made of matter becomes a living, human body; spirit and matter, in man, are not two natures united, but rather their union forms a single nature.

The Church teaches that every spiritual soul is created immediately by God - it is not "produced" by the parents—and also that it is immortal: it does not perish when it separates from the body at death, and it will be reunited with the body at the final Resurrection. [Cf. Pius XII, Humani Generis: DS 3896; Paul VI, CPG § 8; Lateran Council V (1513): DS 1440.]

Sometimes the soul is distinguished from the spirit: St. Paul for instance prays that God may sanctify his people "wholly", with "spirit and soul and body" kept sound and blameless at the Lord's coming. [1 Thess 5:23.] The Church teaches that this distinction does not introduce a duality into the soul. [Cf. Council of Constantinople IV (870): DS 657.] "Spirit" signifies that from creation man is ordered to a supernatural end and that his soul can gratuitously be raised beyond all it deserves to communion with God. [Cf. Vatican Council I, Dei Filius: DS 3005; GS 22 § 5; Humani Generis: DS 3891.]

The spiritual tradition of the Church also emphasizes the heart, in the biblical sense of the depths of one's being, where the person decides for or against God. [Cf. Jer 31:33; Deut 6:5; 29:3; Isa 29:13; Ezek 36:26; Mt 6:21; Lk 8:15; Rom.5:5.]

[14]. MAN IN PARADISE [CCC #374-9]:

The first man was not only created good, but was also established in friendship with his Creator and in harmony with himself and with the creation around him, in a state that would be surpassed only by the glory of the new creation in Christ.

The Church, interpreting the symbolism of biblical language in an authentic way, in the light of the New Testament and Tradition, teaches that our first parents, Adam and Eve, were constituted in an original "state of holiness and justice". [Cf. Council of Trent (1546): DS 1511.] This grace of original holiness was "to share in divine life". [Cf. LG 2.]

By the radiance of this grace all dimensions of man's life were confirmed. As long as he remained in the divine intimacy, man would not have to suffer or die. [Cf. Gen

2:17; 3:16,19.] The inner harmony of the human person, the harmony between man and woman, [Cf. Gen 2:25.] and finally the harmony between the first couple and all creation, comprised the state called "original justice."

The "mastery" over the world that God offered man from the beginning was realized above all within man himself: mastery of self. The first man was unimpaired and ordered in his whole being because he was free from the triple concupiscence [Cf. 1 Jn 2:16.] that subjugates him to the pleasures of the senses, covetousness for earthly goods, and self-assertion, contrary to the dictates of reason.

The sign of man's familiarity with God is that God places him in the garden. [Cf. Gen 2:8.] There he lives "to till it and keep it." Work is not yet a burden [Gen 2:15; cf. 3:17-19] but rather the collaboration of man and woman with God in perfecting the visible creation. This entire harmony of original justice, foreseen for man in God's plan, will be lost by the sin of our first parents.

[15]. For Augustine, the problem was the will, not the body. He came to define Original Sin as narcissism, the turning of the will "to live according to oneself" (secundum se vivere). Here is his classic account from On the City of God, Book 14: (13) Moreover, our first parents fell openly into the sin of disobedience only because, secretly, they had begun to be guilty. Actually, their bad deed of their bad will was nothing else than pride. For "pride is the beginning of all sin" (Sir 10:13). And what is pride but an appetite for inordinate exaltation? Now exaltation is inordinate when the souls cuts itself off from the very Source to which it should keep close and somehow makes itself—and thus becomes—an end in itself. This takes place when the soul becomes inordinately pleased with itself, and such self-pleasing occurs when the soul falls away from the unchangeable Good which ought to please itself. Now this falling away is the soul's own doing, for if the will had merely remained firm in the love of that higher immutable Good which lighted its mind into knowledge and warmed its will into love, it would not have turned away in search of satisfaction in itself and, by so doing, have lost that light and warmth. And thus Eve would not have believed that the serpent's lie was true, nor would Adam have preferred the will of his wife to the will of God or have supposed this transgression of God's command was venial when he refused to abandon the partner of his life even if it meant a partnership of sin.

Our first parents, then, must have already fallen before they could do the evil deed, before they could commit the sin of eating the forbidden fruit. For such bad fruit could come only from a bad tree. That the tree became bad was contrary to its nature, because such a condition could come about only because of a defect of the will—and a defect is whatever goes against nature. Notice, however, that such worsening by reason of a defect is possible only in a nature that had been created out of nothing. In a word, a nature is a nature because it is something made by God, but a nature falls away from That Which Is because the nature was made out of nothing." William Harmless, SJ, Augustine In His Own Words (Washington, DC: The Catholic University of America Press, 2010),351-2.

[16]. Ignatius was a great admirer of St. Francis of Assisi and it was the Franciscans who managed the holy sites in Jerusalem. There he could be near the sons of St. Francis and walk in the footsteps of Jesus.

. "Brothers and sisters: The Spirit scrutinizes everything, even the depths of God. Among men, who knows what pertains to the man except his spirit that is within? Similarly, no one knows what pertains to God except the Spirit of God. We have not received the spirit of the world but the Spirit who is from God, so that we may understand the things freely given us by God. And we speak about them not with words taught by human wisdom, but with words taught by the Spirit, describing spiritual realities in spiritual terms. Now the natural man does not accept what pertains to the Spirit of God, for to him it is foolishness, and he cannot understand it, because it is judged spiritually. The one who is spiritual, however, can judge everything but is not subject to judgment by anyone. For "who has known the mind of the Lord, so as to counsel him?" But we have the mind of Christ." (I Corinthians 2: 10b–16)

A sermon by Pope St Leo the Great: I SHALL PUT MY LAWS WITHIN THEM:

Dearly beloved, when our Lord Jesus Christ was preaching the Gospel of the kingdom and healing various illnesses throughout the whole of Galilee, the fame of his mighty works spread into all of Syria, and great crowds from all parts of Judea flocked to the heavenly physician.

Because human ignorance is slow to believe what it does not see, and equally slow to hope for what it does not know, those who were to be instructed in the divine teaching had first to be aroused by bodily benefits and visible miracles so that, once they had experienced his gracious power, they would no longer doubt the wholesome effect of his doctrine. In order, therefore, to transform outward healings into inward remedies, and to cure men's souls now that he had healed their bodies, our Lord separated himself from the surrounding crowds, climbed to the solitude of a neighboring mountain, and called the apostles to himself.

From the height of this mystical site he then instructed them in the most lofty doctrines, suggesting both by the very nature of the place and by what he was doing that it was he who long ago had honored Moses by speaking to him. At that time, his words showed a terrifying justice, but now they reveal a sacred compassion, in order to fulfill what was promised in the words of the prophet Jeremiah: Behold the days are coming, says the Lord, when I shall establish a new covenant with the house of Israel and with the house of Judah. After those days, says the Lord, I shall put my laws within them and write them on their hearts.

And so it was that he who had spoken to Moses spoke also to the apostles. Writing in the hearts of his disciples, the swift hand of the Word composed the ordinances of the new covenant. And this was not done as formerly, in the midst of dense clouds, amid terrifying sounds and lightning, so that the people were frightened away from approaching the mountain. Instead, there was a tranquil discourse which clearly reached the ears of all who stood nearby so that the harshness of the law might be softened by the gentleness of grace, and the spirit of adoption might dispel the terror of slavery.

Concerning the content of Christ's teaching, his own sacred words bear witness; thus whoever longs to attain eternal blessedness can now recognize the steps that lead to that high happiness. Blessed, he says, are the poor in spirit, for theirs is the kingdom of heaven. It might have been unclear to which poor he was referring, if after the words Blessed are the poor, he had not added anything about the kind of poor he had in mind. For then the poverty that many suffer because of grave and harsh necessity might seem sufficient to merit the kingdom of heaven.

But when he says: Blessed are the poor in spirit, he shows that the kingdom of heaven is to be given to those who are distinguished by their humility of soul rather than by their lack of worldly goods. (Taken from Roman Catholic Office of Readings, book III, weeks of the year 6–34).

[18]. People today often form judgments about human nature based on the experience of human nature in its fallen state. We forget that at one point human nature, as a unity of body and spirit, was undivided: Our hearts were undivided. With the Fall, our hearts are divided and we can no longer easily determine right and wrong: "Ignorance of the fact that man has a wounded nature, inclined to the evil, gives rise to serious errors in the areas of education, politics, social action and morals." [CCC #407].

[19]. THE PRIMACY OF THE SPIRITUAL OVER THE MATERIAL:

Every year science grounded in a materialist-only view of the universe confronts inexplicable phenomena, indicating the primacy of the spiritual realm as the main animator of the physical world. Mario Beauregard's The Spiritual Brain is a work on this topic and the source of some of the ideas below. See also the classic work, The Healing Light by Agnes Sanford. Sanford's Christian healing ministry helped launch the Catholic Charismatic Renewal movement.

✠ Why does the placebo effect work, in which the mind creates curative processes reducing or eliminating ill and diseased states in the human organism?

✠ Why do repeated studies show that some persons are able to mentally affect physical objects outside themselves when the odds of this being mere chance are a trillion to one?

✠ Why are the neurological brain maps of individuals in deep prayer states (feeling connected to a reality outside themselves) identical to individuals actually in direct contact to other persons— with both maps displaying the radically complex neural brain states of real experiences involving human emotion, body representation, visual, motor imagery and spiritual perception?

✠ Why do deep spiritual experiences rewire the neural networks of the brain and lead to deep, long-lasting, attitudinal and behavioral changes such as growth in compassion, love for others, willingness to forgive and awareness of the unity of creation?

✠ Why, when persons are revived after clinical death (zero heart or brainwave activity), do they frequently possess vivid recall of all the events that took place while they were "dead"?

✠ Why, since the discovery of quantum theory, do some physicists affirm that the universe is more mental than physical in the way it behaves? (Richard Conn Henry "The Mental Universe," Nature 436, no. 29, July 7, 2005).

✠ Why can people with certain mental disorders be trained to rewire their neural networks using attentive consciousness (demonstrating that the mind creates the brain and not the other way around)?

[20]. From a sermon by St Bernard of Clairvaux, "On the Stages of Contemplation:"

Let us take our stand on the tower, leaning with all our strength on Christ, the most solid rock, as it is written: He has set my feet on a rock, he has guided my steps. Thus firmly established, let us begin to contemplate, to see what he is saying to us and what reply we ought to make to him. The first stage of contemplation, my dear brothers, is to consider constantly what God wants, what is pleasing to him, and what is acceptable in his eyes. We all offend in many things; our strength cannot match the rightness of God's will and cannot be joined to it or made to fit with it. So let us humble ourselves under the powerful hand of the most high God and make an effort to show ourselves unworthy before his merciful gaze, saying, "Heal me, Lord, and I shall be healed; save me and I shall be saved." And again, "Lord, have mercy on me; heal my soul because I have sinned against you."

Once the eye of the soul has been purified by such considerations, we no longer abide within our spirit in a sense of sorrow, but abide rather in the Spirit of God with great delight. No longer do we consider what is the will of God for us, but rather what it is in itself.

For our life is in his will. Thus we are convinced that what is according to his will is in every way better for us, and more fitting. And so, if we are concerned to preserve the life of our soul, we must be equally concerned to deviate as little as possible from his will.

Thus having made some progress in our spiritual exercise under the guidance of the Spirit who gazes into the deep things of God, let us reflect how gracious the Lord is and how good he is in himself. Let us join the Prophet in praying that we may see the Lord's will and frequent not our own hearts but the Lord's temple; and let us also say, My soul is humbled within me, therefore I shall be mindful of you.

These two stages sum up the whole of the spiritual life: when we contemplate ourselves we are troubled, and our sadness saves us and brings us to contemplate God; that contemplation in turn gives us the consolation of the joy of the Holy Spirit. Contemplating ourselves brings fear and humility; contemplating God brings us hope and love. (Sermo 5 de diversis, 4-5:: Opera omnia, Edit. Cisterc. 6, 1 [1970], 103-4) Used in the Roman Catholic Office of Readings for Wednesday of the 23rd week in Ordinary Time with the accompanying biblical reading taken from Habakkuk 2:5-20).

From Gaudium et Spes

Although he was made by God in a state of holiness, from the very onset of his history man abused his liberty, at the urging of the Evil One. Man set himself against God and sought to attain his goal apart from God. Therefore man is split within himself. As a result, all of human life, whether individual or collective, shows itself to be a dramatic struggle between good and evil, between light and darkness. Indeed, man finds that by himself he is incapable of battling the assaults of evil successfully, so that everyone feels as though he is bound by chains. But the Lord Himself came to free and strengthen man, renewing him inwardly and casting out that "prince of this world" (John 12:31) who held him in the bondage of sin. For sin has diminished man, blocking his path to fulfillment.

The call to grandeur and the depths of misery, both of which are a part of human experience, find their ultimate and simultaneous explanation in the light of this revelation.

Though made of body and soul, man is one. Through his bodily composition he gathers to himself the elements of the material world; thus they reach their crown through him, and through him raise their voice in free praise of the Creator. For this reason man is not allowed to despise his bodily life, rather he is obliged to regard his body as good and honorable since God has created it and will raise it up on the last day. Nevertheless, wounded by sin, man experiences rebellious stirrings in his body. But the very dignity of man postulates that man glorify God in his body and forbid it to serve the evil inclinations of his heart.

Now, man is not wrong when he regards himself as superior to bodily concerns, and as more than a speck of nature or a nameless constituent of the city of man. For by his interior qualities he outstrips the whole sum of mere things. He plunges into the depths of reality whenever he enters into his own heart; God, Who probes the heart, awaits him there; there he discerns his proper destiny beneath the eyes of God. Thus, when he recognizes in himself a spiritual and immortal soul, he is not being mocked by a fantasy born only of physical or social influences, but is rather laying hold of the proper truth of the matter.

Man judges rightly that by his intellect he surpasses the material universe, for he shares in the light of the divine mind. By relentlessly employing his talents through the ages he has indeed made progress in the practical sciences and in technology and the liberal arts. In our times he has won superlative victories, especially in his probing of the material world and in subjecting it to himself. Still he has always searched for more penetrating truths, and finds them. For his intelligence is not confined to observable data alone, but can with genuine certitude attain to reality itself as knowable, though in consequence of sin that certitude is partly obscured and weakened.

The intellectual nature of the human person is perfected by wisdom and needs to be, for wisdom gently attracts the mind of man to a quest and a love for what is true and good. Steeped in wisdom, man passes through visible realities to those which are unseen.

Our era needs such wisdom more than bygone ages if the discoveries made by man are to be further humanized. For the future of the world stands in peril unless wiser men are forthcoming. It should also be pointed out that many nations, poorer in economic goods, are quite rich in wisdom and can offer noteworthy advantages to others.

It is, finally, through the gift of the Holy Spirit that man comes by faith to the contemplation and appreciation of the divine plan. (Vatican II—Gaudium et Spes: The Dignity of the Human Person (13-15).

[21]. The following section from the Church's Code of Canon Law describes the types of beliefs that are non-negotiable for faithful Catholics. This is not intended as a list of all those things one must adhere to in order to be considered a "faithful Catholic." The most important aspect is the docility of spirit granted by God that enables one to approach the teachings and the authority of the Church with trust, instead of a spirit of obstinacy. The spirit of docility, trust, humility and obedience characterize God's presence in one's soul.

A person must believe with divine and Catholic faith all those things contained in the word of God, written or handed on, that is, in the one deposit of faith entrusted to the Church, and at the same time proposed as divinely revealed either by the solemn magisterium of the Church or by its ordinary and universal magisterium which is manifested by the common adherence of the Christian faithful under the leadership of the sacred magisterium; therefore all are bound to avoid any doctrines whatsoever contrary to them. Each and every thing which is proposed definitively by the magisterium of the Church concerning the doctrine of faith and morals, that is, each and every thing which is required to safeguard reverently and to expound faithfully the same deposit of faith, is also to be firmly embraced and retained; therefore, one who rejects those propositions which are to be held definitively is opposed to the doctrine of the Catholic Church. [Can. 750 §1, §2].

[22]. Ignatius provides wise counsel for those tempted by evil thoughts and feelings and helps us know how to conduct ourselves during such times. He writes this advice to Sister Theresa Rejadell:

"I insist that you think of God as loving you, as I have no doubt He does, and that you correspond with this love and pay no attention whatever to the evil thoughts, even if they are obscene or sensual (when they are not deliberate), nor of your cowardice or tepidity. For even St. Peter and St. Paul did not succeed in escaping all or some of these thoughts. Even when we do not succeed fully, we gain much by paying no attention to them. I am not going to save myself by the good works of the good angels, and I am not going to be condemned because of the evil thoughts and weaknesses which bad angels, the flesh, and the world bring before my mind. God asks only one thing of me, that my soul seek to be conformed with His Divine Majesty. And the soul so conformed makes the body conformed, whether it wish it or not, to the divine will. In this is our greatest battle, and here the good pleasure of the eternal and sovereign Goodness. May our Lord by His infinite kindness and grace hold us always in His hand." Ignatius of Loyola: Letters and Instructions (St. Louis: The Institute of Jesuit Sources, 2006), 25.

[23]. Such panic attacks and terrors are similar to aspects of what psychologists refer to as "catastrophic thinking," often suffered by those with serious anxiety disorders. The "racing thoughts" of catastrophic thinking may lead to ideas of self-wounding or other

types of bodily harm, similar to what Ignatius experienced at Manresa when, in the grip of severe scruples, he had an urge to throw himself off a cliff.

[24]. Those suffering from biochemical addictions would be wise to seek professional guidance on extracting oneself from their grip. It is notable however that because of our mind-body connection, people who are withdrawing from spiritual darkness and spiritual addictions often "feel" a dread that is similar to the feelings experienced during biochemical withdrawals. It is obvious that eliminating physical addictions will be a tremendous benefit to one's overall health, but despite this knowledge, the biochemical addict still "feels" afraid of letting go of the addiction. It is clear that the fear and dread we experience when withdrawing from sinful addictions is very similar. Despite the painful emotions, we know that withdrawal from spiritual and physical addiction only leads to life.

[25]. Review the definition of counter-inspirations; see week 3.

[26]. See week 37 "E&W" at www.sacredstory.net.

[27]. See endnote 16.

[28]. For a modern example of these types of temptations, see week 38 "E&W" at www.sacredstory.net.

[29] William Johnston, SJ, Mystical Theology: The Science of Love (New York: HarperCollins, 1995).

[30]. The following section from the Church's Code of Canon Law describes the types of beliefs that are non-negotiable for faithful Catholics. This is not intended as a list of all those things one must adhere to in order to be considered a "faithful Catholic." The most important aspect is the docility of spirit granted by God that enables one to approach the teachings and the authority of the Church with trust, instead of a spirit of obstinacy. The spirit of docility, trust, humility and obedience characterize God's presence in one's soul.

A person must believe with divine and Catholic faith all those things contained in the word of God, written or handed on, that is, in the one deposit of faith entrusted to the Church, and at the same time proposed as divinely revealed either by the solemn magisterium of the Church or by its ordinary and universal magisterium which is manifested by the common adherence of the Christian faithful under the leadership of the sacred magisterium; therefore all are bound to avoid any doctrines whatsoever contrary to them. Each and every thing which is proposed definitively by the magisterium of the Church concerning the doctrine of faith and morals, that is, each and every thing which is required to safeguard reverently and to expound faithfully the same deposit of faith, is also to be firmly embraced and retained; therefore, one who rejects those propositions which are to be held definitively is opposed to the doctrine of the Catholic Church. [Can. 750 §1, §2].

[31]. Thomas M. King, SJ, Teilhard's Mass: Approaches to The Mass on the World (Mahwah: Paulist Press, 2005) 120.

FORTY WEEKS ~ Letters from Prison